The Signs of
James Bond

The Signs of James Bond

Semiotic Explorations in the World of 007

DANIEL FERRERAS SAVOYE
Foreword by James Chapman

McFarland & Company, Inc., Publishers
Jefferson, North Carolina, and London

To Bond lovers everywhere

LIBRARY OF CONGRESS CATALOGUING-IN-PUBLICATION DATA

Savoye, Daniel Ferreras, 1962–
    The signs of James Bond : semiotic explorations in the world of 007 / Daniel Ferreras Savoye ; foreword by James Chapman.
        p.   cm.
    Includes bibliographical references and index.

    ISBN 978-0-7864-7056-3
    softcover : acid free paper ∞

    1. James Bond films history and criticism. 2. Fleming, Ian, 1908–1964 — Characters — James Bond. 3. Bond, James (Fictitious character) 4. Popular culture. I. Title.
PN1995.9.J3S25 2013
791.43'651—dc23   2012046921

BRITISH LIBRARY CATALOGUING DATA ARE AVAILABLE

© 2013 Daniel F. Ferreras. All rights reserved

No part of this book may be reproduced or transmitted in any form or by any means, electronic or mechanical, including photocopying or recording, or by any information storage and retrieval system, without permission in writing from the publisher.

Front cover images © 2013 Shutterstock

Manufactured in the United States of America

McFarland & Company, Inc., Publishers
   Box 611, Jefferson, North Carolina 28640
   www.mcfarlandpub.com

Table of Contents

Acknowledgments   viii
Foreword by James Chapman   1
Introduction: The Last Spy Standing   3

1. Dr. Bond   11
2. The Names of the Order   32
3. Positions and Oppositions   56
4. Primal Forces   91
5. Bondian Art   115
6. Bonding the New World Order   151

Conclusion: The Runaway Narrative Structure   176
Chapter Notes   181
Works Cited   193
Index   197

Acknowledgments

No book exists on its own, even at the time of its writing, and this one is no exception. My deepest gratitude goes to all those who have encouraged me during its composition, by discussing some of its aspects, offering suggestions, and, most of all, patiently listening to my incessant speculations about the signs of James Bond. If there are any bad ideas in this book, they are doubtlessly mine.

I thank the great Bondologist James Chapman for his kind foreword, as well as for his openness and encouragement; it is not every day that a historian endorses a semiotician, and in these times of theoretical sectarianism, his receptiveness and generosity are the unmistakable signs of a true, great scholar. There wouldn't indeed be any *Signs of James Bond* if it weren't for *Licence to Thrill*.

I thank Felicia Campbell for showing me the path to popular culture studies and being an inspiration for my endeavors in the field, as well as for her constant and generous assistance throughout my career. This book would not have been written without her.

I thank Ángel Tuninetti for his continuous encouragement and support, which have allowed me to complete this work.

And I thank Hanna Lin, Robert Brennan, Robert Lewis, John H. Hagen, Jennifer Lawrence, Matt Marble, Kevin Frieson, Fernando Moreno, Ivana Palibrk, Hugo Martínez and Erea Fernández, with whom I have discovered sides of James Bond that I never thought existed.

Foreword by James Chapman

It's nearly sixty years since James Bond made his first appearance in *Casino Royale*, and half a century since the first big-screen outing of Britain's most famous "secret" agent in *Dr No*. A fascinating question for the analyst of popular culture is why this rather absurd figure, an ideological construct of Austerity Britain and the Cold War, has maintained his popularity and cultural visibility into the twenty-first century. One explanation, emphasizing the historical contexts in which the Bond books and films have been created, is that Bond has responded to the changing geopolitical order and cultural environment: the decline of the British Empire, the emergence of the permissive society, the rise of second-wave feminism, the end of the Cold War and the onset of the era of globalization. Another explanation turns to the tools of cultural theory: Bond as a "shifting signifier" whose meaning changes over time and is reconfigured according to different cultural and ideological circumstances. Indeed, there has been a long tradition of theoretical engagements with Bond, starting with Umberto Eco, whose essay on the novels of Ian Fleming remains one of the pioneering examples of the structuralist analysis of narrative (even if Eco ignores those stories — amounting to about a third of the canon — that do not fit his paradigm), while Tony Bennett and Janet Woollacott's *Bond and Beyond: The Political Career of a Popular Hero* is one of the foundational texts of modern cultural studies.

Daniel Ferreras Savoye's insightful new study, *The Signs of James Bond*, is a worthy successor to Eco and the other scholars who have trodden this path. I can happily recommend this book for three reasons. The first is its accessibility. Too much of what passes for cultural studies is blighted by theoretical jargon that requires a dictionary of critical theory to decode it; what struck me about reading Ferreras Savoye's manuscript was his ability to deal with the complex language of semiotics and structuralism in a manner that will not turn off the lay reader. The second reason is that, unlike some other writers on the subject, Ferreras Savoye realizes the need to consider all the Bond texts, including both Fleming's books and the films. In particular, he does not follow the snobbery of some Fleming purists in regarding the films as inferior works but rather as Bond narratives in their own right — and he shows how the films have maintained their connection to the literary Bond even as the original texts were exhausted. Third — and perhaps most importantly — there is Ferreras Savoye's attention to detail and his close knowledge of the texts. Any methodological apparatus needs to be empirically demonstrated if it is worth its salt, and this depends on close, and accurate, textual analysis. I have read too many studies of popular culture that have been let down by basic factual errors and a slipshod approach to the texts. But it is immediately apparent that here is an author who knows his Bond — and who does not let his scholarship detract from his enjoyment of the texts.

The Signs of James Bond is a worthy addition to the growing body of Bond scholarship and should find a place on the bookshelf of every Bond fan and critic.

James Chapman is a professor of film studies at the University of Leicester, specializing in the history of British popular culture, including films, television and comics. He is the author of *Licence to Thrill: A Cultural History of the James Bond Films.*

Introduction:
The Last Spy Standing

The resilience of the James Bond narration prompts an apparently simple yet still unanswered question: How can this be possible? After the collapse of the Soviet Union, the cybernetic revolution and the rise of a new globalized consciousness, how can a narration born in 1953 still function past the first decade of the 21st century without undergoing any major changes other than occasional paradigmatic adjustments? In short, what in the world could James Bond still have to say?[1] Evidently quite a lot if we are to consider the success of the two latest installments of the series, *Casino Royale* (film, 2007) and *Quantum of Solace* (2009), which cast a blond Daniel Craig as the fearless secret agent and re-tell the same story yet again, adding a touch of narrative tension through the recycling of a few narrative paradigms that do not alter the fundamental premises of what has often been called the "Bond formula."

After 22 installments and a 23rd around the corner,[2] the success of James Bond on the screen could only be compared to that of Tarzan, Sherlock Holmes or Dracula, although, contrary to popular belief, the 22 installments of the Bond series do pale in comparison to the 48 films which tell the adventures of Edgar Rice Burroughs' ape-man, or to the staggering 200-plus features dedicated to Arthur Conan Doyle's sleuth. However, what seems quite unprecedented is the currency of James Bond when compared to that of Tarzan or Sherlock Holmes. Whereas the last four Tarzan films have been animated features, and the latest Sherlock Holmes movies strays considerably from the original narration to the point of denaturing both the characters and the plot, James Bond has remained current and loyal to himself throughout the last five decades on the silver screen. When compared to the laborious comeback attempts of other modern popular figures, such as Indiana Jones or Batman, 22 Bond features and counting indicate a remarkable staying power.

Not only has the James Bond narration been able to adapt to continuous geo-political re-configurations, aesthetic shifts and deep societal changes, it has shown as well a striking resistance to parody. With the exception of Dracula, few popular heroes have been parodied as much as James Bond 007, and in a variety of media — not only in texts (Michael K. Frith and Christopher B. Cerf's *Alligator by I*n Fl*mm*ng*, Cyril Connolly's "Bond Strikes Camp") and films (*Casino Royale*, *Spy Hard*, *Johnny English*, the *Austin Powers* series), but in TV shows (*Get Smart*) and comic books as well. To the already virtually endless list of James Bond parodies and caricatures we must add the recent French comedies *Le Caire, nid d'espions* (*Cairo, Nest of Spies*) and its sequel, *Rio ne répond plus* (*Rio Is Not Answering*, released in English as *Lost in Rio*), which, in spite of using another figure of popular spy literature, OSS 117 (created by French writer Jean Bruce), are clearly subversions of the James Bond universe; the sequel's title in French, *Rio ne répond plus*, is indeed reminiscent of the first Bond cinematic installment, which precisely begins with the unexplainable silence of the MI6 station in Jamaica. A precursor to the Bond-inspired OSS 117 parodies can be found in the 1975 French comedy *Bons Baisers de Hong-Kong* (*From Hong Kong with Love*), which went as far as reversing the iconic gun barrel scene by showing the incompetent agent's silhouette unable to pull out his weapon and being shot by his invisible enemy. We should also mention the usually ignored but extremely popular comic books from Spain, *Anacleto, agente secreto*, by Manuel Vázquez,[3] as well as the too often overlooked but brilliantly conceived Belgian comic books *Les Aventures de Steve Pops, agent très spécial* (*The Adventures of Steve Pops, Very Special Agent*) by Jacques Devos, perhaps one of the most appealing spoofs of 007. The two available comic books of the series,[4] *Steve Pop contre Dr. Yes* (*Steve Pops vs. Dr. Yes*) and *Opération Éclair*, imply in their titles[5] the parodic intention and play out most of the important paradigms of the James Bond universe: a terrorist network called SMASH, a super villain called "Dr. Yes" and a Mini-Cooper loaded with homemade gadgets.

The fact that Devos' *Steve Pops contre Dr. Yes* was published in 1966, one year before the first "serious" filmic parody of the James Bond universe, *Casino Royale* (film, 1967), was released, is in itself structurally significant, for it means that by the mid-sixties the "Bond formula" had already been assimilated by audiences everywhere. Rather than defamiliarizing, the Bond narration had become so familiar that it could safely be parodied without running the risk of losing the recipient. When a narration (or an entire narrative genre, for that matter) becomes overly familiar, it naturally prompts parodies, which create another level of defamiliarization in order to sustain narrative authority — that is, to maintain the interest of the receptor. Often the result is the disappearance of said narration or narrative genre in that particular modality, as can be observed in the case of the Spanish chivalry novel, efficiently liquidated by Cervantes' ruthless parody of the genre, *El Ingenioso Hidalgo Don Quijote de la Mancha*, or in that of the "Spaghetti Western," which eventually produced its own parodies with films such as the *Trinita* series before simply ceasing to exist. However, this does not seem to apply to James Bond, who, after being ridiculed more or less directly for the last forty years, has proven his invulnerability and has returned once again, in a more primal form than ever: in comparison to the detached tone of Roger Moore's interpretation and the boyish charms of Pierce Brosnan, Daniel Craig's 007 appears to be much more of an elementary Alpha Male with little sense of humor,[6] proving once and for all that, no matter how hard we try, James Bond 007 is simply no laughing matter.

And so, naturally, the main question remains: How can this be? What does the Bond narration possess to be at the same time rigid enough to re-tell the same narrative syntagm over and over with total impunity and flexible enough to adapt effortlessly to deep cultural changes? Contextual data will be of no help, since what distinguishes the character of James Bond from his most immediate competitors, such as Sherlock Holmes or Dracula, is his ability to remain mostly uncorrupted by historical and cultural changes without losing his fundamental appeal. While the vampire genre has taken a definite turn towards a fusion with the romance novel, as shown by the success of Stephenie Meyer's *Twilight* series,[7] and while the recent resurrection of Sherlock Holmes has implied turning the cold, middle-aged detective and his companion, the respectable Dr. Watson, into rowdy sentimental young men barely more sophisticated than the thugs they beat up,[8] James Bond has remained more or less his usual self throughout the last four decades, just as any of his adventures is more or less identical to the one before and to the one after. From a strictly narratological point of view, to attempt an explanation of the James Bond phenomenon based upon contextual evidence does not necessarily lead to a description of its most significant aspects; what sets the James Bond narration apart are not the changes it has undergone over the last fifty years but rather the remarkable consistency of its narrative syntagm which seems to function on its own, independent of any specific sending entity. It is plain to see that the James Bond narration can no longer be explained in function of its original author, nor can it be explained according to its current producers, since actors and directors are interchangeable, as are the social and historical backgrounds at play within the plot. The senders — anyone involved in the production of a James Bond film — appear to be simple operators whose input consists mainly in updating non-determining paradigms; they are not active senders. We can add a touch of blackness to *Live and Let Die* (film), a bit of kung-fu to *The Man with the Golden Gun*, a measure of space opera to *Moonraker* (film) or a splash of postmodern *Matrix*-like special effects to *Die Another Day* (film) without ever turning the James Bond universe into a martial arts story or a science fiction adventure. The Bond story is already an entire narrative genre by itself, able to incorporate a great diversity of narrative paradigms without altering its essential structure; and thus we can trade an elegant characterization, such as that of Roger Moore, for a much rougher one, such as that of Daniel Craig, without upsetting in the least the narrative balance.

James Bond has defeated time, and social and cultural evolution, as well as Mr. Bean and Austin Powers, and stands as a fairly unique illustration of Roland Barthes' famous statement regarding the death of the author[9]: indeed, one of the first important kills of agent 007 has been Ian Fleming himself, who has been quickly dispossessed of his creation, unable to foresee the unthinkable trajectory of his hero into the 21st century. It seems therefore logical to tackle the James Bond phenomenon from the inside — that is, from message to context rather than the other way around — and to re-phrase our original question: How is the message "James Bond 007" delivered and which clues within the signs themselves can help us understand its remarkable staying power?

The endurance of the James Bond narrative syntagm may very well lie in the *way* the message is presented as much, if not more, than in the message itself. By associating form and content on many levels, this particular narrative structure offers a very high degree of internal coherence, which might explain why it has so successfully survived historical, political and cultural changes, as well as countless parodies. The rebooting of the franchise with a virile, un-refined new 007 suggests a need to return to the very basic premises of the story, which in the end seems as old as time itself, for it tells the struggle between good and evil, the difference being that this particular narrative syntagm seems to tell it better. And so, naturally, James Bond always returns.

Since Umberto Eco's famous essay "Narrative Structures in Ian Fleming," the structural and semiotic aspects of the James Bond phenomenon have seldom been touched upon in order to favor theoretically-oriented debates more akin to today's politico-critical trends. Eco's study has various merits, including being among the first to address the James Bond phenomenon in a serious, scholarly manner; however, being restricted to Ian

Fleming's novels, it does not take into account the remarkably successful adaptation of James Bond to the screen. Since the films have become today an integral part of the Bond phenomenon, it seems justified to start where Eco left off, and to propose a semiotic reading of the James Bond phenomenon that includes its textual as well as its cinematographic representations.

The semiotic approach has the advantage of addressing some problematic issues, such as the success of James Bond at the international and trans-chronological levels, which remains enigmatic if we are to accept the contextual determinations of a typical socio-historical analysis. It is, for instance, difficult to explain the fame of agent 007 in Yemen or in Taiwan by invoking the clearly white euro centric politics inherent in his universe; and to present James Bond as the emblematic figure of a certain nostalgia for a past British Imperial greatness might no longer be enough to account for his appeal to 21st century audiences. The efficiency of this key figure of contemporary popular culture and the reasons for its apparently irresistible narrative authority are to be found within its semiotic significant structural components, for the way the story is told is as significant as the story itself, and the analysis of the different relationships between form and content proves in the case of James Bond to be extremely revealing.

The rise of popular culture studies as a credible field of study has justified a renewed critical interest in important popular figures, and James Bond has indeed benefited from this scholarly shift. However, cultural studies still remains an extremely flexible, not to say tragically undefined, field of study, often subjected to ideological trends and political priorities dictated by the almighty postmodern critical theory; hence, any given corpus of study is susceptible to becoming a pretext rather than a text in order to expose and defend a specific theoretical point of view, often to the detriment of the analysis and interpretation of the work at hand. As we will see shortly (Chapter 1: "Dr. Bond"), this regrettable tendency of current criticism has not spared Agent 007, and recent years have seen an abundance of critical studies on the subject which appear to be more concerned in demonstrating the significance of their own theories than in analyzing and interpreting the James Bond phenomenon. As happens often with postmodern/post-structuralist inquiries, the true subject of most recent essays devoted to James Bond is not really James Bond but rather theoretical claims of an ideological nature.

The importance given to theory in literary and cultural studies has worked to the detriment of the works themselves, and rather than interpreting further the different elements of the James Bond narration, most current criticism has separated us from our corpus of study by using it in a synecdochical manner in order to present another subject, usually of an ideological nature, dressed in the attire of theory. We have yet, for instance, to interpret the significance of elementary paradigms such as James Bond's name or number in regard to the fundamental structural components of the narration (Chapter 2: "The Names of the Order"),[10] or to analyze the evolution and fluidity of the binary oppositions that support the narrative conflict and their relationship with different levels of defamiliarization (Chapter 3: "Positions and Oppositions"). We are still to define the specific roles played by the four primal elements in the James Bond narrative syntagm, which go a long way in explaining its quasi-universal appeal (Chapter 4: "Primal Forces"), or to evaluate the aesthetic merits of the Bond universe, both textual and cinematic, from the point of view of their ability to induce narrative authority (Chapter 5: "Bondian Art"). In short, we are still to understand the inner mechanisms of this particular narration which has successfully transcended its historical, cultural and political contexts without losing its fundamental appeal, and which still purports a very specific ideological content that may not be as conservative and reactionary as it is usually believed (chapter 6: "Bonding the New World Order").

For my demonstration, I will concentrate upon what can be understood as the canonical Bond corpus of study — i.e., Ian Fleming's novels and the EON films. The other by-products of the James Bond phenomenon — imitations, pastiches and parodies — are highly significant; however, they would constitute in themselves the basis for another study, the object of which would be to trace and analyze the remarkable influence the James Bond narration has had upon textual and cinematic production. I will use generally accepted concepts from formalism, structuralism and semiotics, such as "defamiliarization," i.e., "the act of making strange," which is a staple in traditional formalism, as well as "narrative authority," which is the equivalent of "textual authority" (that is, the capacity of a text to capture the attention of the reader, albeit extended to the narrative level to include films as well as texts). I will also distinguish between "narrative syntagm," which refers to the sequential organization of the narrated elements within the structure, and "narrative paradigm," which designate the separate components of the narration. I will, as well, mark the difference between the textual Bond and his cinematic counterpart; although it has become fashionable to merge any type of artistic or cultural manifestation into the postmodern notion of "the Great Text," I do believe that specific terminology is crucial to our endeavor. A text is a written artifact, and to consider (as do, for instance, Bennett and Woollacott) the entire James Bond phenomenon as one "text" often leads to a metaphorical approach that, rather than simplifying matters, tends to add unnecessary confusion.

The language of criticism has to thrive towards the always elusive monosemic relationship between signifier and signified and avoid polysemic complacency, for, as stated elsewhere, "one simply cannot interpret a metaphor with another metaphor."[11]

By tracing the evolution of the fundamental narrative paradigms associated with the Bond universe from text to film, we will be able to better comprehend the remarkable power this specific narrative structure holds upon our collective consciousness, and perhaps understand how we can tolerate the telling of the same story over and over again.

Chapter 1

Dr. Bond

Although current trends in postmodern, theoretically-oriented criticism tend to eliminate the necessity of situating one's endeavor within the pre-existing body of scholarly research in order to favor the promotion of specific philosophical or ideological concerns, a brief review of the existing research concerning any corpus of study remains a logical step if we are to produce a coherent contribution to any area of inquiry. The following pages are therefore a critical classification of the different scholarly efforts that have been devoted so far to the James Bond phenomenon, which can stand to be innocently skipped by anyone more interested in James Bond than in Bondology.

The increasing visibility of popular culture as a credible field of study has naturally generated an ample, if fairly recent, bibliography surrounding its great popular figures and myths; and, logically, James Bond has not escaped such an intense critical scrutiny. The amount of literature dedicated to 007's universe has become almost as overwhelming as the object of study itself, and the cultural scholar is confronted today with a massive amount of information that could appear difficult, if not impossible, to manage. From books to collections of essays to websites and blogs, James Bond has inspired a great deal of comments and commentaries, and I do not intend in these few pages to present and analyze the integrality of Bond's bibliography; rather, I will proceed to a functional classification which will allow us to conceptualize this maze of more or less valuable information regarding the figure of the most well-known spy in the Occidental world. In general terms, the extensive bibliography dedicated to Ian Fleming and James Bond can be divided into four main tendencies: the Descriptive, the Subjective, the Educated and the Scholarly. The first three are strongly mediated by their commercial function, while the fourth one is mainly determined by its academic intent.

Commercial Bond

The first category, strictly commercial and virtually devoid of scholarly interest other than that of providing raw information, consists of descriptive, fan-oriented literature, and is presented mainly under the form of different guides to the James Bond universe. It tends to compile all factual information related to James Bond, which, when considering Ian Fleming's privileged relationship with his character, as well as the success of 007 on the screen, is bound to be a virtually endless task. From the similarities between Fleming and Bond to minute anecdotes from the movie sets, the James Bond phenomenon can indeed stand to be described and documented over and over again, so long as the text is slightly refreshed, the photographs renewed and new people interviewed. For instance, publications such as Dougall's *James Bond: The Secret World of 007*, Cork and Stutz's *James Bond Encyclopedia*, Benson's *The James Bond Bedside Companion*, Abo and Cork's *Bond Girls Are Forever: The Women of James Bond*, Pfeiffer and Worrall's *The Essential Bond: The Authorized Guide to the World of 007*, Macintyre's *For Your Eyes Only: Ian Fleming and James Bond*, Simpson's *The Rough Guide to James Bond*, Henry Chancellor's *James Bond: The Man and His World* and Bouzerau's *The Art of Bond* offer a wealth of data concerning Ian Fleming's life and James Bond's universe, and relatively little in terms of analysis.

Personal Bond

The second category, at the opposite side of the spectrum in terms of output, concerns personal, "educated" accounts of the James Bond phenomenon, and is best represented by Kingsley Amis' *The James Bond Dossier* and the more recent *James Bond: The Man Who Saved England* by Simon Windler. Amis, a novelist himself who published a James Bond's adventure, *Colonel Sun*, in 1968 under the pseudonym of Robert Markham, and who insisted that he was the ghostwriter behind Fleming's last novel, *The Man with the Golden Gun*, naturally identifies strongly with the subject of his inquiry, and this closeness undermines the otherwise undeniable scholarly value of his essay.

In a very personal, appealingly self-indulgent tone, Amis reflects upon James Bond and the Bond universe, mostly guided by the notion of self-identification. The facility with which the recipient can identify with the narrative universe is indeed an important feature of the Bond novels, and it should be pointed out that, in regard to this issue, Amis reaches similar conclusions to those presented by Eco less than a year later in his well-known structuralist analysis of Ian Fleming's novels. Both observe, for instance, that normal, pleasant activities, such as playing golf, skiing or scuba diving, are as important in the economy of the text as the truly adventurous, life-threatening episodes, and naturally promote the identification of the reader with the text (Amis 8, Eco 165). Nonetheless, and it spite of his engaging tone, Amis' *James Bond Dossier* appears today lacking the necessary rigor of a scholarly essay, and its openly subjective approach tends to render it a tad dated, as the following quote illustrates: "Although I quite enjoy being annoyed by M and wouldn't really want him any different, I do wish he would lay off this particular piece of boy's paper bullshit" (65). Amis seems more concerned with defending James Bond against criticism than analyzing and interpreting the novels in a methodical manner, and may sometimes appear to adopt a sexist point of view in order to defend his idol from well-deserved criticism, in particular in chapter five, "Beautiful Firm Breasts" (44–51).

Whereas Amis offers interesting insights into the readings of the Bond novels, and his study is mainly centered on the literary corpus, Windler's *James Bond: The Man Who Saved Britain*, on the other hand, appears to be more a personal memoir than a scholarly consideration of the James Bond phenomenon. Although the main idea, suggested by the title (i.e., that the icon of James Bond has served to console the British from their loss of international political significance), might seem to indicate an historical perspective, very reminiscent of that already suggested by cinema historian Chapman, Windler's highly subjective approach undermines his observations even more than in the case of Amis, for the subject of the study appears to be the author himself rather than James Bond.

Amis and Windler's essays, albeit not easy to use from a strictly scholarly point of view (in particular Windler's), do underline the cultural weight of James Bond, both as a vehicle for personal expression and as a publishing commodity. Chances are that Windler's book would have been more difficult to publish and distribute had it been called *My Life and James Bond*.

Educated Bond

The third category of Bond's bibliography is devoted to a more culturally inclined recipient and relates accepted cultural values and names to the world of James Bond, as epitomized by Yeffet's *James Bond in the 21st Century: Why We Still Need 007* and South's *James Bond and Philosophy*.

Being, for the most part, more humorous than analytical, Yeffet's book could be placed into the first category; it does include, however, some more intellectually challenging parts, such as a study of James Bond's Oedipal complex as represented by the *Goldfinger* narrative, a notion explored in depth by Bennett and Woollacott in *Bond and Beyond*. *James Bond and Philosophy* aims to be far more critical; unfortunately, its format, which consists of short sections, each devoted to a specific philosophical current and its possible connections with the James Bond universe, does not allow its contributors to explore in depth the issues they raise. The definitions of the different philosophical concepts and their implications are necessarily hurried, hence, their application to the Bond narration remains somewhat unsatisfactory, as if the James Bond universe had just been a pretext to expose some fundamental philosophical concepts from Plato or Nietzsche. The openly playful overall tone of the collection also tends to weaken its scholarly intent, for it seems to imply that looking at the universe of James Bond through the prism of the Great Epistemologists is not to be considered in the end as a truly serious endeavor; indeed, most of the essays are based upon partial, not always accurate knowledge of the Bond corpus, as the priority of *James Bond and Philosophy* is to serve philosophy through Bond rather than the other way around.

Scholarly Bond

The fourth category of Bond's bibliography, doubtlessly much more serious and critically viable than the three mentioned above, is susceptible to subdividing itself into three different tendencies: the historical/contextual approach, the critical inquiry, and the structuralist/semiotic analysis. The contextual studies examine the James Bond narration in function of their context, whether historical, social, cultural or cinematographic; the critical inquiries, for lack of a better name, tackle the Bond narrative from the highly theorized perspective of post- and post-post-structuralist thought; and the structural/semiotic analyses explore the internal laws of the James Bond narration in relationship to the universal axis of communication.

Bond in Context

Bennett and Woollacott's *Bond and Beyond*, along with Chapman's *License to Thrill* and Black's *The Politics of James Bond* aim to contextualize the Bond phenomenon within cultural, cinematographic and political history, respectively. Bennett and Woollacott's essay, which is considered by Chapman as "the best academic study of the Bond phenomenon taking into account both the novels and the films" (*License* 15), sets out to examine the James Bond — phenomenon from an "intertextual" point of view and is more concerned with the transmission, evolution and reception of the James Bond narrative than with the narrative itself. Bennett and Woollacott distinguish two levels of intertextuality: "intertextuality" and "inter-textuality." Intertextuality refers to "a set of signifying relations that is alleged to be manifest within a text, the product of the permutation of texts it deploys," while "inter-textuality" points to "the ways in which the relations between texts are socially organized within the objective disposition of a reading formation" (86). Such a distinction is a bit peculiar since the authors of *Bond and Beyond* do not consider the Bond corpus of study (i.e., the novels and films) as an objective cultural reality but rather as the product of an incessant intertextual exchange between sender and recipient. It appears difficult then, given these premises, to conceive of the existence of a possible "objective disposition of reading formation"; if the sender and the message are not fixed values but mobile signifiers in constant mutation, one would suppose that the third element of the axis of communication — that is, the recipient and its reading formation — is equally fluid and undefined.[1] In order to "adequately account for Bond's peculiar status as a popular hero," Bennett and Woollacott deem it necessary to "consider not merely the novels and the films taken separately" (17), nor their relationship to each other, but rather the entire corpus of cultural artifacts revolving around the figure of James Bond:

> Our concern is not with the novels and films "in themselves" but with the mobile and shifting nature of the cultural and ideological business that has been conducted around, by means of and through them, as a consequence of the ways in which transformations in the wider functioning of the figure of Bond — in fanzines, magazine articles, advertisement and the like — have subtly altered the horizons of meaning within which the novels and the films have been activated for consumption [19].

The authors of *Bond and Beyond* go to great lengths to locate the meaning and importance of the James Bond phenomenon outside the narration itself and within the structures of social and ideological exchange that determine its ever-mutating nature. Such approach yields the risk of separating the analysis from the actual corpus of study, which in the end appears quite inapprehensible:

> The analysis must also encompass and take account of the vast range of other texts — advertisements, fanzine articles on Bond, interviews with

Sean Connery, Roger Moore and Ian Fleming, features on "the Bond girls" in men's magazines, spoofs and parodies — in which the figure of Bond, severed, to a degree, from the films and novels, has been constructed and put into broader distribution. It is within the circulations and exchanges between such texts and the films and the novels that the figure of James Bond has achieved the wider popular currency we have described [18].

Besides establishing the fairly obvious notion that the Bond narration — or any other, for that matter — depends naturally upon "circulation and exchanges" in order to exist, it must be noted that Bennett and Woollacott do not dwell much on the "spoofs and parodies," ignoring, for instance, Guest/Hughes' 1967 movie *Casino Royale*; and that if they do bring some of Connery's or Broccoli's remarks into the discussion, their scope is far from encompassing all the "texts" of Bond, a task which in itself represents quite an impossible challenge. It could also be argued that comments from producers, actors and directors, while doubtlessly informative, are of a very uneven value when it comes to their critical insights and should probably be taken with a grain of salt. When Lewis Gilbert, the director of *The Spy Who Loved Me*, states that "they've [the Bond films] disproved every law in cinema, they've done everything wrong and they're a huge success" (179), one can question his motivations as well as the accuracy of his views. It is a given that any film director tends to promote the film on which he or she is working. And in the case of Bond, to purport the idea that in spite of their formulaic elements, the James Bond films go somehow against the grain resembles more a marketing strategy than an objective evaluation, for the Bond films have precisely shown a propensity to follow rather than set commercial cinematic trends for at least the last two decades. *Live and Let Die* (film) assimilated characteristic paradigms of the then-popular "blaxploitation" films; *The Man with the Golden Gun* (film), released one year after the first internationally successful kung-fu feature (namely, *Enter the Dragon*), included its share of would-be martial arts scenes; and *Moonraker* benefited from the enthusiasm for deep space adventures created by Lucas' *Star Wars*. Similarly, the technological excesses of the two last installments of the Pierce Brosnan period, *The World Is Not Enough* and *Die Another Day*, emulate the visual feats of the Wachowski brothers' *Matrix*; and the choice of an actor affiliated with independent cinema, Daniel Craig, for the recent rebooting of the series is obviously a reflection of today's fashion for "indie cinema."[2] So it does appear that the Bond films have not "done everything wrong," nor have they "disproved every law in cinema"— quite the contrary. The Bond narrative syntagm has simply adapted non-determining paradigms, often at a very superficial level,[3] in order to keep up with the most obvious developments of commercial cinema.

By basing their argument upon a very undefined corpus of study (i.e., this apparently abstract-to-the-point-of-inapprehensibility "cultural space" where "the business of cultural exchange is conducted") and conferring equal importance to any more or less relevant comment from every possible origin, the authors of *Bond and Beyond* fail to organize their sources, which eventually undermine each other. Their conception of the cultural object as an ever elusive notion floating amidst other "texts"[4] in an endless intertextual relationship naturally leads Bennett and Woollacott to reject basic structural premises as they deem it "necessary to abandon the assumption that texts, in themselves, constitute the place where the business of culture is conducted, or that they can be construed as the sources of meaning or effect which can be deduced from an analysis of their formal properties"(59). Such a statement may appear perplexing — all the more when it is applied to the James Bond narration. Whereas no one could deny the fundamental role of the receiver within the universal axis of communication, to discard the formal characteristics of the James Bond narrative syntagm as non-significant is a daring move to say the least. While it is plain to see that no narration exists without a receiver, it is equally obvious that the message itself participates in the meaning it conveys; the receiver is not the only entity at play within the communicative structure and does not simply create meaning independently of the message — rather, meaning could be conceived as the dialectic relationship between sender(s), message and receiver(s).[5]

By searching the significance of the Bond phenomenon outside the actual novels and films, the authors distance themselves from the actual corpus of study — that which motivates their analysis in the first place — i.e., the Bond narration. Although the authors dismiss "Derrida's project of deconstruction" somewhat hurriedly, based upon Terry Eagleton's views (254), the theoretical framework of *Bond and Beyond* is firmly anchored upon theorists usually located within the post-modern tendency, such as Lacan and Foucault,[6] and is decidedly closer to post- structuralism than to traditional Marxism. Foucault's notion of the author, as presented in the third chapter (46–7) and repeated in chapter 7 (233), is indeed interesting but contributes to further distance the authors of *Bond and Beyond* from their corpus of study. As to the use of Jacques Lacan's concept of *"point de capiton"* (35), it presents some problems from the point of view of its interpretation: *"point de capiton"* in French means "upholstery button"; however, Bennett and Woollacott, following the psychoanalytical tradition, choose to use "point of anchorage" (297), hence considerably altering the connotations of the original French, which included the notion of pad or padding ("*capiton*"). The liberties Lacan takes with the French language are well documented (see Sebreli, *El olvido de la razón*) and do not necessarily help to interpret his discourse, let alone in translation, rendering their direct application to any corpus of study a very uneasy task. The connotations of "pad" are indeed very different from those of "anchorage" and should be reflected in the English version in order to understand and use the concept according to the French original: the "*point de capiton*" not only anchors, but muffles and absorbs as well.

Furthermore, Bennett and Woollacott's view of the text in reference to the context is quite reminiscent of Derrida's well-known declaration "there is no outside the text," [7] for they "attempt to rethink the concept of context such that ... neither text nor context are conceivable as entities separable from one another" (262). Ultimately, and again very much along the lines of post-structuralism, *Bond and Beyond* denies any intrinsic properties to the James Bond narration, which is considered as a "floating" and "mobile" signifier without real or stable signified meaning, even from an ideological point of view:

> *A View to a Kill* attests to a further attenuation in the ideological currency of Bond and, we would guess, a consequent narrowing in the scope of his appeal.... It will do so [make a reasonable profit], however, less because of the cultural and ideological resonances of the hero or because of the Bond formula than because it is, simply, a Bond film. James Bond, *well past the twilight of his career* [my emphasis], is now, more than anything else, a trademark which, having established a certain degree of brand loyalty among certain sections of the cinema-going public, remains a viable investment in the film industry [294].

Since the authors stated at the beginning of their first chapter that they are "centrally concerned" with the question of "Why has James Bond been so massively and enduringly popular" (15), to conclude that a "Bond film" will do well at the box office "because it is, simply, a Bond film" seems somewhat unsatisfactory. The heavy, often over-conceptualized critical apparatus used by the authors of *Bond and Beyond* does not help the clarity of their exposition and sometimes leads to obvious declarations, such as: "Rather than supplying the center around which such inter-textual references were coordinated, the cultural space within which the figure of Bond operated was incessantly re-negotiated by referring it to new tendencies and developments within popular culture, especially the cinema" (39) — which is to say that the James Bond narration has adapted with the times and not the other way around — hardly a breathtaking discovery. Similarly, the end of the first part of chapter seven barely justifies six pages of demonstration: "Most of the later Bond films rework themes present in other popular fictional forms or in public life in relation to Bond" (210): this fact is indeed known to anyone familiar with the James Bond films. In the end, the authors of *Bond and Beyond* appear more concerned with the "Beyond" than with the "Bond" part of the phenomenon, and the James Bond narration often becomes a pre-text rather than a text in order to theorize about culture and society in a highly conceptualized manner.

Bond and Beyond was published in 1987, and its authors could not foresee the recovery of the franchise after Moore left the role, and its demonstrated renewed appeal beyond "certain sections of the cinema-going public." It appears that the Bond narration is still in the process of adaptation, and that Daniel Craig is not indeed "well past the twilight" of his career. The notion of moving or mobile signifier presented by Bennett and Woollacott allows one to conceive the James Bond universe as a flexible narrative syntagm; however, this flexibility is not unlimited, and the character of James Bond, far from being an empty vehicle reduced to the dimensions of a purely commercial trademark (i.e., the signifier of another signifier), still corresponds to a very defined ideological signifier. For all the changes that he has undergone from film, to film and in spite of Bennett and Woollacott's affirmations, James Bond remains the guardian of the Order and of Western normative values, and corresponds thus to a very determined ideological tendency.

The James Bond narration might be in constant evolution — but as part of a fixed narrative syntagm and within its limits. Let's just imagine the possibility of James Bond smoking a joint at a reggae concert before getting killed five minutes into the film to feel the unshakable weight of his ideological make-up as well as the rigid limits of its narrative structure. As a signifier, James Bond might be highly mobile; as a signified, he doesn't travel much.[8]

In comparison with Bennett and Woollacott's highly theorized and ultimately inconclusive study, both Chapman's and Black's essays appear refreshingly straightforward. In his highly documented *License to Thrill*, Chapman seeks to contextualize the Bond films within British cinema and film studies, and presents the origins of the spy thriller genre before proceeding to a very detailed analysis of the Bond movies and their cinematographic particularities, in which he addresses the conditions of production and the critical and public reception of the Bond movies, as well as their cultural and political content. For Chapman, the Bond universe expresses a notion of "Britishness," a somewhat nostalgic reminiscence of the Great Albion's glorious past, carefully packaged for international consumption. Its staying power is due to the ability of its producers to continuously adapt the formula to political and social change: "The longevity of the series is due, in large measure, to the strategies which the filmmakers have adopted for renewing and updating the Bond formula" (*License to Thrill* 17).[9] Although this is undeniably true, the remarkable endurance and high profile of James Bond in our cultural landscape cannot be altogether explained by the business savvy of any given production company—we should then have to deduce that the makers of *Indiana Jones* or *Die Hard* simply have not thought yet about adapting their product to the necessities of the market. When we compare the recent and quite laborious comeback of Indiana Jones, or that of Superman or Batman for that matter, to the apparently effortless repeated resurrections of 007 over the last forty-odd years, we have no other choice but to accept the fact that the James Bond narration possesses some specific particularities which allow it to occupy a very privileged status among other modern filmic heroes. Nonetheless, Chapman's essay remains perhaps the most informative essay to date the inception and reception of the James Bond films, as well as their cultural and cinematographic contexts.[10]

Some of Chapman's observations, such as the classlessness that characterizes James Bond, implicitly suggested as well by Amis in *The James Bond Dossier* (84–88), and the high level of response from the franchise to the changes in the film industry, are echoed in Black's *The Politics of James Bond*, which consists in relating the political content in Bond's novels and films to their context: "Bond is a virile, classless character who combines the suave sophistication of the traditional British gentleman-hero with the toughness and sexual magnetism of the Hollywood leading man" (Chapman, *License* 274; and "License to Thrill" in Lindner 97); "[Bond] is apparently at home in any social situation, knows what drinks to order and what is regarded as inappropriate or stupid and what is not, creating an image that appeals to many" (Black 86).[11] Black presents, as well, the transition from the novels to the films, the alterations the narrative universe had to undergo in order to remain current and meaningful, and the relationship between Bond and the evolution of the geo-political and cultural contexts. Curiously, it appears that the James Bond narration sometimes reflects its environment, anticipates it, or simply misses it altogether. For instance, the Soviet SMERSH yields to the a-national SPECTRE when "ironically these were years in which the Cold War itself heated up again" (49). If the threat of rockets upon England in the novel *Moonraker* might have been a premonition of possible menaces looming ahead, the elimination of SMERSH might seem a bit precipitated if we are to establish an interpretation of the James Bond universe based upon its correlation with its historical context. Black observes that "politics plays a smaller role in the films, or rather a smaller explicit role" (92), which brings up the question of the semiotic weight of the visual medium by opposition to the text and the myriad of connotations it might convey in a single frame. For instance, the killing of black antagonists in two different scenes of the recent adaptation of *Casino Royale* by a blond, blue-eyed Daniel Craig does carry a very heavy political content; however, whether this content is explicit or implicit will mainly depend upon the recipient's sensitivity. Jeremy Black obviously refers to external political events in relation to the films rather than to the inner politics of the James Bond universe, which are inseparable from its narrative syntagm.

Critical Bond

Unlike Chapman's and Black's contextual analysis, which are both well-documented and informative, most of the critical inquiries devoted to James Bond prove to be rather problematic as to their actual scholarly usefulness, due for the most part to the partiality of their ideological slants and to their inclination towards over-conceptualized theorizing, which, as we have already observed in the case of Bennett and Woollacott's study, tends to separate the analysis from its very object of inquiry. As stated in its introduction, the collection of essays edited by Christopher Lindner in *The James Bond Phenomenon: A Critical Reader* aims to "collect for the very first time a lively and diverse body of criticism on the Bond novels, the Bond films, and their tangled relationship with popular culture" (2). The essays which compose the volume are intended to study the James Bond corpus from "different theoretical perspectives, including structuralism, Marxism, feminism, post-colonialism, and psychoanalysis" (2). Such a vast array of points of view works somewhat against the cohesion of the volume; whereas structuralist and sociological approaches can be considered as methods of narrative interpretation, feminism and post-colonialism are indeed much more thematically than methodologically oriented and usually imply a strong ideological agenda, which can sometimes distance the analysis from the object of study.[12] The collection includes Eco's well-known "Narrative Structures in Fleming," as well as the first chapter of Bennett and Woollacott's *Bond and Beyond*, along with other essays of a diverse nature and of very inconsistent quality. For instance, Michael Denning's essay "Licenced to Look: James Bond and the Heroism of Consumption" tends to repeat the main points of Eco's study, including the notion of game (60, 62), the comparison between Bond's stories and those written by Mickey Spillane (61), the peculiar organization of *Goldfinger*'s narrative syntagm (63), which devotes three times as many pages to a game of golf than to the attack on Fort Knox, and the text's imperialist ideology (66).

Christopher Lindner's "Criminal Vision and the Ideology of Detection in Fleming's 007 Series" is based upon the notion that the Bond novels express a new vision of criminality in accord with the new world geopolitical configuration, and by opposition to the traditional detective stories: "For just as Fleming conceives crime and criminality in the context of Britain's Cold-War ideology and post-war geopolitics, so too does he conceive the figure of the detective. The detective now becomes the secret agent" (84). The criminal has become a master mind, and the threat is now global. It could be argued that this sounds a bit like Dr. Fu Manchu, who started as an assassin but soon became the head of his evil organization and aimed to weigh upon international politics, supporting himself through typical criminal activities. However, Lindner relates this change of crime and criminal vision to historical factors, while basing his argument in relationship to the detective story — a common position which does not go without serious questioning, since the narrative structure of the detective story is centered on the notion of detection, while that of a typical James Bond narration relies only peripherally upon the collecting of clues. The main conflict, which sustains the entire narrative syntagm, is the binary opposition between Bond and the Villain, and not between the enigma and its resolution, as is the case with the detective story. We are confronted with two distinct narrative genres — the detective story and the spy adventure — and the presence of occasional common paradigms in both does not lead to identify one with the other. We do find gangsters in Ian Fleming's James Bond novels, as early as *Live and Let Die* (1954) and *Diamonds Are Forever* (1956), and as late as *The Man with the Golden Gun* (1965); however, neither Mr. Big, the ruling hood in Harlem from *Live and Let Die,* nor Jack Spang of the Spangled Mob from *Diamonds Are Forever,* nor the high-priced hit man Scaramanga and his extensive connections (which include heads of crime families as well as Russian spies) in *The Man with the Golden Gun* need to be discovered as criminals. They are identified as such from the very beginning of the narration, and therefore the discovery of their identity does not create the narrative tension at the core of any detective story. We do not need to know "Who did it" since we already know; the question is rather "Can we stop him from doing it." Whereas the detective usually reconstructs the past in order to resolve an enigma and identify the criminal, the spy is perfectly familiar with the past, which includes the identity of the culprit, and his function is to act upon the future. The engine of the narration is the mission rather than the search for a truth which has already been established from the start.[13]

These two types of narration co-exist in a parallel manner rather than in a process of substitution, and it suffices to observe the enduring and very current success of the detective genre under its multiple forms to deduce that the "new vision" of criminality has not replaced the "old one," as Lindner's essay seems to suggest.

Current theoretical inquiries tend to display a certain nonchalance towards the concrete objects they use for their demonstrations, which usually privilege theoretical speculations over close and comprehensive readings. Many recent studies dedicated to James Bond seem to extrapolate epistemologically powerful albeit often abstruse conclusions based upon a fraction of the available corpus. Hence, Paul Stock's article included in the same collection, "Dial 'M' for Metonym: Universal Exports, M's Office Space and Empire," appears to be based upon a somewhat partial knowledge of the James Bond universe. This leads its author to very questionable statements, such as "Away from his office, M has diminished powers" (218), and to a downright esoteric conclusion: "But while 'The World Is Not Enough' for Robert Carlyle's Renard, perhaps the same is true for Bond as well" (229). Stock seems to attribute this motto to Renard, the villain from the 1999 film *The World Is Not Enough*, while actually it is Bond's reply to Elektra when she states that "I could have given you the world" (1:39:03–1:39:04), and Bond indeed adds "old family motto" (1:39:11–1:39:12). This confusion is all the more puzzling when we consider that the question of heraldry is an important narrative paradigm of *On Her Majesty's Secret Service*, in both novel and film. In the novel, Bond's filiation to Sir Thomas Bond, baronet, is not quite established as James Bond dissuades Griffon Or to pursue his genealogical researches to concentrate on the matter at hand, which is the infiltration of Blofeld's organization. However, the motto "The World Is Not Enough" is indeed mentioned and qualified as charming by Griffon Or, and Bond decides to appropriate it rather casually: "'It is an excellent motto which I shall certainly adopt,' said Bond curtly" (74). In the filmed version, Hilary Bray, the fellow Bond is to impersonate, shows him the Bond coat of arms which bears the motto *Orbis Non Sufficit* and translates it into English; while in the novel, Bond's filiation with the famous baronet Thomas Bond, baronet of Pekham, appears doubtful, it is somewhat taken for granted in the film. Thus, to associate this very motto with the character of Renard is to openly ignore its importance within the Bond narrative tradition and severely undermines the textual authority of the essay.

Similarly, some remarks from the otherwise interesting essay by Elisabeth Ladenson such as "all the Bond girls respond generically to this name [Pussy Galore]" (199), might appear to be founded upon a somewhat reductive view of the Bond text. Nonetheless, Ladenson's perceptive remarks regarding the linguistic aspects of the novel *Goldfinger* make her essay one of the most convincing of the collection, notwithstanding a certain propensity for post-structuralist over-conceptualization which complicates rather than clarifies matters, a tendency we find as well in Toby Miller's essay "James Bond's Penis," which appears more dogmatic than convincing: "Bond's penis is a threat to him — a mean of being known and of losing authority, a site of the potentially abject that must be objectified as an index of self-control and autotelic satisfaction" (233). Miller attempts to present Bond "in the avant garde of weak, commodified male beauty" (233), relying on a heavy conceptual psychoanalytical apparatus rather than on the James Bond narrations themselves. He ultimately fails to prove his point, again due to an apparently incomplete knowledge of the Bond corpus, as the following quote demonstrates: "For all the supposed association with fast living, high-octane sex, and a dazzling life, *Bond basically runs away from fucking in the novels* [my emphasis], leaving the desiring women who surround him in a state of great anxiety" (235). This is, of course, far from true, for Bond is indeed highly sexually proactive throughout every novel; in some cases he is even the one to be left in a state of sexual frustration, such as at the end of *Moonraker* (novel) after Gala informs him that she has a fiancé.

Beyond the inconsistent quality of the essays which compose it, *The James Bond Phenomenon: A Critical Reader* also presents a quite perplexing editorial flaw: Eco's study, "Narrative Structures in Fleming," presented in the volume as a reprint from *The Role of the Reader*, has been amputated without any explanations of its second part, "Play Situations and the Story as a 'Game'" (*Reader* 155–161), as well as of its introductory outline and of the definition of its corpus (*Reader* 146–147). Eco's essay, originally published in *Il Caso Bond* in 1965, has been reprinted since then in other compilations, which have not always reproduced the entire text, as was the case for the volume devoted to crime and detective stories edited by William W. Stowe and Glenn W. Most, *Poetics of Murder*, published by Harcourt in 1983; however, its editors do mention the fact in their introduction and furthermore choose to do away with the last part of Eco's study rather than the second, a decision that appears to be both more rational and less misleading. The elimination of the paragraph that presents the outline and of the entire second part, as is done in the *Bond Phenomenon*, seriously undermines the value of Eco's study, which is all the more unsettling when we consider that it is perhaps one of the best essays of the collection, as David Lancaster states in his review of *The Bond Phenomenon*[14]: The missing part is precisely the one where Eco analyzes the structural formula of the James Bond novels and can be considered as one of the most important of his essay, not mentioning the base for the following two developments; its elimination without any explanation from this particular reprint poses serious questions as to the scholarly coherence of the volume."[15]

Just as *The James Bond Phenomenon: A Critical Reader* does, *Ian Fleming and James Bond: The Cultural Politics of 007*, one of the most recent collections of essays devoted to James Bond, displays a vast array of modern theoretical interpretations which are not always convincing nor particularly enlightening. The disparate nature of both compilations, somewhat suggested by the all-inclusive vagueness of their respective titles, makes it difficult at times to distinguish between legitimate scholarly inquiries and mere academic opportunism. Indeed, the stated purpose of *The Cultural Politics of 007*, as described in the foreword, goes a long way in further complicating the matter, for it is to examine Ian Fleming's creation "from different scholarly perspectives including history, geography, sociology, philosophy, and gay and cultural studies" (Lycett, viii). This raises immediately the question of critical definition, since it could be argued that gay studies could be included within the post-modern conception of cultural studies, and that "geography" in itself does not point to any specific interpretative method.

Cultural studies, it seems, much as literary studies, are suffering from the overuse of theory and from the self-indulgence of subjective, ideological interpretations. The Indiana University conference on *The Cultural Politics of 007* (2003), during which the papers included in the volume were originally delivered, appears to have been an open field to push forward different political or theoretical agendas, to the detriment of the alleged corpus of study. As the editors put it unwillingly in their introduction, "Importantly, *The Cultural Politics of 007* addresses not only what academics can do for Bond, but also what Bond does for academics" (xiii). Just as any cultural object, James Bond has easily become an academic commodity to emit highly theoretical, when not lyrical, declarations, often based on partial knowledge of the works at hand, as are Judith Roof's "Living the James Bond Lifestyle," Allen's "'Alimentary, Dr. Leiter': Anal Anxiety in *Diamonds Are Forever*," and Hovey's "Lesbian Bondage, or Why Dykes Like 007." Roof's essay is mainly composed of declarations without real foundation, expressed in an obscure, over-conceptualized theoretical discourse: "The Bond figure's performance of stylistic efficacy, mummified retroaction, and homeopathic opposition enact and salvage the Law of the Godfathers, securing those things — certainty, identity, history — we seem to have lost" (71). This conception of Bond allows Roof to draw relationships between Bond and the Mummy (82) or Bond and Frank Sinatra (71, 81), and to make sometimes solemn statements such as: "What is important is not that we might read Bond as the Phallic signifier of desire (and Law), but that the figure of Bond always in itself plays out the flirtation of veiling in such a way that we know that the Phallus and Law are there" (83). Beyond the fairly obvious fact that Bond is to be considered as a representative figure of male sex appeal and of the Western order, and that his political message is mediated by the narration, this apparently powerful statement sheds little light upon the Bond phenomenon.

Allen's ideological framework and his desire to locate "anxiety about the masculine identity" within the James Bond universe, based on Freud's well-known case of the Rat Man, even leads him to adopt a somewhat cavalier attitude regarding the narration of *Diamonds Are Forever* (film) as he qualifies the narrative paradigm of Blofeld's doubles as irrelevant "diegetically speaking" (26). This can be construed as a very questionable value judgment, for the concept of doubles and fakes is an inherent part of the narrative conflict, a fact already observed by Chapman:

> In an ironic reflection of the artificiality of Las Vegas, so many things in the film turn out to be fake: Blofeld's doubles, the diamonds which Bond smuggles in for the villains, the circus sideshow in which a girl supposedly turns into a gorilla, the cat which Bond kicks to determine which is the real Blofeld ... even what appears to be the landscape of the moon turns out to be a mock-up at a space research centre" [*Licence* 135].

To state that this particular, highly coherent narrative paradigm is "irrelevant" and "largely incidental to the plot of the movie" (26), and ignoring the significant semiotic correlations pointed out by Chapman, as Allen does in order to better serve his particular interpretation, reveals the limits of purely thematically oriented interpretations, as well as the shortcomings of excessively politicized readings, to the detriment of the corpus itself. If James Bond exhibits signs of male anxiety, as Allen sets out to demonstrate, they might be more convincingly represented in other instances of the Bond narration, such as in chapter 3 of *The Man with the Golden Gun* (novel), "'Pistols Scaramanga,'" which consists mainly in the report of a psychological profiler enigmatically named "C.C." about professional assassin Paco Scaramanga, and which explicitly states the relationship between guns, penises and male uncertainties, mentioning Freud as well as Adler. One could also think of the famous description of Honeychile Rider coming out of the water in *Dr. No*, which provides ample ammunition for a gender-based analysis: "The gentle curve of the backbone was deeply indented, suggesting more powerful muscles than is usual in a woman, and the behind was almost as firm and rounded as a boy's" (104–105). Both C.C.'s report regarding guns and latent homosexuality, as well as this ambiguous description of a clear object of desire first seen from behind, would allow one to speculate upon Bond's possible male anxiety without the need to resort to an overly interpretive mode. As to the rat becoming a "central symbol of anal intercourse" (31), based on Freud's case of the Rat Man, it remains a narrow parameter of interpretation that would be difficult to apply to other instances of the James Bond narration, such as that of the confrontation with the rodents that happens in *From Russia with Love* (film) as Bond and Tatiana Romanova run in the underground of the Russian embassy after the explosion provoked by Kerim Bey to facilitate their escape with the Lektor (1.03.09–1.03.30).

As announced perhaps a little imprudently in its introduction, the main object of *The Cultural Politics of 007* is "How can we put him [Bond] to work for *us?*" (xv); it is therefore more a matter of putting James Bond to work for cultural scholars rather that of cultural scholars applying their expertise to interpret and explain the remarkable James Bond phenomenon, as if the latter had simply become a pretext to present and defend any given theoretical or ideological agenda. The events that took place during the Bloomington symposium where the essays composing *The Cultural Politics of 007* were originally presented illustrate quite clearly the erasure of a given corpus of study, in this case that of Ian Fleming and the James Bond narration, in favor of obscure and ultimately fruitless theoretical debates. During his keynote address, Jeremy Black was apparently quite critical of the different postmodern approaches adopted by some of the presenters and openly criticized their tendency to neglect contextual information and primary sources in order to favor theoretical and political agendas. As a result, a group of participants generated a manifesto to protest Black's position, in which they announced their intention to boycott a round table discussion that was to take place on the following morning and where Black was to be present. The manifesto stated that its authors were "firm believers in unfettered academic exchange," and that they therefore refused to participate "in an exchange that [was] no exchange, but merely the rehearsal of stereotypes, unexamined prejudices and anti-intellectual posturing" (xv). It could, of course, be argued that rejecting any possibility of dialog is in itself quite an anti-intellectual stand, and one could infer from such an attitude that the Manifesto Party did not have many valid objections to Black's critical view of postmodern theoretical practices and thus chose to denounce it rather than confront it. In other words, this particular group of postmodern thinkers opposed a prejudiced stand to what they conceived as another prejudiced stand.[16] This paradoxical, and a bit puerile, dispute is symptomatic of the uneasiness of cultural studies in the aftermath of post-structuralism. The scholars of the postmodern persuasion who participated to the symposium on Ian Fleming and James Bond were doubtlessly more interested in defending their territoriality than in reading and interpreting Ian Fleming and James Bond, as theoretical discourse substituted the object of study and eclipsed its importance. The outcome of the symposium on Ian Fleming and James Bond clearly shows how an object of study can be turned into a mere product for academic consumption by the empire of theory and ideological agendas.

The re-packaging of Lindner's study mentioned above, "Criminal Vision and the Ideology of Detection in Fleming's 007 Series" from the *James Bond Phenomenon* under a different, more fashionable title ("Why Size Matters") in *The Cultural Politics of 007* also raises the question of the overall validity of the James Bond bibliography from the point of view of its scholarly functionality. Whether anyone involved professionally with academia today is highly conscious of the publication factor, and whether the fully enforced "Publish or Perish" rule might lead to the temptation of recycling some already used ideas, are not the only issues at stake here.[17] What might be more concerning is the lack of discernment on the recipient's part, both in editors and scholars. Although Lindner states in a note that his essay "draws on material revised" from his previous study, published in *The Bond Phenomenon* (237), it remains unclear what has been added to the "revised" version. The central idea of "Why Size Matters" (i.e., the emergence of new crime and new crime detection as reflected in the Bond narrations) is the same as that of "Criminal Vision and the Ideology of Detection," and its demonstration relies upon the same quotes. Just as in his previous essay, Lindner explains the popularity of the James Bond narration, arguing that "Fleming among others developed a variation on the popular genre of detective fiction that registered and responded to specifically post-war concerns about crime, conspiracy, and human agency" (226), and reaches identical conclusions: "In the 007 series as a whole, then, the size and sophistication of the various criminal conspiracies mirrors the size of their criminal conspiracy"(*Phenomenon* 82, *Politics* 230). We must deduce that neither the participants at the James Bond and Ian Fleming symposium nor the editors of *The Cultural Politics of 007* were familiar with Lindner's previous essay, the title of which, interestingly, is omitted from his note and simply referred to as "chapter 4 of Lindner, *The James Bond Phenomenon*" (237), a somewhat confusing way to present an essay coming from a multi-authored collection. Popular culture studies, just as literary studies, are suffering from the over-production of critical material which prevents its assimilation and ultimately favors repetition, not to say recycling.

If Chapman's and Black's studies exhibit a firm grasp upon their object of study (i.e., the James Bond narration in its textual as well as cinematographic modalities), and succeed in contextualizing it in a well-documented and convincing manner, the same cannot be said regarding many of the critical inquiries included in *The James Bond Phenomenon* and *The Cultural Politics of 007*, which exhibit a disconcerting lack of rigor in both form and content. It is as if while becoming an academically acceptable field of research, popular culture studies also implied a tongue-in-cheek attitude, not to say a certain lack of seriousness as well as of discrimination in terms of linguistic registers. This attitude is naturally reflected in the choice of vocabulary used by some critics, as shown in some of the aforementioned quotes; and to the already elegant Allen's "fucking" (*Phenomenon* 234) and Hovey's "dyke" (*Cultural Politics* 42), we can add Bennett and Woollacott's sophisticated view of romance in the James Bond narration: "Bond and the 'Bond girl' are, in effect, pure cock and cunt" (*Beyond* 123). One cannot help wondering if these words are indeed the *mots justes* or if postmodern cultural scholars are merely attempting to display their postmodernity by using nasty signifiers.

The corpus of the James Bond narration is indeed vast, and to attempt to elaborate a convincing analysis based upon two or three novels or films is to run the risk of overstating one's intentions and expertise, for neither the most sophisticated conceptual apparatus nor the use of unsavory expressions will be able to compensate for the vagueness of over-conceptualized postmodern rhetoric or for a limited knowledge of any given object of study. This is not to say that any particular instance of the James Bond narration cannot be fruitfully studied apart from the others; however, such partial analysis can hardly warrant the comprehensive conclusions that are so easily drawn by postmodern discourse.

Structural Bond

In comparison with the contextual approaches and the critical inquiries, the structural and semiotic analyses of the Bond narration are much less in terms of quantity, albeit not necessarily in terms of importance. Due to its close relationship to its environment, as well as to the "literary" qualities of its historical author, the James Bond narration has mainly inspired a context-to-text analysis rather than a purely textual one, and Umberto Eco's "Narrative Structures in Ian Fleming," originally published in 1965, remains, in spite of its venerable age, the only structuralist essay on the subject, i.e., the only attempt to comprehend James Bond starting from the text outward rather than from its context, or from the over-conceptualized apparatus of postmodern theory. More disconcerting is the fact that some of the conclusions reached by Eco regarding the political, colonialist, racist and sexist connotations of the James Bond novels' narrative structures have become the basis for much of what postmodern criticism had to say, or to repeat, for that matter. Considering that most, if not all, critical attention devoted to James Bond since Eco's essay has started from the outside, either from the historical context (Chapman, Black) or from any given flavor-of-the-week revolutionary theory, it appears logical, given the tremendous evolution of the James Bond phenomenon beyond the Ian Fleming novels in the last five decades, to examine anew its narrative structures in order to point out some of their relevant features in terms of semiotic functions.

The project of identifying the dominant semiotic structures in the James Bond universe could seem today a more difficult task than it was in Eco's time, if for nothing else than because the object of study itself has grown exponentially to become a colossal cultural artifact, encompassing a variety of media. Eco dealt exclusively with Ian Fleming's novels, excluding from his analysis *The Spy Who Loved Me*, which he considered "somewhat atypical," and some of the short stories included in *Octopussy and The Living Daylights*, a comfortable point of view that singularly simplified the task of identifying recurrent narrative patterns. It could be argued that such exclusion from an already fairly limited corpus of study goes against the very premises of structuralism and somewhat undermines the stated intent; if *The Spy Who Loved Me* appears indeed as a non-typical Bond narration, a fact acknowledged by Ian Fleming himself, the two volumes of short stories, on the other hand, do belong to the James Bond corpus, for, unlike *The Spy Who Loved Me*, they feature James Bond 007 as the main protagonist and should logically be included in the analysis. Today we must, as well, take into account the 22 films from the Eon series as an integral part of the James Bond sign, which renders the task of any bondologist more overwhelming than ever. However, when translated to the screen, the overall narrative structure has been simplified in terms of conflicts and tensions, which facilitates its analysis and allows us to identify more fundamental and comprehensive binary oppositions and semiotic functions than those pointed out by Eco. Cinema has highlighted the most meaningful narrative elements of James Bond by concentrating them in a more systematic message, while further underlining the different correlations between form and content. It appears that the author is more dead than ever, for Ian Fleming has been eliminated by his hero as the story was taking on a life of its own, and the Bond case can thus be considered as a perfect illustration of two fundamental structuralist premises: the author has become external to his work, and it is not the story that counts but the way it is told, which is precisely what this essay intends to tackle.

Chapter 2

The Names of the Order

Bond ... James Bond

Along with "Shaken, not stirred," "Bond ... James Bond" might be the most well-known sound bite associated with 007, and it is probably not a coincidence that these words happen to be the initial words pronounced by Sean Connery when facing the camera in *Dr. No*, the first film adaptation of an Ian Fleming novel: The Bond filmic saga starts with the secret agent introducing himself. Since then, this self-introduction has become a trademark of the character and has been repeated throughout every installment, prompting the question of its actual significance. As James Bond moved from the text to the screen, and hence became a true popular culture phenomenon, these words acquired a new semiotic content beyond their direct, semantic value, and the name of James Bond 007 has come to suggest the entire content of the narration to which it is associated.

After all, except for the slightly surrealistic notion of a secret agent apparently always eager to introduce himself, this sequence offers very little meaning, hardly enough to justify becoming one of the most famous lines of modern cinematographic history. This celebrated one liner — as well as the "shaken, not stirred" Martini bit — is far from occupying the same importance in Fleming's text as it does in the films, and was never considered a trademark of the protagonist until the story crossed from literature to cinema. On the screen, these words found themselves magnified to the point of becoming a micro-structure of the entire narration, and suggesting by themselves the entire James Bond universe; we have come to expect them in every installment of his adventures, regardless of time and trends, and they appear symbolically at the very end of the recent installment, *Casino Royale* (which can be considered a new beginning for the series), living up to the phrase's status as one of the most famous one-liners of all time. The name Bond has thus acquired a greater importance as it moved from a literary to a cinematographic universe, and this could be explained by its very strong relationship with the content of the story itself, a relationship that so far has eluded the critics and most likely Ian Fleming himself.[1]

It has been established how and why Ian Fleming chose the name of James Bond for his hero; as a fervent bird watcher, he owned a copy of *A Field Guide to the Birds of the West Indies*, whose author is precisely James Bond. The name appealed to him for being "the simplest, dullest, plainest-sounding name I could find.... Exotic things would happen to and around him [the protagonist], but he would be a neutral figure — an anonymous, blunt instrument wielded by a government department."[2] What is less known, however, is that the name "James Bond" has already been associated with plainness and bluntness in British popular literature, specifically by Agatha Christie in her short story "The Rajah's Emerald,"[3] which plays out the relationship between the commonality of the name and of its bearer: Christie's James Bond is indeed a simple fellow whose lack of sophistication is underlined throughout the story by the condescending attitude his would-be fiancée, Clara, and her high-class friends adopt vis-à-vis him. As the plot develops, the humble James Bond will turn out to be more righteous than the members of the supposedly "higher-class," and "The Rajah's Emerald" can be read as the triumph of simple honesty — that is true class — over the hypocritical schemes of the rich and morally bankrupt. The association between the name "James Bond" and an ordinary, most undistinguished protagonist hence complements the narration, which is founded mainly upon a binary opposition between a common but moral man and a higher-class but immoral environment. However, when applied to 007, this particular connotation, apparently the one that seduced Ian Fleming,[4] no longer corresponds to the narration, as is the case in Christie's short story. If her James Bond is indeed a most common fellow whose existence is governed by his lack of exceptional qualities, Fleming's hero is precisely the opposite, and his exceptional qualities shine more apparently as we move from the novels into the Eon film series. The fact that the name Bond sounded most "flat" to the ears of Fleming,[5] as it must have to those of Agatha Christie, is no longer necessarily relevant, for James Bond 007 is, in effect, the complete opposite of a common man. If his name sounded plain and boring to Christie and Fleming, its connotations have changed to the point of meaning exactly the contrary today; the sign "James Bond 007" immediately implies a world of adventures made of casinos, tuxedos, fast cars, faster women, deadly threats, and the Greater Good. Whether the name James Bond came from *Birds of the West Indies* or from a memory of reading Agatha Christie (which Ian Fleming did not acknowledge) will remain an unsolved mystery, showing, in passing, the limitations of biographically-oriented historical criticism; Ian Fleming might have concealed the fact that the name "James Bond" had already been used in detective fiction in order to prevent any type of relationship with another best-selling author, or simply because he considered the *Birds of the West Indies* bit both more exotic and more literary (and it is, of course, also possible that the creator of 007 honestly did not remember having read "The Rajah's Emerald" nor the name of its main character). Approaching the issue from a structuralist point of view might in the end be more revealing than any biographical considerations, for the texts themselves provide us with at least a possible lead: Fleming's short story "The Hildebrand Rarity" exhibits a similar narrative structure to that of *Murder on the Orient Express*, and uses the same setting as *Death on the Nile*, which suggests a very tangible filiation between Agatha Christie and Ian Fleming's respective conceptions of murder and suspense, regardless of biographical uncertainties and declared or un-declared authorial intentions.

The text of the James Bond novels is onomastically very self-conscious, sometimes within the title itself (*Goldfinger, Dr. No*), and often regarding the choice of names for the main characters, usually recycled in the films, such as Honeychile Rider, Pussy Galore, Tiffany Case, Mary Goodnight, or Solitaire. These names are usually related to the narration: Solitaire reads the future in the cards, Goldfinger is a gold fetishist, Dr. No opposes the values of the Western world, Pussy Galore loves women, and so on. Logically, the name of James Bond itself, even though it happened to belong historically to a distinguished ornithologist, has acquired a new meaning beyond its original common semiotic content — that of blunt and ordinary — which supports its content rather than undermines it. Eco remarks that it evokes "the luxuries of Bond Street or treasury bonds"(116) but does not go any further in his onomastic interpretation. Now that the sign Bond has been further structured through the Eon film series, its fundamental connotations appear clearer than ever and work in perfect harmony with the narrative structure. James Bond 007 is not only the name of the hero, it is also his function within the narrative structure: he is literally the *bonding agent* of a social and political order that threatens to become *un-bonded*.

The Bonding Agent

When considered at its primary structural level, any James Bond adventure, either literary or filmic, could be summed up within the basic opposition between Order and Disorder. The beginning of the conflict establishes the existence of a threat to the social and political order, usually involving an organization the hierarchy of which appears to be of a totalitarian nature. This organization can be quite involved, as are those of Dr. No, Goldfinger, Drax, and, of course, Blofeld, or apparently less complex, as that of Scaramanga from *The Man with the Golden Gun*. In both cases, however, the villain has the right of life and death over his accomplices and intends to impose a new order — a basic opposition to the notion of the allegedly "free world" James Bond represents — upon society. This substitution of orders logically implies the destabilization of the accepted order, and therefore manifests itself by disordering the basic balance of society: Scaramanga in *The Man with the Golden Gun* (novel) is scheming different plots with both the underworld and the KGB to destabilize the West by controlling cane sugar exports and flooding the U.S. with drugs. In the film, Scaramanga has developed a sun-powered laser canon that upsets the balance of sheer firepower and challenges the hegemony of Western muscle. Hence, the only real structural changes between the novel and the film, in spite of their apparently vast dissimilarities, concern exclusively the paradigmatic aspects of the narration. The threat has become both more technological and spectacular in the film, but the basic binary opposition upon which the narrative syntagm relies remains identical: The Order is under attack and must be defended. Both the novel and the film end with a duel between Bond and Scaramanga, and although the circumstances are very different (one takes place in a mangrove swamp and the other in Scaramanga's personal fun house), the basic opposition between ordered good, represented by James Bond, and disorderly evil, incarnated by Paco Scaramanga, is respected and satisfactorily resolved.

James Bond's function will be that of eliminating the threat — of *bonding* the order back together. By an interesting semiotic shift, the bonding with a female is often the conclusion of the narrative syntagm, for it represents in its simplest form the return to order and harmony. Present in several of Fleming's novels and short stories (i.e., with Solitaire in *Live and Let Die*, Tiffany Case in *Diamonds Are Forever*, Honeychile in *Dr. No*, Domino in *Thunderball*, Mary Ann in "A View to a Kill," or Lisl in "Risico"), it has been systematized on the screen to become a staple of the new and improved Bond narrative structure for universal consumption. This bonding must remain provisional, as demonstrated by the unfortunate demise of the Bond girl at the end of *Casino Royale* and *On Her Majesty's Secret Service*, which show an extremely strong bonding in process between Bond and the main female protagonist: 007 intends to marry Vesper Lynn in the novel *Casino Royale*, and he actually marries Tracy in *On Her Majesty's Secret Service* (in the novel as well as in the film). In both cases a new order — that of marriage — threatens the integrity of the narrative structure, which is based upon the preservation of a collective order rather than the construction of a localized, private one, such as that represented by the family. And so, naturally, both Vesper Lynn and Mrs. Tracy Bond must be eliminated from the narrative syntagm, the former before formalizing her engagement to James Bond and the latter on the way to her honeymoon. At the end of the novel *Moonraker*, Gala reveals to Bond that she is engaged to be married, and in spite of the strong attraction he feels towards her and against his womanizing habits, 007 lets her go without much resistance, suggesting by his very resignation the self-excluding parallel existence of both orders, the general and the particular. As a representative of the Greater Order, Bond will never be allowed to partake in the sacred institution of marriage, and the ending of *On Her Majesty's Secret Service* is the most obvious demonstration of this impossibility. His final thoughts, if we are to believe the accepted chronology of Ian Fleming's works, are those expressed at the end of *The Man with the Golden Gun* and revolve precisely around the possibility of a steady relationship with a woman: "At the same time, he knew, deep down, that love from Mary Goodnight, or from any other woman, was not enough for him. It would be like taking a 'room with a view.' For James Bond, the same view would always pall" (200). Bond cannot be bonded by marriage, for he is already bonded to MI6, queen and country.

The sign "Bond" implies, therefore, the basic purpose of the protagonist, that of *bonding* reality, and functions both semantically, as a name and an identity, and semiotically — that is, suggestively — as a role, which in itself represents a micro-structure of the entire narrative conflict between Order and Disorder as well as its satisfactory resolution. The values represented by this bonding agent appropriately named James Bond are accepted as absolute truths: 007 can kill without experiencing any type of guilt, his righteousness is beyond doubt and his Christian name underlines his unquestionable ethical status, for the King James Bible has been the authoritative version of the Good Book in the English language long enough to become an institution. Any bonding performed by James serves an unquestionable good, and the narration will never let us doubt 007's essentially pure intentions; his license to kill is in the secular world the administrative equivalent of the Angel of Death's godly orders.

The Power of 00

James Bond's section number, 007, is just as efficiently and coherently related to the content of the narration as his name. In *The Bond Code: The*

Dark World of Ian Fleming and James Bond, Gardiner reveals that the number 007 was used as a signature by 16th century thinker and mathematician John Dee, when he worked as a spy for Queen Elisabeth I, a fact already pointed out by Anthony Burgess in his 1988 essay "The James Bond Novels: An Introduction" (4), and that Her Majesty in turn signed her replies by the letter "M." Gardiner's position appears biographically justified, since Ian Fleming is known to have been reading a memoir on the life of John Dee at the time he set off to write the first installment of the adventures of James Bond, *Casino Royale*. Nevertheless, this particular association, however founded it might be upon the reading habits of Ian Fleming, is more supplementary than complementary[6] and does not inform us upon the content of the narration nor participate to the overall message. Any existing similarity between John Dee and James Bond remains somewhat esoteric, for it is not at work within the narration itself, and any reader or spectator can relate to the James Bond universe without being aware of John Dee's intellectual achievements and undercover work. Furthermore, an analysis of a James Bond adventure according to the life and times of John Dee might even prove counterproductive, for it would irremediably distract us from the narration itself to concentrate upon an important and influential figure from a radically different historical period to that in which James Bond exists — just as concentrating upon the ornithologist named James Bond would shed little light upon secret agent James Bond 007. One could muse as well about the striking similarity between Bond's license number and that of French writer Jean Bruce's hero, OSS 117. It is established that Bruce borrowed the code number of an actual agent from the Office of Strategic Services (William Leonard Langer); hence his selection cannot be deemed to be semiotically motivated but rather the result of sheer coincidence. Since the first OSS 117 novel was published in 1949, four years before Fleming's *Casino Royale*, we can certainly entertain the possibility that Fleming might have been aware of its existence and was influenced by Bruce's choice of digits for his protagonist's license number. Regardless of how plausible this hypothesis may seem — Fleming was both fond and knowledgeable of French culture, a fact which is clearly reflected in the adventures of James Bond — it only informs us upon the genesis of the sign "007" and not upon its semiotic function in the narrative universe. Whether or not Fleming imitated Bruce's numerological choice does not necessarily help understand how and why the sign "007" has acquired such a symbolic weight.

The complementary meaning of James Bond's section number, inseparable from his character,[7] must be found elsewhere, independently from its biographical sources, functioning at a connotative level and completing rather than competing with the content of the narration by underlining some of its most characteristic features.

The character of James Bond is immediately associated with courage and virility, and these two qualities could be considered the determining conditions of his narrative function. The narration presents a fearless hero, brave to the point of recklessness and impervious to torture, as demonstrated in *Casino Royale* (novel and film) *Live and Let Die* (novel and film) or *Tomorrow Never Dies* (film and novelization). In *Dr. No* (novel), in spite of being at the mercy the evil Julius No and his murdering "Chigro" thugs, Bond does not hesitate to insult his adversary: "It's the same old business of thinking you're the King of England or the President of the United State, or God. The asylums are full of them.... Why does sitting shut up in this cell give you the illusion of power?" (213). This is quite characteristic of Bond's interactions with the enemy, for neither Le Chiffre or Mr. Big, nor Drax, Blofeld or Scaramanga will prove anymore successful in bullying 007. In the films, as the narrative structure is reduced to its more functional elements, James Bond's courage tends to be over-emphasized, as illustrated by his famous one-liners, often placed after the hero has escaped life-threatening circumstances, which underline his ability to overcome emotional distress as well as his indomitable bravery: 007 literally laughs in the face of death.

In the schematic representation of the would-be superhero that James Bond has become as he evolved on the screen, Bond's courage now includes the audacity of defying the hierarchy of his own organization,[8] the very reason for his existence in the first place, and leads him, starting with *License to Kill*, the second and last of the Timothy Dalton series, to directly disobey his superior's orders. In the novels, as well as in the early films featuring Connery and Moore as 007, Bond's interaction with M is that of an inferior with his superior; James Bond is respectful and compliant, whether he disagrees with M or not, as when ordered to leave his Beretta behind to adopt a Walther PPK in *Dr. No* (novel and film), or when requested to spend a reinvigorating week at the health spa Shrublands in *Thunderball* (novel). The Lazenby parenthesis presents the most serious friction between Bond and M to be found in the earlier films, as 007, after a vigorous exchange with M, storms out of the office and dictates a letter of resignation from the Service to Moneypenny; in the novel, the letter of resignation, which Bond composes in his head while cruising the French countryside in his Bentley, remains an amiable fantasy and never reaches the level of tangibility it does in the film. The Moore installments show a more distant, almost ironical relationship between Bond and M; however, Moore 007 never actually defies the authority of his superior, and his most daring act of disobedience is to occasionally interrupt his final report in order to devote his undivided attention to the current Bond girl, as shown at the end of *The Man with the Golden Gun* and *Moonraker*. He does go after Scaramanga unofficially in *The Man with the Golden Gun* (film); however, he has the full acknowledgment, if not the blessings, of his superior, which is no longer the case with *License to Kill* (film and novelization), where 007 starts showing more serious discipline problems as he openly disobeys direct orders from M and goes after the villain on his own as a rogue agent in order to avenge his long-time friend, C.I.A. agent Felix Leiter.

This new narrative tension is accentuated throughout the Brosnan series and culminates with the agent going temporarily rogue after having been suspended by M in *Die Another Day*. This tension between 007 and M has by now become a new staple of the filmic Bond, and the first two installments of the series' recent rebooting, *Casino Royale* and *Quantum of Solace*, present an open conflict between M and James Bond, as "young 007" appears somewhat difficult to control (the very opposite of a "blunt instrument"). In *Casino Royale*, he refuses to report, breaks into M's house, and must have a microchip locator inserted into his forearm in order for his superior to keep track of her agent. In *Quantum of Solace*, he openly disobeys M's direct orders, seduces Fields, the agent in charge of sending him from Bolivia back to the U.K., and pursues his objective against M's specific instructions. Following the death of Strawberry Fields, M relieves Bond from duty and suspends him, pending further investigation; as could be expected, Bond quickly eludes the guards M has assigned to escort him back to London and pursues what can be perceived by then as a self-appointed mission.

However, we cannot deduce from this opposition between Bond and M, and, by extension, MI6, that agent 007 is actually capable of transcending the order that he incarnates, but rather that the narrative syntagm has simply adapted a contemporary cinematic paradigm — that of the rebellious but righteous loose cannon who may have some problems with authority made popular by the *Lethal Weapon* and *Die Hard* series, among others. This narrative development, specific to the filmic Bond, is to be considered as an evolution of the textual Bond's most determining feature — that is, manly courage. The Bond narration has already demonstrated its remarkable capacity to assimilate external trends without ever losing its cohesion, and the evolution of a respectful and obedient James Bond into a tougher, non-conformist character merely follows a common trend in popular cinema, that of the maverick. Needless to say, Bond will never be a true maverick, for this would upset the balance of the narrative syntagm beyond repair. Bond represents the Greater Order and remains, for all his exceptional personal qualities, a representative figure of collective priorities whose existence depends upon his capacity to defend and restore Order. M's attitude when confronted by Bond's disciplinary problems is in this sense highly significant, for he/she is indeed never totally convinced that his/her agent has actually gone rogue and can go so far as bypassing regulations in order to protect him. In *License to Kill*, which presents the first real instance of Bond disobeying specific orders, M prevents one of his men from shooting him as he escapes. The camera focuses then on M's face, and his expression is that of a concerned father as he mutters to himself, "God help you, commander" (0:34:42–0:34:44). We find a very similar scene in *Quantum of Solace* when M decides to cover her agent vis-à-vis the "Americans" after he has just knocked out the escort she had assigned to him. She explicitly justifies her position to her secretary with, "I don't give a shit about the C.I.A. [1:17:16–1:17:17].... He's my agent and I trust him" (1:17:19–1:17:20).

The rupture between Bond and MI6 can thus never be definitive; as the incarnation of Order, James Bond's ties with MI6 cannot be severed, for it would mean the disintegration of both the character and the narrative syntagm. Hence, the natural conclusion of the narrative instance which might have revealed some tension between Bond and M is an understated reconciliation, as illustrated at the end of the latest installment to date, *Quantum of Solace*, when Bond, after a final prank,[9] confirms his undying loyalty to the service: "[M]:Bond. I need you back. [Bond:] I never left" (1:37:03–1:37:07).

Bond's opposition to M adds a touch of narrative tension by assimilating a staple of contemporary commercial cinema without, however, compromising the integrity of the narrative syntagm. For 007 remains, in spite of all appearances, a tool of the establishment, and therefore his acts of disobedience underline his bravery rather than suggest a possible appetite for independence. As the archetypal bonding agent of Order, Bond cannot be conceived outside of the ruling structure.[10]

Besides his undeniable courage, James Bond is also characterized by his appetite for and success with women, in the novels as well as in the movies. Miller's affirmation that "elsewhere in the movies [besides *Dr. No* and in opposition to the novels], however, the penis comes out of this protective sheath, just as the literary Bond's ambivalence about commodities bursts onto the screen as joy through consumption" (236–7) is debatable, regarding both sex and "commodities" of consumption. James Bond in the novels is indeed sensitive to both, as illustrated in the opening chapters of *On Her Majesty's Secret Service* and throughout the short story "007 in New York," which precisely follows Bond's inner monologue concerning the consumption of food, objects and a woman, Solange. Although Ian Fleming did not present Bond's sexuality as simplistically as the films do, sex in general, and the sexually attractive, sometimes dangerous female and her direct effect upon James Bond, are constant paradigms in the novels, since the very first installment, *Casino Royale*, which shows Vesper and Bond's sexual activity in a most explicit manner: "The succeeding days were a shambles of falseness and hypocrisy, mingled with her tears and moments of animal passion to which she abandoned herself with a greed made indecent by the hollowness of their days" (195). Similarly, Tracy's invitation to Bond in *On Her Majesty's Secret Service* is quite unequivocal: "Do anything you like. And tell me what you like and what you would like from me. Be rough with me. Treat me like the lowest whore in creation. Forget everything else. No questions. Take me" (38).

It should be noted that, contrary to Miller's position, Tracy is far from being as crude in the filmic adaptation, in which the scene's sexual tension is represented in a more spectacular yet less mature fashion, relying mostly upon the exhibition of Diana Rigg's impressive bust in an undersized bra. The film's dialogue does not reflect the notion of prostitution put forth by the novel, nor does it translate Tracy's desperation reflected in the quote mentioned above. As for making love, the camera moves away during the first kiss to a bouquet above the protagonists before a quick change of scene (0:17:34).

In the novels, sexuality is an integral part of the James Bond universe and concerns more aspects of the narration than just the relationship between Bond and the girl. A recurrent figure in the texts concerns the business of sex, which is downplayed in the films but emphasized throughout the novels. It can be of a collective nature, as in *Dr. No*, where the situation of the girls "imported" once a month in order to fill the needs of the working crews is described at length:

> They [the Chinese Negroes] too would have their drinking and dancing, and there would be a new monthly batch of girls from "inside." Some "marriages" from the last lot would continue for further months or weeks according to the taste of the "husband," but for the others there would be a fresh choice. There would be some of the older girls who had had their babies in the crèche and were coming back for a fresh spell of duty "outside," and there would be a sprinkling of young ones who had come of age and would be 'coming out' for the first time. There would be fights over these and blood would be shed, but in the end the officer's quarters would settle down for another month of communal life, each officer with his woman to look after his needs [197].

We find a similar notion in *Goldfinger* where the sexual needs of the help, as well as the means to relieve them, are equally kept in mind by Goldfinger himself: "'They are well paid and well fed and housed. When they want women, street women are brought down from London, well remunerated for their services and sent back'" (171–2). Honeychile's project of becoming a call girl in *Dr. No* represents a more individualized type of prostitution: "'I thought I'd be a call girl.' She said it as she might have said 'nurse' or 'secretary'" (*Dr. No* 157). And so does the dialogue between Bond and the barmaid of the Kingston brothel in *The Man with the Golden Gun*, which discusses openly the physical merits of the available girls:

> "There's Sarah up there now. Care to meet up with her?"
>
> "Not today, thanks. It's too hot. But you only have one at a time?"
>
> "There's Lindy, but she's engaged. She's a big girl. If you like them big. She'll be free in half an hour" [60].

In the films the sexual paradigm is more pervasive than it is in the novels — Bond appears more successful yet with the fair sex — but is however presented in a much lighter, cleaner manner. The first visualization of the archetypical Bond girl, namely Ursula Andress as Honey Rider walking out of the sea in *Dr. No*, sets the tone for most future representations. Sexuality and sexual tensions have been stereotyped for mass consumption, and it is no surprise to find this very scene recycled in the last of the Brosnan installments, when Bond watches Jinx, played by Halle Berry, emerging from the water just as Honey Rider did in *Dr. No*, as well as in the first episode of the series' recent re-booting, *Casino Royale* (film, 2006), albeit in a reversed mode since it is Daniel Craig 007 who emerges from the sea under the admiring gaze of Dimitrios' girlfriend, Solange. All three, Honey Rider, Jinx and Solange succumb to 007's charm, but none of them ever considers a possible career in prostitution. In *The Man with the Golden Gun* film adaptation, the Jamaican brothel has become a Lebanese cabaret, and the prostitutes a belly dancer from France who has indeed relatively loose morals but is still not a working girl of the type evoked in the novel. Later in the film the business of sex is clearly suggested, although never explicitly shown, by the presence of scantily dressed hostesses with whom James Bond has no direct contact. It is therefore a sanitized vision of sex that prevails in the films, and sexual tension is usually concentrated around the main characters, protagonist and antagonist. Nevertheless, it is safe to conclude that whether directly expressed in the text or spectacularly denoted in the films, a strong, convincing sexual activity on the part of 007 is required as an essential element of the narrative syntagm.

Undying courage and sexual tension are hence two necessary components of the James Bond narrative syntagm, as pervasive as they are fundamental, be it in the text or on the screen and both can be related semiotically to the sign "007," which graphically suggests male genitalia: the famous double–O connotes the testicles, and the 7, which quickly became a stylized gun in its visual representation, is indeed, and without much need of Freudian theory, a phallic symbol.[11] The testicles are naturally associated with courage, as illustrated by common metaphorical expressions to be found in a variety of languages besides English,[12] and, along with the gun, can as well be read as clear metonymies of sexual activity. This meaningful convergence is clearly illustrated by the very first torture scene ever to be introduced in the Bond narration, which is when Le Chiffre interrogates 007 to find the missing check in *Casino Royale* (novel): Bond is tied up to a chair with no seat, "his buttocks and the underpart of his body" (132) protruding; and with a carpet-beater, Le Chiffre targets his "sensitive parts" in an explicit attempt to break both his courage and his virility: "It is not only the immediate agony, but also the thought that your manhood is being gradually destroyed and that at the end, if you will not yield, you will no longer be a man" (137). Bond's testicles represent more than just his will and his virility, they are Bond 007 himself,[13] and it is highly significant that the first test the hero must endure is a direct attack against the very metonymy of his section number. We find a similar scene in *You Only Live Twice* when Bond is ordered to sit on a geyser that erupts every fifteen minutes in order to determine if he truly is who he claims to be:

> Blofeld looked behind him and turned back. "You will therefore observe that you have exactly eleven minutes before the next eruption. If you cannot hear me, or the translation that will follow, if you are a deaf and dumb Japanese as you maintain, you will not move from that chair and, at the fifteenth minute past eleven, you will suffer a most dreadful death by the incineration of your lower body [238].

The mineral throne formed by the geyser is reminiscent of the arm-chair with the cut-off cane seat used by Le Chiffre to torture Bond in *Casino Royale* and has the same function — that of forcing Bond to talk by facilitating a direct threat against his lower parts.

The films have adapted the most collectively significant elements of the textual Bond, and thus the filmic Bond has had his testicles threatened on at least three different occasions before *Casino Royale* (film, 2006) was released: in *Goldfinger* (film), *Live and Let Die* (film), and *Never Say Never Again*.[14] In *Goldfinger*, Bond finds himself prisoner of Goldfinger, tied to a table as a laser beam progresses up between his legs (0:49:42); in *Live and Let Die* he is tied to a chair, and Kananga/Mr. Big orders his henchman to start cutting off his finger before moving on to more "sensitive parts" (1:12:27–

1:12:29); and in the most canonical of the non-canonical films, *Never Say Never Again*, when the leather-clad, stiletto-wearing Fatima has 007 at her mercy, she orders him to spread his legs before ostensibly aiming her gun in the direction of his crotch, asking casually if he can guess where the "first bullet" will hit (1:23:37). This fascination for punishing Bond's testicles is directly related to the importance of his double–O status, abundantly mentioned throughout the narration, which is both the administrative justification of his power and the symbolic representation of his courage. Not only do M and MI6, as well as the villains themselves, sooner or later refer to James Bond's 00's, but the hero himself seems irremediably committed to his license number. In *You Only Live Twice* (novel), Bond's reaction when M informs him that he is relieved from 00 duty is that of immediate rejection:

> [M:] "As for the last two assignments, anyone can make mistakes. But I can't have idle hands around the place, so I'm taking you out of the Double-O Section." Bond's heart had temporarily risen. Now it plummeted again. The old man was being kind, trying to let him down lightly. He said, "Then, if it's all the same to you, sir, I'd still like to put in my resignation. I've held the Double-O number for too long. I'm not interested in staff work, I'm afraid, sir. And no good at it either" [30].

In actuality, M intends to promote Bond to the diplomatic section, and the reasons for this promotion are very much along the lines of Bond's abilities, which go hand in hand with his original section number, as confirmed by the ensuing dialogue between Bond and Bill Tanner, the chief of staff who is supposed to brief him about his new mission, which consists of luring Tiger Tanaka, the head of the Japanese secret services, into sharing information with MI6:

> [BOND:] "This man Tanaka sounds a tough nut, and I'm no great hand at diplomacy. But why did M pick on me, Bill? ... Now, be a good chap and tell me what's the real score." Bill Tanner had been ready for that one. He said easily, "Balls, James.... M just thought you'd be the best man for the job.... Anyway, it'll be a change from your usual rough-housing. Time you moved up out of that damned Double-O Section of yours. Don't you ever think about promotion?" "Absolutely not," said Bond with fervour. "As soon as I get back from this caper, I'll ask for my old number back again" [36–7].

So, not only has Bond been chosen for this particularly perilous mission on the bases of his courage, but he is so fervently attached to his "old number" that he intends to recuperate it as soon as the job is done, proving once again that James Bond is not complete without 007.

The 00 question, which we can now safely equate to that of male virility, arises logically during the initial encounter between Bond and the new M in the first film of the Brosnan series (*GoldenEye*) when M states, "If you think I don't have *the balls* [my emphasis] to send a man to die, you're dead wrong" (0:45:14–0:45:18). Although the casting of a female M might be perceived as a radical paradigmatic change, it does not affect the narrative syntagm, based upon a very primal, not to say reptilian virility, emphasized by a female M's choice of words as if to compensate for her gender. Whether M is represented by an older, asexualized man or by a stern, equally asexualized woman, MI6 is still all about courage and strength — that is, testicles. It is indeed highly significant that the first installment of the series' recent rebooting, *Casino Royale*, not only follows the novel closely when it comes to torturing the secret agent's testicles but emphasizes both notions as well — courage and testicles — through supplementary dialogue: "Now, the whole world is going to know that you died scratching my balls" says a defiant Bond to Le Chiffre, demonstrating yet again his heroic bravery (1:47:29–0:1:47:33). Similarly, the imminent castration from which Bond is saved in extremis by the intervention of the SMERSH operative, only suggested in the novel, becomes much more explicit in the film. As Le Chiffre states: "I'll feed you what seem not to mind" (1:48:50–1:48:53). When we consider that the very beginning of the films shows us James Bond earning his double-O status by making his two mandatory kills — one for each O — we can deduce that his latest comeback is therefore more than ever depending on his determination, his courage and, of course, his 00s.

As to the number "7," it is plain to see that it is the only digit which looks like a stylized gun, and it naturally becomes the logical complement of the 00s. Any iconographic representation of James Bond includes a gun, traditionally pointed up, symbolizing both his strength and his virility which had to be magnified for the latest installment to date if we are to judge by the size of the machine gun Daniel Craig is holding up in some of the posters for *Quantum of Solace*. Of course, one could wonder why James Bond's section number is not directly 070 rather than 007; however, such disposition would prevent the pervasiveness of the double-O bit throughout the narration, in both the novels and the movies, and therefore would not allow the constant equivalence between Bond's section number and raw, alpha-male-grade courage and virility.

We are therefore able to establish a first series of meaningful correlations between the sign "James Bond 007" and the content of the narrative syntagm to which it refers: the biblically authoritative *James*, soldier of king and country, *bonds* the order back together thanks to his *00s* and his *gun*, and his function as well as his two major attributes are already semiotically included in his name and section number. The title of 007's very first adventure, *Casino Royale*, can be considered in itself as a perfect microstructure of the James Bond narrative syntagm, for it suggests its two fundamental semiotic domains: *Royale* designates the definitive order implied by the fossilized social hierarchy contained within the idea of royalty — the order James Bond is in charge of defending while *Casino* points to the danger and uncertainties which characterize gambling. "*Royale*" signifies Order, "*casino*" the possibility of Disorder, and James Bond appears as the natural link between both, being at the same time sanctified by the ruling order and constantly dealing with disorderly threats. It is not a coincidence that the very first appearance of James Bond onscreen in *Dr. No* shows the secret agent precisely playing — and, of course, winning — a game of baccarat. This correspondence between the notion of game and the eternal fight between Order and Disorder is concretized in the narration by the competition that traditionally opposes Bond to the villain previous to the final confrontation, and which has become somewhat of a Bond cliché; we find it represented in the novels, as in *Moonraker* and *Goldfinger*, which include, respectively, a game of cards and one of golf, and it has been systematized in the films under a variety of forms, from backgammon in *Octopussy* to fencing in *Die Another Day*. By winning a game of some sort against the villain, Bond demonstrates his ability to impose order, in parallel with his reliability as the essential bonding agent of World Order.

James Bomb

Beyond its direct connotative associations, the sign "Bond" also has the phonetic value of a detonation; although the last name "Bond" is unremarkable, almost common, and can even be found within the crew and cast involved in the Bond films (the animation credits of *Dr. No* and the title design of *From Russia with Love* are credited to Trevor Bond, while the role of Miss Moneypenny in the Brosnan installments is played by Samantha Bond), it acquires complementary meaning in this particular context for its sound — that of a detonation — which harmonizes the content of the syntagm. The closeness between the words "Bond" and "bomb" is indeed underlined by the narration itself in *Goldfinger* (novel) where Auric Goldfinger addresses 007 as "Mr. Bomb" on three separate occasions, forcing James Bond to actually spell out his last name for him: " [GOLDFINGER:] 'Will you be staying long, Mr. Bomb?' Bond smiled. 'It's Bond, B-O-N-D'" (40). The name of the hero thus acquires a second level of connotative meaning through this immediate and spontaneous phonetic opposition, more open and universal than that of the direct English linguistic associations mentioned above.

007's name bears traces of the explosive and hence is in direct semiotic relation to the narration itself, for the paradigm of the explosion is not only the logical conclusion of the narrative syntagm (i.e., the manner in which each adventure of James Bond is concluded), it is also a characteristic visual trademark of the filmic narration, often appearing as early as in the pre-credits opening sequence, as it does in *Goldfinger, The Man with the Golden Gun* and *Tomorrow Never Dies*. In some textual instances, the act of bombing can even signify the integrality of the typical Bond narration, as illustrated by the short story "Quantum of Solace," the object of which, far from being an adventure of James Bond, is an implicit dismissal of his occupation: After blowing up a couple of boats with thermite bombs, Bond is invited to the governor's mansion for an evening that he anticipates will be most uneventful and finds himself in actuality treated to a gripping story of conjugal betrayal and revenge. This leaves him perplexed about the intensity of his own occupation:

> Bond laughed. Suddenly the violent dramatics of his own life seemed very hollow. The affair of the Castro rebels and the burned out yachts was the stuff of an adventure-strip in a cheap newspaper.... He reflected on the conference he would be having in the morning with the Coastguards and the FBI in Miami. The prospect, which had previously interested, even excited him, was now edged with boredom and futility" (129).

The entire James Bond adventure is hence reduced to the bombing of two boats, barely a paragraph at the beginning of the story, which, just like the final explosion that characterizes the end of the typical narrative syntagm, is enough to suggest the entire mission. In "Quantum of Solace," the intensity of everyday life seems to defeat Bond's adventurous existence, which is contained within an undercover bombing, a simple prologue to a real story with real protagonists. More than ever, Bond appears to be nothing but a bomber.

Spectacular by nature, the narrative motif of the bomb is generously administered throughout every film, and it is not surprising to find it in the opening sequence of *GoldenEye*, the first installment of the Brosnan period, as Bond and Alec are setting bombs in a Russian facility (0:03:59–0:04:00). "For England, James," declares Alec emphatically — and not without irony, since he will turn out to be a traitor — implying by this very statement that the sacrosanct mission of the elite 00 section is indeed that of setting bombs. *GoldenEye* can be seen as a new start for the series which had been silent for six years following the somewhat disappointing last installment of the Moore period, *A View to a Kill*.[15] It is therefore significant that its first scene would precisely present 007 setting bombs. Besides being the first film with Brosnan as 007, *GoldenEye* also includes several important paradigmatic changes, for not only the Russians have become friendly, but M has changed sex; however, the bomb and its subsequent explosion remain very much at the core of the Bond universe.

The explosive quality of Bond's name naturally transcends the English language to acquire the value of an onomatopoeia for a vast international recipient. The phonetic association between "Bond" and "bomb" precedes by far that of Bond with a common English name, for it is most likely that the vast majority of foreign spectators will never be acquainted enough with the subtleties of English last names to recognize it as such. Internationally, the sign "Bond" is more of a detonation than a typical British name and fits the hero as perfectly as it does the narrative syntagm, just as the importance of Bond's 00s can be understood in function of the narration without much need of subtitles. The sign "James Bond 007" is thus loaded with semiotic markers which function in harmony with the content of the narration in a variety of languages, and which, when emphasized in the filmic adaptations, have contributed to its worldwide success.[16]

As the narration moved from text towards film, it was filtered by a variety of senders, and its most relevant structural components acquired greater importance. Whereas a literary author is perceived usually as one sender, sometimes two,[17] filmic authorship necessarily implies a fragmentation of the sending entity; from the director to the actors, from the music composer to the scriptwriter(s), from the prop master to the sponsors, the message is filtered by a long chain of subjectivities and must be perceived as the product of a collective rather than individual consciousness. The cinematic adaptation of a novel implies a more or less collective interpretation of the original text[18] and tends naturally to retain and emphasize the most collectively significant elements of the narrative universe. In the case of James Bond, when transposed to the screen, the narration shows a propensity to become exclusively a matter of explosions and 00s, for most attempts to complicate Bond's life on film — that is, to add some depth to his one-dimensional character — have been, until the very recent rebooting of the series, met with some resistance by the critics as well as the public at large. George Lazenby's and Timothy Dalton's tenures as 007, which presented radical changes in a Bond narration already simplified for cinematographic mass appeal, were indeed short-lived, the former lasting one single installment (*On Her Majesty's Secret Service*) and the later only two (*The Living Daylights* and *License to Kill*). By closely following the novel,

On Her Majesty's Secret Service (film) paradoxically strayed from an already established James Bond cinematographic formula and was considered a failure — to the extent that Sean Connery himself had to be recalled for the very next installment, *Diamonds Are Forever*, in order to quickly erase his would-be replacement's legacy. Besides introducing meta-fictitious elements to the narration, such as Lazenby turning towards the camera at the end of the opening sequence to assure the spectators that "this never happened to the other fellow" (0:06:30–0:06:33), or alluding to the previous installments of the series by playing fragments of their soundtracks (0:27:27–0:27:45), *On Her Majesty's Secret Service* (film) also concluded with Bond's defeat, for young Mrs. Bond is murdered by Blofeld's accomplice, Irma Blunt, while the Bonds are on their way to their honeymoon. Such variations from the usual Bond film pattern frustrated public expectations and proved downright counterproductive; the Bond universe as it has been structured by a collective sender for a collective recipient only admits a reduced amount of modernist narrative twists, such as meta-fictitious winks, and does not tolerate the possibility of Bond not being victorious at the end of the episode. By the time *On Her Majesty's Secret Service* (film) was released, the commercial Bond structure had already been firmly established upon the most primal elements of Ian Fleming's narrative universe, and it simply would not do to conclude the syntagm with James Bond 007 sobbing over the corpse of his wife, regardless of how close this particular ending was to Ian Fleming's original text. Limited to the immediate and most elementary connotations of the James Bond universe, the commercial narrative structure could only end with the celebration of Bond's courage and virility — that is, of his well-deserving 00s.

If *On Her Majesty's Secret Service* presented an unacceptable syntagmatic change, the alterations observed in *The Living Daylights* and *License to Kill* were more of a paradigmatic nature, for Timothy Dalton 007 simply appeared closer to the character in the novels — tougher and definitely more serious, again against the logics of the already independent narrative structure generated by the films. In other words, the complexities of Ian Fleming's character simply got in the way of James Bond 007's natural filmic evolution, as it had been structured independently of the original texts through the exchange between sender and recipient.

Although, as we saw, the textual Bond is all about courage and virility, he appears far more vulnerable than his filmic counterpart — to the point of crying like a child, as he does at the end of *Live and Let Die* (novel) when he sees Quarrel coming to rescue him: "The first tears since his childhood came into James Bond's blue-grey eyes and ran down his drawn cheeks into the bloodstained sea" (274). The filmic James Bond, on the other hand, appears more defined by his 00s and the explosions that he provokes than by his emotional depth; after all, crying did cost George Lazenby the job.

We can distinguish chronological markers in the EON series which do not only correspond to a change of actor but also to the spacing between productions. From 1963 to 1989, the James Bond films were produced usually every two years, sometimes three or two years in a row, and on two separate occasions, the same director was kept from one actor to the next: John Hamilton directed the last official installment with Sean Connery as 007 (*Diamonds Are Forever*) as well as the first two films featuring Roger Moore, and John Glen directed the last three Moore Bonds as well as the two installments of Dalton's short tenure. The transition from Connery to Lazenby to Connery again and then to Moore as 007 was fairly seamless, for the basic supporting cast — M, Miss Moneypenny and Q — remained the same. However, six years separate the last Moore film from the first installment with Brosnan as 007, and the last Brosnan feature is four years apart from the promising debut of Daniel Craig in the leading role, therefore each of these instances can be considered as a re-activation of the series, which includes important paradigmatic changes: *GoldenEye*, the first of the Brosnan Bonds, includes a female M and the last two installments of the series featuring Daniel Craig (*Casino Royale* and *Quantum of Solace*) have eliminated the characters of Miss Moneypenny and Q and introduced an African American as Felix Leiter. While the re-activation of the series featuring Brosnan as 007 attempted to add some complexity to the character and the plot by including an ongoing tension between 007 and MI6, the recent rebooting has accentuated said tension as well as removed some narrative staples, such as the usual visit to the Q branch and the final, sexually gratifying scene. However, Bond still triumphs at the end of the narration.

Taken into logical sequence, the novels of James Bond present the psychological degeneration of the character, a progression altogether ignored in the EON film series. After the murder of his wife in *On Her Majesty's Secret Service*, James Bond becomes a shadow of his former self, and if M assigns him yet one more mission in *You Only Live Twice*, it is following the advice of Sir James Molony, the "most prestigious neurologist in England," as a last attempt to cure Bond from the neurosis he has developed. In the words of Sir James Molony himself:

> He [Bond] admitted to me that all his zest had gone. That he wasn't interested in his job any more, or even in his life.... It's a form of psycho-neurosis, and it can grow slowly or suddenly. In your man's case, it was brought on out of the blue by an intolerable life-situation — or one

that he found intolerable because he had never encountered it before —
the loss of a loved one, aggravated in his case by the fact that he blamed
himself for her death.... But haven't you got something really sticky,
some apparently hopeless assignment you can give this man?... He's a
patriotic sort of a chap. Give him something that really matters to his
country [21].

By the end of *On Her Majesty's Secret Service*, Bond has thus become a sick man, unable to relate to reality, a rather delicate and vulnerable individual who seems unable to overcome his sentimental problems. M is ready to retire him to some obscure filing cabinet where former secret agents are left to die, and only Molony's expert advice convinces him otherwise. The following and last novel of the series, *The Man with the Golden Gun*, begins with more proof of 007's mental decay, for, after having being brainwashed by Colonel Boris from the KGB, James Bond attempts to assassinate M, who, in turn, once the "de-brainwashing" is complete, decides to send him on the ultimate suicidal mission: the elimination of top hit man, Paco Scaramanga:

> [M:] "After lunch, give me the file on Scaramanga. If we can get him fit again, that's the right-sized target for 007." The Chief of Staff protested, "But that's suicide, sir! Even 007 could never take him." M said coldly, "What would 007 get for this morning's bit of work? Twenty years? As a minimum, I'd say. Better for him to fall on the battlefield" [22].

Such ruthlessness is altogether absent from the somewhat tense but always human relationship between Bond and M we find in the films. As the narrative structure began to evolve by itself within the specific axis of communication of commercial cinema beyond the control of its original sender, Ian Fleming, some important paradigmatic and syntagmatic nuances introduced in the novels were erased, among which were the logical degeneration of Bond's psyche and the administrative priorities of a surprisingly cold M, in order to favor a more humanized narrative universe better suited for the taste of a wide-ranging public[19] and that emphasized James Bond's most characteristic features — that is, the power of his 00s and the explosive connotations of his name.

M, MI6 and the Motherland

M, the microstructure of MI6, and his direct extension, both physical and semiotic, Moneypenny, present a highly coherent relationship between their functions within the narrative syntagm and their very names. M, more than just a mere father figure, is also a metonymy for the Motherland and literally gives birth to the narration by charging Bond with a mission. Just as a penny is a metonymy for money (i.e., a part for the whole), Moneypenny is a metonymy of M and functions as a natural relay between M and Bond. M's office, located in the heart of London, in Regent's Park, is both the origin of the story and of James Bond 007, who represents and acts on behalf of queen and country. Indeed, the word "park" can be lexically associated with the country (countryside, going to the country), and the notion of royalty is naturally signified by the word "Regent." Even the name of the front for MI6, *Universal Exports*, semiotically complements the narrative syntagm, since it is by now a given that the main role of James Bond 007 is to export the values of Great Britain and the Western World throughout the rest of the planet.[20]

We find in the text of *Casino Royale* a perfect formal binary opposition between the unquestionable righteousness of M (that is, of the Motherland and its priorities) and the no less unquestionable wrongness of the enemy. After the SMERSH operative swiftly dispatches Le Chiffre, he carves a symbol on the back of Bond's right hand:

> "But I shall leave you my visiting-card…. The point of the stiletto executed three quick straight slashes. A fourth slash crossed them where they ended, just short of the knuckles. Blood in the shape of an inverted 'M' welled out and slowly started to drip on to the floor" [145].

The reference to gambling, as well as the inverted "M"—*Sh* in Cyrillic characters to signify *Shpion* ("spy" in Russian)—acquire thus a connotative function which parallels the entire syntagm of *Casino Royale* as well as the fundamental binary opposition at the heart of the Bond narrative conflict. It is, after all, always a question of the Motherland against the agents of Disorder in an endless game of life and death.[21]

At a very primal level, the bilabial nasal consonant "M" connotes the first articulated word by a young child, such as "mum" or "mom,"[22] and some aspects of the interaction between 007 and his superior can be reminiscent of that between a child and a parent/teacher figure. For instance, in *Goldfinger* (novel), Bond can barely contain a juvenile hilarity when charged to investigate Auric Goldfinger, as he has already started the very same mission on his own: " 'What's the matter?' M's voice was testy. 'What in hell is there to laugh about?' 'I'm sorry, sir.' Bond got hold of himself…. M was getting angry. 'What the hell's all this about? Stop behaving like a bloody schoolboy'" (68–9). The word "schoolboy," as well as M's tone of reprimand, suggest the hierarchy of a pupil and a headmaster, or that of a child and a parent. We find another example of this adult/boy relationship in *On Her Majesty's Secret Service*, when M invites Bond to his mansion for a Christmas dinner:

> M continued with his stories about the Navy which Bond could listen to all day — stories of battles, tornadoes, bizarre happenings, narrow shaves, courts martial, eccentric officers, neatly-worded signals.... Perhaps it was all just the stuff of boys' adventure books, but it was all true and it was about a great navy that was no more and a great breed of officers and seamen that would never be seen again [247].

This scene evokes the type of fascination the stories of a well traveled uncle would hold upon an imaginative nephew, a notion underlined by the use of the expression "boy's adventure books," which suggests a family-oriented hierarchical structure beyond the professional relationship between the leader of MI6 and his employee. Perhaps one of the most "motherly" moments of M is to be found at the beginning of *Thunderball* (novel) when, concerned about James Bond's general state of health, he orders him to undertake a cure at a health spa, Shrublands, after lecturing him about healthy eating and living habits. M addresses him as "James" rather than double–O seven, which tends to discourage Bond: "It was never a good sign when M addressed him by his Christian name instead of by his number. This didn't look like a job — more like something personal." The separation between "James" and "007" corresponds indeed to that between the administrative and the personal, and in this particular instance, M resembles more a motherly father than a direct superior.

But besides being a mother-like fatherly figure, the textual M is also a symbolic Master who holds the right of life and death over his private slaves, namely the 00 section, a characteristic which has been altogether ignored in the films. M is ready to send Bond to certain doom in order to resolve was appears to be a problem of reputation in *The Man with the Golden Gun*, and his nonchalance in doing so, similar to that of a master disposing of the lives of his subjects, prompts his own chief of staff to mutter, "You cold hearted bastard."[23] M's harsh attitude is justified in the novels by the burden of his responsibilities, and it is not uncommon to find entire chapters devoted to his brooding over Bond's next mission, weighing the pros and the cons of any possible action in a most administrative-like manner.

This bureaucratic heaviness disappears on the screen, as M is no longer a stern Master but only a would-be strict Mother who does not hold the same authority over James Bond as his/her textual counterpart. While the filmic M is still authoritative, he/she no longer represents the administrative rigidity of his office, and often appears as concerned with the security of his/her agent as he/she is with preserving World Order. In the narrative economy of the films, M yields to 007, who becomes more of an independent protagonist, allowing eventually for another level of tension to appear, that which opposes — albeit always provisionally — 007 to M.

The filmic Bond being in constant motion from film to film, we can observe an evolution in the relationship between Bond and M which never took place in the textual Bond. Whereas M in the novels remains a rigid, sometimes cold-hearted military type, the cinematographic M, portrayed right from the beginning as more human and understanding, has evolved considerably with the Brosnan period. Although the Moore Bond acted in a more detached, ironic manner with his superior than his Connery counterpart, and notwithstanding the occasional friction between both, the nature of their relationship with M did not change in any essential way during both actors' tenures. M remained within the stereotype of the righteous superior, sometimes gruff, but certainly never eager to send his favorite agent to slaughter, as he appears to be in the last two textual installments.

The gender shift introduced in the Brosnan series, which feature Judi Dench as M, is more than a simple paradigmatic substitution, for it alters drastically the relationship between Bond and his superior. Most likely due to production decisions destined to offset the recognized sexist content of the James Bond narrations in these times of political correctness, this change has paradoxically brought forward a new misogynistic dimension to the interaction between 007 and M, as Bond, living up to his 00s, adopts a much more contemptuous attitude towards his superior than his predecessors. M is, from now on, addressed as "M," in opposition to the traditional and respectful "sir," and seems on a constant defensive vis-à-vis Bond, who, in turn, as shown in the last installment of the Brosnan series, allows himself to reprimand her: "Maybe it's time you let me get on with my job" (1.00.18–1.00.21). We are indeed far from the bewildered boy-like textual Bond who could listen to the old man's tales forever. We do observe, however, that the boyishness is rescued in the Brosnan series through the relationship between Bond and Q, who must often call 007 to order, as the latter behaves like a disobedient pupil, picking up and trying out different pieces of equipment without authorization during his ritual visit to the Q branch workshop. Q's most well-known one-liners — "Please, be serious 007!"— is precisely a parent-like reprimand.

The disappearance of Q in the recent re-booting of the series has done away with a certain level of childishness in the Bond universe, as the narration had to adapt to the new, decidedly harder and more mature trends of modern action cinema which leave little room for silliness. However, the function of M as the Mother has never been so explicit, somewhat magnified by M's gender change, and appears directly in the dialogue of *Quantum of Solace*: As Camille, unknowingly referring to M, inquires if the person 007 is seeking to avenge is his mother, Bond responds, "She'd like to think so" (1:03:42–1:03:43). The fatherly aspects of the first filmic M have therefore been replaced by the motherly attitude of his female successor, and it comes as no surprise if the second line we hear from the brand new female M in the initial installment of the Brosnan's series, *GoldenEye*, as she appears behind the officer who is briefing Bond and who has just called her "the evil queen of numbers," refers to her family life: "If I want sarcasm ... I'll talk to my children, thank you very much" (0:36:27–0:36:31). The M from the novels was a confirmed bachelor, and the male filmic M never alluded to any type of life outside the office; She-M's very first statement is therefore connotatively significant of traditional gender markings that associate woman and family, and can be directly related to the aforementioned quote from *Quantum of Solace*. Living up to the connotations of her initial, M has officially become Bond's Mother.

The transition from novel to film, and the subsequent constant adaptations to new cinematographic trends, have altered (when not denaturized) some aspects of the original textual Bond while emphasizing its most semiotically significant elements: James Bond is more 00 than ever, and M is still the Motherland, for, regardless of the new level of conflict introduced during the Dalton period which opposes Bond to M and continues throughout the Brosnan and the Craig series, 007 still remains inseparable from his mother — that is, MI6 — which is the condition *sine qua non* for his existence. Unlike the stereotypical rebellious loose cannon but good guy of contemporary commercial cinema whose relationship with Order might be problematic, Bond not only defends the structures of the establishment but identifies with it — he may display his 00s with all their might but always in the name of M, MI6 and the Motherland.

There is, therefore, a linguistic *order* at the heart of the Bond narration when it comes to its most narratively significant elements, such as the protagonist's name or his section number, which enforces the coherence between form and content and contributes to the overall narrative authority of the fictitious universe. Beyond the paradigmatic level, we must now move into the analysis of the narrative syntagm to see how these elements are organized within the highly efficient Bond narrative structure.

Chapter 3

Positions and Oppositions

The Terms of the Conflict

Following the basic structure of most popular imaginary universes, the Bond narration organizes the main paradigms of the conflict in a series of simple binary oppositions, which tend to be, according to Eco, resolved in a Manichean manner: Bond embodies all that is Good, while his enemy is the epitome of Evil and presents no redeeming feature, neither moral nor physical.[1] Rather than conceiving the struggle between Bond and the Villain as the fundamental opposition between Order and Disorder, which, as we have seen, works in semiotic harmony with the form of the message since Bond is indeed the *bonding* agent of Order, Eco sees the minimal pair Bond/Villain as a representation of the opposition between *Eros* and *Thanatos*, which he identifies as the principles of pleasure and that of reality, respectively. Eco illustrates his view by analyzing the somewhat sado-masochistic relationship the Villain typically entertains with the Bond girl: Blofeld manipulates Domino, Mr. Big "owns" Solitaire, the Spangled Mob controls Tiffany, etc.[2] Notwithstanding the validity of such a remark, we must observe, however, that it displaces the basic terms of the narrative conflict, for it substitutes Bond with the Bond girl in opposition to the Villain, as if the Bond girl functioned as a mere metonymy of 007. If we can indeed consider any active element of the narration as a microstructural representation of the opposing forces upon which the conflict is established, this shift from Bond to the Bond girl tends to undermine the specific role of both characters within the economy of the narration, all the more so when we consider the evolution of the Bond girl on the screen.[3]

Eco enumerates fourteen binary oppositions — Bond/M, Bond Villain, Villain/Woman, Woman/Bond, Free World/Soviet Union, Great Britain/Non-Anglo-Saxon Countries, Duty/Sacrifice, Cupidity/Ideals, Love/Death, Chance/Planning, Luxury/Discomfort, Excess/Moderation,

Perversion/Innocence, and Loyalty/Disloyalty — which compose what he sees mainly as a narrative support to express a rather conservative ideology. Whereas some of the aforementioned oppositions appear quite valid, such as Woman/Bond, Loyalty/Disloyalty, and, of course, Bond/Villain, some others, such as Duty/Sacrifice and Love/Death, seem a tad arbitrary. Opposing Duty to Sacrifice, for instance, is problematic since both values belong to the same semantic field and one usually implies the other. Similarly, if the opposition between Love and Death is indeed diegetically relevant in some instances (*Casino Royale, On Her Majesty's Secret Service* and *Goldfinger*), it has a more reduced function in several novels (*From Russia with Love, You Only Live Twice* and *The Man with the Golden Gun*) and does not influence the narrative syntagm. As to the geo-politically defined oppositions — i.e., Free World/Soviet Union and Great Britain/Non-Anglo-Saxon Countries — historical and cultural changes have rendered them much less significant than they once were. The transition from text to screen has meant a much wider diffusion of the Bond universe among the "Non-Anglo-Saxon Countries," which coincided with a cultural pre-globalization period, and, naturally, the original political paradigms of the narration have been adapted to a new world consciousness.

Some of the oppositions pointed out by Eco, which might have been operative before Bond became more important than Fleming, and his adventures transcended time, geo-political configurations and primal ethnocentrism, are no longer as functional and can stand to be completed in accordance with the new limits of our object of study and its multi-mediatic nature.

Beyond the basic axis of the narrative structure presented earlier between Order and Disorder, which could be associated directly with the struggle between Bond and the Villain, and in addition to those listed by Eco, we can establish thirteen structurally significant oppositions that have met different fates as the narration moved from the text to the screen: M/W; Reality/Imagination; Paperwork/Action; Gentleman/Thug; Obedience/Independence; Secrecy/Disclosure (Anonymity/Naming); War/Love; Sexual frustration/Sexual satisfaction; Savior/Murderer; Bond/Bond (Bluntness/Emotion, Instrument/Man); Installment/Saga (open vs. closed structures); Realism/Credibility; and Defamiliarization/Over-Defamiliarization. Each of these oppositions represents an axis of conflict that sustains narrative authority at a specific level. The first two, and in the lesser measure, the third, concern the novels, while the remaining ten can be found in both the textual and the cinematographic Bonds, albeit not always given the same importance. Whereas most affect directly the narrative syntagm, others, such as Installment/Saga, Realism/Credibility and Defamiliarization/Over-Defamiliarization, affect the very peculiar relationship the Bond universe establishes with its recipient.

The Lost Oppositions

If some of the above-enunciated oppositions have become more semiotically relevant when the Bond narration has been transposed to the screen, some others have entirely disappeared, mostly due (albeit not always) to the specificities of the medium. As the Bond universe turns more into a commodity in terms of public reception through the cinematic adaptations of the novels, its narrative structure tends to become more commercialized — that is, less problematic in terms of content. However, such simplification is only related to the change of medium in a superficial manner, and the cinematographic adaptation of any written narration does not necessarily imply a betrayal of the original intent; on the contrary, it can be perceived as a possible interpretation of the text, susceptible to produce itself a new array of connotations and to be as aesthetically convincing and as semiotically coherent as its literary counterpart. In some cases it might even surpass the model, as shown, for instance, by Roman Polansky's adaptation of Spanish author Arturo Pérez Reverte's novel *El Club Dumas, The Ninth Gate*, or by Mary Harron's cinematographic version of Brett Easton Ellis' *American Psycho*[4]; therefore, the intrinsic properties of the medium have little to do with the overall cultural quality of the project, however this value may be defined. A cinematic adaptation can be conceived as a semiotic translation based upon a specific interpretation, and its signification depends more upon the validity of said interpretation than upon the particularities of the medium itself.

In some instances the cinematographic Bond universe appears to have become almost schematic, and this is especially true when considering some installments of Roger Moore's tenure, which exhibited so many overly self-conscious elements that they threatened to become their own caricatures.[5] However, this tendency was not due to the specific qualities of the medium as much to the commercial priorities of the producers: The character of James Bond belonging to popular literature, its cinematographic adaptations were necessarily conceived as commercial cinema, and hence their content was altered in function of a wider, less discriminate recipient. As a result, some meaningful binary oppositions present in the novels were lost in the films, due sometimes to medium-oriented practical reasons but also frequently to the interpretive choices of the producers.

Such is the case for one particularly symbolic opposition present in

Casino Royale, which has been eliminated from its recent filmic adaptation in spite of its high semiotic value as a microstructural metonymy — namely, the above mentioned "W" that the agent of SMERSH carves on the back of Bond's hand after he eliminates Le Chiffre. This narrative paradigm symbolizes perfectly the underlining axis of conflict between Order and Disorder, M and the World, which is at the root of any James Bond story, and the choice of discarding it from the film is not due to the technical difficulty of translating it into visual communication but rather has more to do with the producers overlooking its importance. By now the reading of the textual Bond is most likely preceded, and therefore influenced, by its filmic counterpart, and thus the semiotic importance of its intricacies becomes naturally increasingly elusive, especially to a collective entity such as a Bond film production team.

Similarly, the tension between action and paperwork, present at the beginning of several novels, such as *Moonraker* and *Thunderball*, has been all but omitted in the filmic Bond. We might recall M vaguely threatening Bond with boring desk activities at the beginning of *Dr. No* (film) in order to convince him to trade his Beretta for a Walther PPK — M: "You'll carry the Walther. Unless, of course, you'd prefer to go back to standard intelligence duties." BOND: "No, sir, I would not" (0.13.02–0.13.07). Nevertheless, this simple allusion and its immediate dismissal are about as close as the filmic 007 will ever get to doing office work. This first level of simple defamiliarization, for MI6 paperwork remains a special kind of paperwork that might produce some type of narrative authority within the confines of a highly credible environment, was replaced in the films until the last rebooting of the series, with the staple scene in which 007 is receiving sexual gratification, thus creating a new opposition (one perhaps more convincing than Eco's Duty/Sacrifice) — that of Pleasure/Duty, which can also be formulated as Pleasure/Action, for sexual entertainment has replaced the much more tedious tasks of paperwork. Structurally, both oppositions, Paperwork/Action and its filmic equivalent, Leisurely Sexual Activity/Action, function very much in the same manner: They both oppose predictable everyday life to the unpredictability of the adventure and prepare the irruption of the crisis within a balanced order, favoring the dynamics of the narration and thus contributing to establish narrative authority. What has been lost in translation, however, is the realistic dimension suggested by the original opposition, Paperwork/Action, which adds credibility to the narrative universe by introducing a down-to-earth note without exactly surrendering textual authority, since that type of paperwork (the secret kind) is susceptible to produce a certain level of defamiliarization by itself. The substitution of the tedious sides of any government job —

even in the secret branch — with non-committal sex with a stranger takes one more step towards the construction of James Bond beyond Ian Fleming, as the popular myth begins structuring itself independently of its original sender. We can no longer conceive of James Bond sitting at a desk doing paperwork and answering the phone, for the disciplined government employee from the text has given way to the flamboyant ladykiller who waits for his next mission by having sex with some anonymous young woman rather than filling out official forms for Her Majesty's Secret Service. In the narrative balance of the novels, the presence of paperwork and Bond's distaste for it creates a tension between the uneventful and the eventful; the boredom suggested by paperwork duties accentuates the contrast between the routine (essentially boring) and the adventurous (essentially entertaining). One can muse that when the text was created — that is, when the initial connection between the sender, Ian Fleming, and the receiver, his public, was established — having sex with anonymous young women was not exactly considered to be a routine activity, and therefore such a paradigm could not be used in order to suggest some type of everyday life activity. Although our perception of sexual activity has changed considerably, having casual sex is still a far cry from filling out official documents, even secret ones; therefore the original dynamics based on the tension between the two contradicting aspects of the secret agent's occupation disappear in order to favor a more spectacular, perhaps less aesthetically convincing but more satisfying opposition between casual sex (pleasure) and action (duty). Furthermore, the original tension between paperwork and action included a more fundamental, purely spatial opposition, especially significant when we consider that along with characters and conflict, the setting is among the three most basic elements of any narration.[6] When confined to administrative duties, James Bond is also confined spatially, for he only evolves in a strictly localized setting — namely, his office, with all the connotations of uninteresting mediocrity that the word implies. As soon as he is given a mission (that is, when the main conflict begins), 007 is on the move, and this change of setting greatly contributes to establishing and maintaining narrative authority — if for nothing else because it introduces an elementary level of spatial defamiliarization at the heart of the action by playing the exotic against the dull.

At a deeper level, the distaste of the textual James Bond for the administrative obligations that come with his profession point to some type of existential angst, for Bond does not really feel alive unless he is on a mission during which he may very well be killed (the members of the 00 section have indeed a short life expectancy) and must therefore implicate himself totally in a struggle, both moral and physical, which falls within the parameters of the Sartrian *engagement*.⁷ There is little chance that the cinematic James Bond of the last quarter of the 20th century could convey any trace of existential angst, and especially not regarding his usual activities in between missions, for casual sex is usually not as conducive to existential considerations as tedious paperwork might be. Consequently, an important aspect of the character's consciousness has been obliterated when adapted to the screen. We can observe that the initial scene of James Bond having sex before being contacted by MI6 to be given a mission has been dropped from the recent rebooting of the series and replaced by his first two kills in *Casino Royale* (that which precisely confers him the status of 00), and by a violent car chase in *Quantum of Solace*. In order to modernize the James Bond narration and to bring it up to the level of 21st century "serious" action cinema, the opposition between casual sex and action, which can be seen structurally as a spectacularized perversion of the original opposition Paperwork/Action, has been substituted with the most basic binary opposition of the narrative syntagm, that which opposes Bond to the Villain, and is represented by two of its most primal narrative motifs: murder and chase.

A related opposition, Reality/Imagination, has also disappeared from the cinematographic Bond, due in part to the semiotic specificities of the cinematographic language, which obviously does not allow the representation of inner thoughts as conveniently as textual narration; consequently, another important dimension, that of imaginative depth, has been all but eliminated from the narration. Unlike the hyperactive and overly self-assured cinematic James Bond, the textual 007 has an inner life of thoughts, doubts and desires, even if they are naturally inhibited by action.⁸ For instance, the short story "007 in New York" consists entirely of James Bond imagining what he will do once his brief mission — establishing contact with a former MI6 operative in New York — is completed, from going to the restaurant to purchasing some goods. His inner monologue reveals a complementary side to his psyche, which we naturally oppose to his duty-oriented, pragmatic mind; there is no direct usefulness in Bond's preoccupations, and thus he escapes the limits of his alleged definition as a "blunt instrument" at the service of the government. The conclusion of "007 in New York" is a perfect narrative representation of the opposition between reality and imagination, as the former imposes itself upon the latter, and reality (that is, the mission) literally dissolves imagination:

> After the scrambled eggs in the Edwardian Room, everything went hopelessly wrong, and, instead of the dream programme, there had to be urgent and embarrassing telephone calls with London headquarters, and then only by the greatest of good luck, an untidy meeting at mid-

night beside the skating rink at Rockefeller Center with tears and threats of suicide from the English girl [131].

Bond does not achieve any of the goals to which he had been looking forward because he fails to establish the routine contact that justifies his presence in New York in the first place and spends the entirety of his stay attempting to compensate for a simple — and somewhat silly — topographic blunder: the meeting was supposed to takes place at the Reptile House at the Central Park Zoo; however, "One can hardly credit the deficiency, but there is no Reptile House at the Central Park Zoo" (131). The entire narrative syntagm is therefore based upon the opposition Reality/Imagination, with the ever-present conflict between Order and Disorder as a narrative frame, for 007 is in New York on a mission, specifically to inform an ex–MI6 agent that she is co-habitating with a Soviet KGB spy, and that both the FBI and the CIA are close to identifying her.

Similarly, in "From a View to a Kill," as Bond waits for his contact, sitting at a café in Paris, he muses about seducing a woman and imagines what may ensue:

> He [Bond] would somehow find himself a girl who was a real girl, and he would take her to dinner at some make-believe place in the Bois like the Armenonville.... He would say to her: "I propose to call you Donatienne, or possibly Solange, because these are names that suit my mood and the evening. We knew each other before and you lent me this money because I was in a jam. Here it is, and now we will tell each other what we have been doing since we last met in St. Tropez just a year ago." And there they would be, started on the myth of "Paris in the Spring." And, by God, by the end of the evening it would not be his fault if it transpired that there was in fact no shred of stuffing left in the hoary old fairytale of "A good time in Paris."
> Sitting in Fouquet's, waiting for his Americano, Bond smiled at his vehemence. He knew that he was only playing at this fantasy.... Since 1945, he had not had a happy day in Paris [7–8].

This elaborate projection reveals Bond's capacity for imagination, as does the conclusion of "The Living Daylights" (short story), in which Bond lives out a romance in his mind that might even cost him his 00 status:

> Bond got up. He suddenly didn't want to leave the stinking little smashed-up flat, leave the place from which, for three days, he had had this long-range, onesided romance with an unknown girl — an unknown enemy agent with much the same job in her outfit as he had in his. Poor little bitch! She would be in worse trouble now than he was! She'd certainly be court-martialed for muffing this job. Probably be kicked out of the KGB. He shrugged. At least they'd stop short of

killing her—as he himself had done. James Bond said wearily, "Okay. With any luck it'll cost me my Double-O number. But tell Head of Station not to worry. That girl won't do any more sniping. Probably lost her left hand. Certainly broke her nerve for that kind of work. Scared the living daylights out of her. In my book, that was enough. Let's go" [117].

The imaginary dimension of Bond represents a departure from the psychological profile that we traditionally associate with an action hero, and it has naturally disappeared on the screen. Although the above scene was recycled at the beginning of the eponymous film, as Bond protects the escape of a Russian asset by disarming a sniper, neither the brisk dialogues with his partner, nor his apparent nonchalance when informed that his unprofessional attitude will be reported, are able to translate the imaginary dimension found in the original short story. The opposition between reality and imagination corresponds roughly to the genesis of the narrative syntagm, for reality is what precedes the mission, and imagination is the development of said mission. At a higher level of semiotic coherence, any adventure of James Bond corresponds to a triumph of imagination over reality, as long as it takes place within a coherent, pseudo-realistic universe.

Driven by spectacular and commercial priorities, most cinematic adaptations of the James Bond novels have done away with the subtle binary opposition that pointed to a possible psychological complexity in the protagonist in order to concentrate upon more direct, primal oppositions. These primal oppositions are essential to the narrative universe of James Bond and much easier to develop and promote, including that of Sexual Frustration/Gratification, which has become arguably the second most fundamental opposition at the base of the James Bond universe and one of its strongest narrative trademarks, demonstrating once again, as if there were any need, that sex is more appealing than existentialism.

Sex, Thugs and Gentlemen

Starting with the titillating movie poster, we are assured that the narration will procure vicarious sexual gratification, and the character of Bond has incarnated until very recently the archetype of the sexually irresistible male who consumes women without any emotional investment. Only since the rebooting of the series have we witnessed a return to a more emotional Bond, who has lost most of his charming arrogance and who is actually capable of falling in love: *Casino Royale* (movie, 2006) and, in a lesser measure, *Quantum of Solace* create a new interpretation of the textual Bond, based upon his least balanced and perhaps darkest elements, which can remind us of the character as interpreted by George Lazenby in the doomed adaptation of *On Her Majesty's Secret Service*, and by Timothy Dalton in the less than successful *The Living Daylights* and *Licence to Kill*, both allegedly closer to the novels than their predecessors. A more one-dimensional Bond was elaborated during the Connery, Moore and Brosnan periods, and this simplification turned the sexual tension of the novels into a simple operation of almost direct gratification. In the novels, contrary to common belief, Bond does not always get the girl, the most notable example being *Moonraker*; and when he does, he usually has to work at it. Whereas in the films, with the notable exception of *On Her Majesty's Secret Service* and the two latest installments which reboot the series, Bond does not crave a woman for very long, in the novels, desire is not as easily satisfied, and separation can actually cause anxiety. The opposition between sexual frustration and its satisfaction has evolved into uncommitted sexual desire versus its immediate satisfaction, and we must deduce that the traditional cinematic Bond thrives upon the sexual frustrations of the recipient, displacing the tension from within the message towards the addressee and emphasizing the cathartic effect over artistic expression.

In the novels, sexual desire produces an underlining narrative tension which is all but eliminated in the films by the logics of the narrative syntagm: It is a given that Bond will seduce the girl(s) and have sex with her, since this is what he does in his spare time. Without establishing any inter-narrative connections, and supposing that we were only to see one Bond movie of the traditional type,[9] we would be exposed to his sexual feats before he even enters the main narrative syntagm. As shown earlier, sex is presented with a grittier tone in the novels, in direct relationship with the consequences of the frustration produced by social rules; and the adventures of the textual James Bond are also those of a sexually liberated individual attempting to fight frustration against social conventions.

Eco sets aside *The Spy Who Loved Me* from his analysis, finding the novel "atypical" and therefore unfit for his structural breakdown. However, the narrative conflict of *The Spy Who Loved Me*, if indeed quite different from that of any other James Bond novel, is based upon the same opposition between desire and fulfillment that we find pervasively represented in the rest of the novels; Vivienne Michel openly expresses her sexual needs and desires, and pays the price of social exclusion for it. Unlike Bond, who, as a man and a government employee specializing in clandestine operations, can indulge in satisfying his sexual drives without consequences, Vivienne has to pay the price for her defiance of social conventions. If both, Bond and Vivienne, exist somewhat on the fringes of society, the agent benefits from his gender as well as from the attributes of his morally legitimized occupation, while Vivienne is utterly isolated by social conventions. Beyond these major but mainly contextual differences, Vivienne could be seen as a double of James Bond in the development of an understated but constant binary opposition present in all the novels, i.e., sexual frustration versus sexual gratification, which is represented by the simplified, albeit pervasive opposition between desire and immediate gratification in the films. *The Spy Who Loved Me* (novel) thus simply presents a reversal of narrative priorities, as the vague but constant theme of sexual frustration/satisfaction, which usually disappears behind the main conflict that opposes Order to Disorder, and consequently Bond to the Villain in the rest of the novels, becomes here the central axis of narration. Rather than merely "atypical," *The Spy Who Loved Me* is structurally and thematically complementary to the other adventures of James Bond, for it expands upon a paradigm that is inherent in the James Bond universe, and probably one of its most significant — that of the constant opposition between sexual desire and sexual satisfaction.

The explicit promotion of the protagonist's sexual instinct in the James Bond universe, justified both narratively and morally by the precariousness of his occupation, which forces him to react mostly on a reptilian level, can be related to a peculiar treatment in the Bond universe of an otherwise common binary opposition — that of Thug versus Gentleman, which should be distinguished from that of Bond/Villain. The sexual behavior of James Bond does not correspond to standard morality, and the way he treats women is not exactly that of a gentleman. Although popular narrations usually establish a direct correspondence between the moral value of a character and his appearance and demeanor (i.e., the Villain is ugly and rude, while the Hero is handsome and polite), the James Bond narration accepts a certain amount of latency between the form and the content of the characters. Consequently, neither the Hero nor the Villains respond necessarily to the typical characteristics of stock book protagonists and antagonists. Eco rightfully remarks that the Villain tends to exhibit some type of physical flaw, thus following the laws of popular narration; however, if this is undeniable for most of the novels — while not necessarily for all the short stories — it no longer applies when it comes to the majority of the films, as the terms of the opposition Thug/Gentleman have become rather fluid. Over the years, the Thug has turned into an elegant and well-spoken fellow, such as Scaramanga of *The Man with the Golden Gun* (film), whose propensity towards sophisticated living and fine cuisine makes us quickly forget the existence of his ever discrete third nipple, or as Zorin from *A View to a Kill* (film), whose lifestyle and attitude are decidedly aristocratic, stables and castles included. There is such a thing as a stereotypical Bond Villain, who does not correspond to the typical antagonist of most popular narrations: a well-educated, elegant and cold-blooded gentleman, vaguely reminiscent of a Nazi officer, and whose only remaining physical handicap might be his foreign accent.

In the novels, the opposition Thug/Gentleman appears more clearly defined along character lines — without excluding, however, a certain amount of latency. In spite of their efforts to appear distinguished, Drax, Goldfinger and Blofeld are not gentlemen, and their demeanor does not correspond to British propriety. It is, for instance, highly significant that both Drax and Goldfinger cheat at gentlemen games, such as bridge and golf, defying the proverbial fair play associated with well-bred English company. Drax and Goldfinger are essentially not English, which means that they cannot be real gentlemen, a characteristic implicitly pointed out by Eco in his typology, and explicitly by Chapman, who emphasizes the importance of James Bond's "Britishness" as one of his most distinctive features, both politically and narratively. However, it can also be observed that when his turn comes, James Bond himself cheats heartily, behaving therefore in the same manner as his opponent. He does not lose his "Britishness" in doing so, for his actions are morally justified; still, the line between what is morally acceptable and what is not — that is, between the Gentleman and the Thug — appears suddenly less clear-cut.

The character of James Bond has the tendency to internalize the binary opposition between thug and gentleman, for he is either, according to the circumstances. This ambivalence is rendered necessary by his very occupation, which consists mainly of pretending to be someone he is not. And so, in *The Man with the Golden Gun*, he reacts very much as any of the thugs with whom he is having dinner when he accepts a challenge that is anything but gentleman-like:

> Scaramanga looked up at him [Bond] under lizard eyelids. "No. If you figure the evening's not going so good, make it go better. That's what you're being paid for. You act as if you know Jamaica. Okay. Get those people off the pad."...
>
> It was many years since James Bond had accepted a dare. He felt the eyes of The Group on him. What he had drunk had made him careless — perhaps wanting to show off, like the man at the party who insists on playing the drums. Stupidly, he wanted to assert his personality over this bunch of tough guys who rated him insignificant. He didn't stop to think that it was bad tactics, that he would be better off being the ineffectual limey [117].

The way Bond resolves the situation is by shooting off a fake pineapple that the singer is wearing as a headdress, creating a commotion in the dining room and terrifying the girl, whom he compensates by slipping a hundred dollar bill in her cleavage, a behavior more typical of a low-class gangster than of a gentleman.

When transposed to the screen, the terms of the opposition Gentleman/Thug have become more fluid yet, as the gentleman is constantly forced to behave like a thug, and the thug insists on appearing like a gentleman. The Brosnan period accentuated this trend, which culminates in the figure of the Villain from *Die Another Day*—young tycoon Graves, who appears just as English and well-bred as any member of Blades could be, in spite of his more than murky origin. In a particularly enlightening scene, Bond and Graves have a ferocious swordfight in a very posh London fencing club—incidentally, also called Blades. Both behave like thugs, albeit among gentlemen and in a classy environment, being therefore thugs and gentlemen at the same time (0:54:25–0:56:25). In this particular instance, the basic binary opposition between Bond and the Villain is more balanced, if overly simplified, than ever and can therefore effortlessly sustain the narrative conflict. Graves is to be seen as an evil double of James Bond—just as daring and successful, and as much of a thug and a gentleman as Bond himself. We will, of course, discover at the end that Graves, very much like Drax from the novel *Moonraker*, is not a "real" Englishman; nonetheless, within the economy of the narration and until its conclusion, his character does act and function as one, providing the perfect term of opposition to the character of Bond.

With the exception of Renard from *The World Is Not Enough*, who suffers from a disturbing physical condition—a bullet on its way to the center of his brain has numbed his senses—and whose appearance is equally disquieting, the Villains from the Brosnan period are more like gentlemen than thugs. In the Bond universe as it has evolved on the screen, Good and Evil are no longer directly related to external appearance and demeanor, and good breeding is no longer a guarantee of moral integrity. After all, not only is Alec, the traitor from the first installment of the Brosnan series, *GoldenEye*, just as English and well-mannered as Bond, but he is also a 00; and, just as Bond himself, he is as treacherous and ruthless as any dedicated thug. In this particular instance, the films have transcended the primary physical opposition between the Hero and the Villain as described by Eco, which attribute some type of deformity or handicap to the latter and follow the traditional rules of stock figures that allow for binary oppositions to be articulated in simple terms of form and content. This transgression of the common popular association between physical appearance and moral make-up is already present in the novels on the side of the protagonist, for Bond does not correspond exactly to the traditional good-looking hero of popular culture, mainly due to the scar on his cheek and the occasional cruelty of his smile; the antagonists, however, do follow the tradition and tend to exhibit some type of physical characteristic that makes them naturally unattractive. This is not always true in the films: Zorin, Alec, Carver, Graves and Greene appear normal, while Scaramanga, Goldfinger and Blofeld (when played by Savallas and Gray) remain within acceptable parameters of physical appearance, if only slightly creepy.

Nevertheless, and along the lines of Eco's typology, the Bond narration seems unable to shake a certain ethnocentric if not racist tone, even though the latter has been somewhat displaced throughout the films towards secondary characters and apparently inconspicuous scenes. The Great Britain/Non-Anglo-Saxon opposition pointed out by Eco, which is often resolved into a White/Non-White conflict, is indeed present in the Bond narrative syntagm. Nonetheless, it functions in a less systematic manner than that suggested by Eco, for in spite of his quasi-ontological "Britishness," Bond is perfectly able to have sexual encounters with non–Anglo-Saxon and even non–White females: Tatiana Romanova (*From Russia with Love*, novel and film), Anya Amasova (*The Spy Who Loved Me*, film) and Pola Ivanova (*A View to a Kill*, film) are Russian; Rosie Carver (*Live and Let Die*, film), May Day (*A View to a Kill*) and Jinx (*Die Another Day*) are African-American; Kissy Suzuki (*You Only Live Twice*, novel and film) is Japanese; and Wai Lin (*Tomorrow Never Dies*, film) is Chinese. Although neither Rosie Carver nor May Day can be deemed to be designated "Bond girls," since they yield to a White, Anglo-Saxon female as the narration progresses, Kissy Suzuki and Jinx do represent the main sexual interest of James Bond in their respective installments. While the underlying ideology of the narrative structure might exhibit ethnocentric tendencies, the sex is anything but racist.

Over the years the representation of cultural and/or race conflict in the James Bond universe has become more nuanced, so as to maintain the ever-so-delicate balance between the naturally ethnocentric values purported by a fairly rigid narrative structure on the one hand and the evolution of social perception on the other. This subtle negotiation between the ideology inherent in the Bond universe and its adaptation to a more politically correct receiver often results in ambiguous or even contradictory messages. In *Octopussy* (film), Bond's ally, Vijay Amritraj is Hindu; nevertheless, his loyalty towards the cause of Bond and MI6 (that is, the Free World) help us quickly forget that he is not British and not quite white. However, he will be murdered by other Hindus, and in a particularly gruesome manner, for he is gutted with a flying circular saw while Bond and Octopussy lay in bed — which is to say that the non-white allies are expendable, while the white protagonists are invulnerable, a typical scheme that echoes the death of Cayman native and Bond's ally, Quarrel, in *Dr. No* (novel and film). In *The Man with the Golden Gun* (film), James Bond is saved by Lt. Hip and his two Kung-Fu expert nieces who allow him to escape from the dojo of Scaramanga's associate, Hai Fat, hence raising the positive cultural value of a non–English, non–White race (0:54:45– 0:55:30). However, when Bond's boat stalls as he flees through the Bangkok canals, Bond, in exchange for 20,000 baths, accepts the help of a Thai child who is attempting to sell a small wooden elephant to the cruise tourists. But Bond throws the child back in the water without paying him as soon as the engine starts again, as if he were disposing of superfluous equipment (0:57:49–0:58:02). Bond has indeed lied to the child all along, since, still clad in kimono, he obviously has no money. This scene exhibits an undeniable complacency towards the notion of child labor related to inferior racial markings, for it is supposed to be a moment of comic relief based upon a lack of identification with the victim: the recipient is supposed to identify with 007, and the narrative function of the surprised look on the child's face as he emerges from the water, still demanding his 20,000 baths, is one of tension release, for the boat has started again and Bond can continue his escape from the Villain's henchmen. Clearly this particular scene was never meant as an invitation to reflect upon the very serious issue of child labor in developing countries.

The first installment of the series' recent rebooting, *Casino Royale*, played extremely delicately with the race opposition by constantly administering contradictory elements within the narrative syntagm. James Bond's first two kills, which confer upon him the 00 status, are perpetrated on white men; however, we soon find him spreading havoc through the Nambutu embassy, the diplomatic headquarters of a fictional African country, before killing his target, who happens to be a black terrorist. Similarly, although the official Villain, Le Chiffre, is white, albeit not Anglo-Saxon, most of the other antagonists are of the Mediterranean type, when not black. One of the bloodiest scenes in the film has Bond battling two members of the African guerrilla group who have entrusted Le Chiffre with their money; and after a relentless fight, Bond properly executes the chief of the guerrillas by strangling him with Vesper's help (1:17:37–1:18:04). The racist undertone of this particular episode is emphasized by the ferocity of the African guerrillas, symbolized by their predilection for the machete to torture their victims, as well as by the secondary importance they occupy in the economy of the narration. This particular faction does not appear in the original novel and is not fundamental to the conflict but rather represents a diegetic digression, which on the other hand functions coherently within the rules of the James Bond narration. As if to offset this quasi-explicit racist message, Felix Leiter is portrayed by a black actor, allowing the narration to achieve an almost perfect balance between the ethnocentric tendencies inherent in the James Bond universe and a contemporary politically-correct sensitivity.

A female M or a black Felix Leiter do not exactly prevent the Bond narration from conveying a certain political incorrectness, either sexual or racial, but rather offsets the strength of the original message by diluting its apparent traditional white male ideology into a certain ambiguity, well illustrated by the relationship between Bond and the different female characters in the latest installment to date, *Quantum of Solace*. Whereas, agent Fields, the MI6 agent from the embassy in La Paz who has been ordered by She-M to send Bond back to London, acts in a stern, severe manner, but spontaneously succumbs to 007's charm with little or no preambles, Camille, the main female protagonist, is strong and independent and does not have a sexual relationship with Bond; however, Bond saves her life several times throughout the film, emerging once again as the promoter of certain patriarchal values — even though he does not possess her, a unique fate for a cinematic Bond girl. As to the female Canadian agent that Yusef Kabira has seduced and that Bond confronts at the end of the film, she appears passive and defenseless, and is quickly dismissed as an insignificant pawn. The authoritarian presence of M in the very last sequence of the film reestablishes some type of balance between the sexes, although it should be pointed out that it is Bond who has the last words, and that his final reply — "I never left" (1.37.07) — tends to indicate that M, who has just pleaded for him to come back, had it wrong all along.

The James Bond universe is hence capable of accommodating somewhat contradictory cultural, racial and sexual paradigms by allowing a great level of latency in the terms of its most basic binary opposition without, however, altering its narrative integrity.

Dual Bond

The radical distinctions established by Eco between Bond and the Villain or Great Britain and Non-Anglo-Saxon countries, if essentially valid, are not as clear-cut as they appear. And if the Villains indeed tend to exhibit a physical anomaly, then again, so does Felix Leiter, Bond's long-time ally from the CIA, after his encounter with the shark in *Live and Let Die* (novel), which costs him literally an arm and a leg, and whose prostheses, when he reappears in subsequent novels, could remind us of Dr. No's artificial hands. The same can be said regarding John Strangways, the MI6 chief agent in the Caribbean (*Live and Let Die*, novel, and *Dr. No*, novel), who wears an eye-patch, a characteristic that we can relate to Le Chiffre's dysfunction of the lachrymal conduct, which causes him to shed tears from one eye (*Casino Royale*, film, 2007). Bond himself is not a typecast hero, and the scar on his cheek, as well as his cruel smile, set him apart from the traditional protagonist of escapist narrations. His body is covered with the traces of his profession — to the point of surprising health professionals, as shown in *Thunderball* (novel): "Mr. Wain asked Bond to remove all his clothes except his shorts. When he saw the many scars he said politely, 'Dear me, you do seem to have been in the wars, Mr. Bond'" (18). The scar on Bond's cheek is to be opposed to his otherwise good looks, an opposition well defined in the following lucid self-evaluation:

> He [Bond] paused for a moment and examined himself levelly in the mirror. His grey-blue eyes looked calmly back with a hint of ironical inquiry. With the thin vertical scar down his right cheek the general effect was faintly piratical. Not much of Hoagy Carmichael there, thought Bond, as he filled a flat, light gunmetal box with fifty of the Morland cigarettes with the triple gold band [*Casino Royale* 58].

If the screen adaptations seemed to have soften Bond's physical traits, they have not tempered his propensity to behave like an aggressive thug. Quite to the contrary, the spectacular priorities of the films have exacerbated his aptitude for ultra-violent behavior; and so 007 breaks more cars and kills more people, and appears more as both a savior and a murderer on the screen than he does in the novels. In *Tomorrow Never Dies* he coldly executes Dr. Kaufman, the assassin that Carver has sent to dispose of him and of his own wife, Mrs. Paris. The henchman pleads for his life, arguing that he is a "professional," and Bond answers that so is he before shooting him in the head at point blank range, demonstrating his ability to behave exactly as a villain would (0:56:18–0:56:27). This scene is a perfect illustration of the interchangeability of moral traits between protagonist (Bond) and antagonist (Dr. Kaufman), for both act in identical ways when confronted with the same situation. The dialogue underlines this ambivalence: Both are "professionals"— that is, executioners at the order of their respective masters, M and Carver — who are willing to carry out their orders without any type of ethical dilemma. Kaufman is about to shoot Bond in cold blood when 007 succeeds in distracting his attention and finds himself in the exact position as his enemy a few seconds before; he then takes full advantage of the situation without any scruples. Contrary to most popular heroes, James Bond is neither generous nor forgiving, and his defects are perhaps his most attaching features, for they establish a constant contrast within the character himself. Bond can afford to be as morally suspicious as the villains that he defeats, for, yet again, he is the messenger of the sacrosanct Order.

The character of James Bond thus embodies several of the fundamental binary oppositions that structure the entire narration: he is both a Gentleman and a Thug, as well as a Savior and an Assassin, and the basic oppositions at the core of the narration — Obedience/Independence, Secrecy/Disclosure, War/Love — revolve around him. James Bond is bound to the service, but, as we observed earlier, his relationship with M and with duty are more problematic than those of a "blunt instrument." Narratively, Bond's profession justifies his independence, since a secret agent is by definition supposed to be on his own during his mission, and as paperwork disappeared from the narrative universe during the transition from text to cinema, the mission itself began to cover nearly the entire narrative syntagm. As a result, Bond became increasingly independent. Besides the traditional meeting with M, which, during the Moore period, tended to exhibit some unmistakable signs of ironic distance on the part of 007, the cinematic Bond has little to do with the administrative side of his profession and therefore eludes the chain of command. Bond is at the service of Her Majesty, but he becomes his own superior once engaged in his mission and can even disobey direct orders, which can lead, as we saw earlier, to serious tensions with M. Nonetheless, he never permanently severs his ties with the service, for in order to fulfill his narrative function, James Bond must be both dependent and independent, just as he is simultaneously a thug and a gentleman.

James Bond incarnates, as well, the tension between Secrecy and Disclosure that is constantly at play in any secret agent adventure, albeit in a paradoxical manner, for 007's covers tend to disappear sooner than later behind the protagonist, especially in the films. The facility with which James Bond's cover is blown should be of some concern to any self-respecting secret intelligence agency, for it would tend to indicate that their intelligence is no longer secret. However, in order to function properly as the ultimate bonding paradigm, James Bond must be James Bond, and cocksureness does not blend well with undercover work. The tension between what is known and what is hidden, on the side of Bond as well as on the side of the Villain, participates fully in the dynamics of the narrative syntagm; however, the truth is disclosed before — sometimes long before — the conclusion of the narrative syntagm in order to serve the balance of the fundamental binary opposition between Bond and the Villain. It is

Bond who must oppose the Villain rather than some uninteresting impersonator, hence 007's tendency to tempt the devil, which has quickly become a staple in the films, as Bond openly provokes his adversary with no apparent care for the supposed secrecy of his mission. The secret agent must no longer be secret in order to become a true popular Hero, and so Bond's cover has to be blown in order for him to transcend his condition of government employee and to emerge as a Hero of epic dimensions. The opposition between Secrecy and Disclosure, a typical paradigm from the narrative palette of the spy genre, is appropriated by the character of James Bond, and his shifting from the realm of secrecy to that of disclosure allows him to reveal his intrinsic qualities and to prepare the resolution of the fundamental opposition between Good and Evil, epitomized by Bond's final confrontation with the designated Villain. After all, James Bond 007 is the most famous *secret* agent in the world, and his peculiar relationship to secrecy is contained within this apparent contradiction: If Bond appears so eager to introduce himself by his real name, it is because Epic Heroes do not work undercover. Due to the uncanny popular reception of the Bond narration, the name itself has come to embody the duality of Secret/Disclosure, for it still signifies both relative anonymity—Trevor Bond, Samantha Bond—and universal recognition, James Bond.

When it comes to the opposition between Love and War, the most basic elements of the narration speak for themselves: Admirably served by his 00s, James Bond is both the ideal lover and the perfect soldier, and his two main functions are evenly distributed throughout the narrative syntagm, producing a constant tension between two opposite poles of human behavior, loving and killing.[10]

These oppositions, which are directly related to the role of James Bond in the narrative syntagm, function harmoniously to establish narrative authority by creating different levels of tension, the resolution of which elicits different types of expectations from the recipient. Along with the basic conflict opposing Order to Disorder, any James Bond adventure is also a love story, albeit highly sexualized and hardly sentimental, a compromise between the obedience of the secret agent vis-à-vis his superiors and the independence of the Epic Hero, and a negotiation between secrecy and disclosure, all either suggested or represented by James Bond himself.

Form and Formula

The Bond narration, again very much along the lines of any popular fictitious narrative universe, tends to repeat a fairly rigid pattern, which is often referred to by critics and journalists alike as "the Bond formula."[11] For Eco, the Bond narration consists of a series of "moves" that present the same type of appeal to the recipient, as a game of chess would do:

> A. M moves and gives a task to Bond;
> B. Villain moves and appears to Bond (perhaps in vicarious forms);
> C. Bond moves and gives first check to villain or villain gives first check to Bond;
> D. Woman moves and shows herself to Bond;
> E. Bond takes woman (possesses her or begins her seduction);
> F. Villain captures Bond (with or without Woman, or at different moments);
> G. Villain tortures Bond (with or without Woman);
> H. Bond beats villain (kills him or kills his representatives or help at their killing);
> I. Bond, convalescing, enjoys woman, whom he then loses [156].

These different moves can be repeated throughout the narration, and some of them can even occupy different moments in the narrative syntagm, although, logically, *A, C, H* and *I* tend to be fixed. Eco's effort of synthesis implies a certain amount of latency in his description, particularly regarding the vicarious function of some characters. In *From Russia with Love* (novel), the seventh move, *G* (Villain tortures Bond), is substituted by the killing of Bond's ally and contact in Istanbul, Darko Kerim, which may seem a bit questionable, since Kerim is simply murdered by Grant, along with his prisoner, and not exactly "tortured." Furthermore, in view of Eco's very own typology, which establishes the basic opposition between Anglo-Saxon and Non-Anglo-Saxon, the character of Darko Kerim does not sit well as a James Bond double due to his mixed racial origin — he is half–Turkish half–English — but rather belongs, along with Quarrel and Vijay, to the type of expendable non–White allies described earlier. In order to function as a set element of the formula, Eco's conception of the torture paradigm in the Bond narration must encompass a wide range of narrative situations, and goes as far as including the taxing ski escape from Piz Gloria in *On Her Majesty's Secret Service*, which again might seem debatable.

It is not clear either if *I* (Bond, convalescing, enjoys Woman, whom he then loses) is as invariable as Eco suggests: we have no news of Bond losing either Solitaire or Domino at the end of *Live and Let Die* and of *Thunderball*. To the contrary, both novels conclude upon suggested promises of tender intimacy:

> "He's [the cook] coming with us on our passionate holiday," said Bond. He told her of M's cable. "We're going to a house on stilts with palm

> trees and five miles of golden sand. And you'll have to look after me very well because I shan't be able to make love with only one arm." There was open sensuality in Solitaire's eyes as she looked up at him. She smiled innocently. "What about my back?" she said [*Live and Let Die*, 278].
>
> Inside the small room, the jalousies threw bands of light and shadow over the bed. Bond staggered over to the bed and knelt down beside it. The small head on the pillow turned toward him. A hand came out and grasped his hair, pulling his head closer to her. Her voice said huskily, "You are to stay here. Do you understand? You are not to go away."
>
> When Bond didn't answer, she feebly shook his head to and fro, "Do you hear me, James? Do you understand?" She felt Bond's body slipping to the floor. When she let go his hair, he slumped down on the rug beside her bed. She carefully shifted her position and looked down at him. He was already asleep with his head cradled on the inside of his forearm. The girl watched the dark, rather cruel face for a moment. Then she gave a small sigh, pulled the pillow to the edge of the bed so that it was just above him, laid her head down so that she could see him whenever she wanted to, and closed her eyes [*Thunderball*, 336].

As we can see, Bond is not exactly about to "lose Woman" in either case but rather to "enjoy" her, as Eco so delicately puts it. The exact place of this particular move in the narrative syntagm of *Moonraker* is more aleatory yet, since Bond never actually gets to "enjoy" the designated Bond girl, Gala Brand, who is already engaged to another man.

The loss of the Woman pointed out by Eco corresponds in reality to the virtual status of her narrative function: She simply does not have any staying power within the economy of the narration. As shown earlier, Bond cannot be committed to any woman in particular, and this impossibility directly benefits the tension between Sexual Frustration and Sexual Satisfaction, a fundamental axis of conflict in the Bond universe, by allowing the introduction of a new sexual interest in every installment.

Eco's analysis can thus stand to be nuanced, although, as he rightfully points out, we can predict a certain amount of narrative instances or "moves" in any given Bond adventure, as we do in most popular narrative genres. The cinematographic adaptations have contributed to the notion of a Bond formula by eliminating the character's evolution as it is portrayed in the novels, and somewhat freezing the hero at his most triumphant moment. The narrative syntagm is consequently simplified, and, emulating Eco's technique, many Bond movies could be described as the following series of specific narrative moments:

A. The Order is threatened;
B. Bond is called upon while having a sexual encounter and given the mission;

C. Bond infiltrates the villain's organization;
D. Bond meets and usually competes with villain in a game;
E. Bond meets woman;
F. Bond is captured by villain;
G. Bond escapes;
H. Bond defeats villain, destroys his lair and saves woman;
I. Order is reestablished and Bond has sex with woman.

However, as is the case with Eco's scheme, this enumeration of doubtlessly fundamental Bond moments cannot be considered exhaustive nor prescriptive. It does not include other narrative instances, such as the customary visit of Bond to the Q branch, the encounter with a first woman usually promised to an untimely death before meeting the main female character, or the contact with MI6 at mid-mission in an unlikely environment. All these may or may not occur depending on the installment, but they are nonetheless metonymically representative of the Bond universe.[12] The elimination of several usual paradigms, such as the initial and final sex scenes (*B*, *H*), the flirting with Moneypenny and the traditional visit to Q in the first two installments of the franchise's recent rebooting can be interpreted as a more or less conscious effort on the part of the production team to break free from the formulaic notion that we generally associate with the Bond universe; however, paradoxically, it consists mainly in returning to the paradigms already present in the novels, which underlines the facility with which the Bond narration can acquire a life of its own, self-generating representative elements that were not part of the original textual Bond to begin with. Even in its simplified cinematographic form, the Bond narration is not susceptible to being reduced to a single formula, but rather could be described as an ensemble of interdependent narrative moments functioning together to create an entire semiotic dimension that eludes, in spite of all appearances, a straight forward linear breakdown. In other words, the narrative authority of the Bond adventures does not rely only upon the endless repetition of the same syntagm but also upon the suggestive power of its paradigms.

Let us examine the function of a simple, albeit fundamental, paradigm — the chase — which can be administered virtually at any moment during the narration and pervades all levels of the action. The chase is directly related to the quest, one of the oldest and most mythical themes of human narration, which is primarily represented in the Bond universe by MI6's all-important mission to preserve the Order. This primordial quest breaks down into a series of chases that not only denote the crucial urgency of 007's task, but allow, as well, the introduction of different degrees of defamiliarization within the Bond narration which greatly contribute to establishing its multifaceted narrative authority.

3. Positions and Oppositions

In the novels, the car chase after Le Chiffre in *Casino Royale* or Bond's escape on skis from Blofeld's Alpine refuge in *On Her Majesty's Secret Service* represent the very basic, traditional type of chase, which also can be overextended, as when Bond follows Goldfinger through Europe. The chase can also be found at the very inception of the action, as in *Thunderball*, where the entire narrative syntagm consists of chasing after the missing plane and the missiles it carried, generating a micro-structural correlation within the story itself when the U.S. submarine Manta chases Largo's *Disco Volante*. In spite of being more resistant to structural breakdown than the novels due to their thematic variety, the short stories also use the narrative figure of the chase. In "For Your Eyes Only," Bond is in charge of tracking down von Hammerstein in a diluted sort of chase; in "Risico," Bond and Colombo track Kristatos to Santa María, and Bond ends up chasing Kristatos before killing him; in "The Property of a Lady," the plot is based upon 007 chasing the employer of the double agent who is selling the payment for her betrayal through the auction. In a more metaphorical but nonetheless persuasive manner, the motif of the chase is central to "The Hildebrand Rarity," since Bond has been hired by Mr. Krest, the owner of the yacht the Wavekrest, in order to capture a rare fish, and is therefore directly related to the plot, although in a parallel manner. In "Octopussy," the actual narrative frame is that of a chase, since 007 has chased Major Dexter Smythe all the way to his refuge in the Caribbean in order to bring him to justice; in a symbolic way, the unfortunate Smythe becomes the victim of the most primordial chase of them all, the chase for food when he falls prey to his own pet octopus.

Both "Quantum of Solace" and "007 in New York," very much on the fringes of Bond's narrative, do not have many paradigmatic elements in common with the James Bond universe, and their narrative syntagm exhibits few similarities by what is conceived as a James Bond narration. Still, from an abstract point of view, both protagonists of "Quantum of Solace," which is more of a social commentary than a spy adventure, are chasing an ideal — romantic in the case of Philip Masters, and decidedly more materialistic and glamorous in the case of Rhoda Llewellyn; the radically different nature of their respective chases creates the tension that sustains the narrative syntagm and determines its existence as well as its evolution. In a similar manner, the entire narrative structure of the ironic "007 in New York" is based upon the conflict of two types of chases, which correspond to the terms of the opposition between reality and imagination described earlier. The first one is of the abstract type, for Bond "chases" after an imaginary good evening in New York for most of the text; and the second, decidedly more down to earth, concerns his original assignment — that is, informing an ex-operative from MI6 that she is sleeping with the enemy. After the original meeting fails, what was supposed to be a routine encounter turns into a desperate chase that prevents 007 from pursuing his quest for a perfect evening. James Bond's personal, imaginary chase is replaced by a very literal chase due to his incomplete knowledge of the Central Park Zoo. We find the chase even in the most atypical installment of the textual Bond, *The Spy Who Loved Me*, which includes a chase in the woods, as Vivienne is trying to escape from Horror and Sluggsy, and one in the motel, as Bond and the two thugs are hunting each other through the Dreamy Pines Motor Court. From a more symbolic point of view, it could be said that most of the novel is dedicated to Vivienne's constant chase of a possible way of life that would suit her natural inclinations towards independence and sexual self-determination.

Naturally, the chase motif is omnipresent in the films and fuels most of its spectacular action scenes. It can be a sophisticated mixture of different types of transportation, such as Bond's Lotus being chased by an helicopter before turning into a pocket-submarine in *The Spy Who Loved Me* (film), or as basic as two cars chasing each other on a narrow road, as at the beginnings of *On Her Majesty's Secret Service* and *GoldenEye*. And judging by the opening sequence of *Quantum of Solace*, the latest installment to date as I write these lines, which includes an intense car chase, this very classic figure of action cinema is still as current as ever in the Bond universe. Alternately predator and prey, James Bond chases or is chased throughout his adventure until the quest is over, until the Order has been restored; however, the administration of the chase in the economy of the narration is highly variable. Furthermore, it is far from being the exclusive property of the Bond narration. What makes it more particular is the great variety of the elements it may involve — from cars to helicopters, from spaceships to wetbikes, the Bond narrative syntagm admits by definition every conceivable motor vehicle, as well as horses if need be, as in *A View to a Kill* (film). More importantly perhaps, it allows the insertion of technological feats, as well as luxury items, into the action, hence reinforcing the authority of the entire Bond narration by creating an appeal that goes beyond the simple tension generated by a car chase and referring to diverse levels of defamiliarization: We are not only interested in the chase but in the car as well.

Just as we expect the traditional detective (Sherlock Holmes or Hercules Poirot) to resolve the enigma in a dramatic manner, usually making his final demonstration in front of all the parties involved, including the culprit, and just as we are not surprised when the hard-boiled gumshoe is roughed up either by the gangsters or the police, we look forward to some specific narrative moments in any James Bond narration. However, unlike traditional or hardboiled detective stories, which are represented by different heroes, James Bond has come to embody an entire genre by itself: There is a Bond *genre* rather than *a formula*, just like there is a detective genre — that is, an entire narrative world built upon the specific organization of a given amount of semiotically cohesive paradigms that accepts variations according to specific, internal rules and establishes a privileged contact with its recipient by creating different levels of defamiliarization within the confines of a would-be realistic narration.[13] Whereas we can associate science fiction or detective stories with a variety of different narrative types, the Bond narration is totally unique and exclusively self-represented: Philip Marlowe, Sam Spade or Mike Hammer may be considered as equally representative of the hard-boiled detective genre, while it is plain to see that there is only one James Bond and a myriad of imitations. The James Bond genre is thus curiously self-sufficient, for it can only admit its own reiterations, and its remarkable influence upon popular narration remains strictly paradigmatic. It is not a coincidence that it has been parodied so abundantly, as early as 1967 in *Casino Royale* and as recently as 2011 with *Johnny English Reborn*. Contrary to hard-boiled detective story parodies, such as the *Naked Gun* series, which are based upon collective narrative clichés drawn from a variety of specific sources, any James Bond parody is exclusively based upon the Bond narration, which has acquired as much semiotic weight as an entire genre, and hence has been easily appropriated by a collective authorship, not only through the film adaptations but through the literary continuations of Robert Markham (Kingsley Amis), John Gardner, Charlie Higson and Raymond Benson.

The Bond narration, as a self-sufficient genre, has created its own self-referential clichés by borrowing different paradigms from several popular genres and combining them in a unique manner. We recognize determining elements from the epic tale, the adventure story and the romance novel, and non-determining narrative paradigms from the detective and the scientific genres. Contrary to what one may believe, and in spite of presenting a fair amount of cops and robbers figures, the Bond narration structurally does not correspond to a detective story: There is no enigma *per se*, since we already know who the Villain is at the beginning of the narration, and Bond's responsibility is to defeat him rather than to identify him — he does not get to detect that much. The only enigma Bond has to elucidate is the exact nature of the Villain's plans and how to cancel the chaotic function (the direct threat to the Order); and the traditional scene where the detective reveals the solution of the enigma is replaced by the Villain exposing the ins and outs of his project, hence providing Bond with the necessary knowledge to be able to thwart it. In other words, Bond does not elucidate a great deal since he needs the Villain to explain the details of his plan before being able to act. Contrary to detective fiction, the narrative tension in the Bond genre is sustained through the physical and psychological opposition between Bond and the Villain or his henchmen rather than between a protagonist and a problem, the solution of which will lead to the identification of a culprit.

The importance of the romance element should not be overlooked, for it allows us to consider *The Spy Who Loved Me* (novel) as an integral part of our corpus; in this particular case, the romance novel paradigms, articulated along the opposition Sexual Frustration/Sexual Gratification, dominate most of the narration until the arrival of James Bond, who, as we have seen, embodies most of the binary oppositions at the core of the narration. His arrival will resolve both the adventure-oriented conflict and the sexual tension created by the text.

By combining specific paradigms from different genres according to its underlining basic binary oppositions, the architecture of the Bond narration allows for multiple narrative tensions to coexist and force authority upon the addressee from a variety of points of view, for, without leaving the realm of reality, the Bond genre creates several degrees of suspension of disbelief.

The Wonders of Reality

The terms "fantasy" and "science fiction" are often mentioned when referring to the James Bond narration; however, the narrative universe of James Bond is definitely and irremediably realistic. The category of fantasy, if we are to consider it as a narrative genre,[14] as well as that of science fiction, implies a different conception of the recipient's identification with the narrative universe. Whereas a fantasy or a science fiction narration take place in a more or less deeply modified reality, the adventures of James Bond take place in our world, and his fight is that of our time.[15] The presence of technological exaggerations — that is, of machines and gadgets which do not actually exist — at the heart of the James Bond universe, which has been magnified on the screen for evident spectacular reasons, does not imply that the narration could be at any moment considered "science fiction," for we never cease to identify the fictitious universe as being an exact replica of ours. Of course, any valid science fiction narration should in theory also constitute a comment upon our world and the human condition,[16] however, the relationship its narrative universe establishes with our own reality is metaphorical rather than literal, for it requires an interpretive effort on the part of the recipient. The same applies to the narrative universe of the still hazy genre of fantasy, which is by nature disconnected from our historical and epistemological frames of reference. *Conan the Barbarian*, *The Lord of the Rings* and *Star Wars* (the genre of space opera is indeed much closer to fantasy that to science fiction) elude our direct frame of references and require a metaphorical reception, forcing us to spontaneously interpret the relationship between this alternative reality and our own if the message is meant to service more than simple escapist tendencies.[17]

On the contrary, a typical detective story — or a spy adventure, for that matter — tends to facilitate a literal identification with a represented reality that allegedly corresponds to our own, i.e., that is subject to the same natural laws and framed within the same historical context as ours. Contextual elements thus acquire a direct referential value and contribute to structure the type of narration we understand as realistic. Whereas the important works of science fiction tend to introduce questions of an epistemological nature, such as the nature of reality or the limits of our perception, the detective story is more conducive to a sociologically-oriented reflection, for its narrative universe tends to represent the same social tensions that we encounter in our reality.

The boundaries between these different categories are naturally porous, for popular narrations are often structured according to intergeneric combinations that Eco elegantly relates to the classical *ars combinatoria* (155). Consequently we can find paradigms traditionally associated with one specific genre within another genre without observing any major change in the essential nature of a given narrative syntagm. For instance, James Bond can be led to exercise some degree of deduction during his mission, such as sneaking into the Villain's lab to gather evidence, without ever turning into a detective. In the same manner, if the narrative motifs of *Moonraker* (film and novel), or the highly unlikely technological feats of the Q branch, tend to be associated with the genre of science fiction, they do not alter the essentially realistic nature of the Bond narrative universe, which is subjected to the same fundamental laws as our reality. They may not be achievable with the means at our disposal today, but they are nonetheless based upon current scientific progress and aim to reflect what could be perceived as the state of the art. The excess of technological wonders even proves to be counterproductive in the case of the Bond genre, and some of the Brosnan installments, especially the last one, *Die Another Day*, have received their share of criticism for having overly indulged in spectacular gadgetry. It is significant that the recent rebooting of the series has done away with the traditional visit to the Q branch, opting to represent high technology in a more subtle way so as not to interfere with the realistic pretension of the narrative universe.

If the Bond genre is realistic (i.e., is set to happen in a reality identical to ours), it is not, however, credible, for many events it presents are simply not believable — if nothing else, James Bond 007 should have been killed long ago. Like any other so-called realistic fiction, it is confronted with the typical paradox of the mode,[18] which consists of achieving a compromise between credibility and narrative authority. Realism cannot be, of course, a mere copy of reality, which, for starters, would be simply unachievable, for there exists no absolute objective point of view that could render such a copy possible.[19] Furthermore, it would be devoid of any aesthetic qualities and be unable to produce any tension to establish narrative authority; in effect, it would be boring. In order to elicit attention along the specific parameters of its mode, a realistic narration must organize reality in a manner that generates authority — without, however, undermining its original ambition to represent our world faithfully. Popular narrations oriented towards escapism naturally tend to seek a very primal narrative authority by representing incredible events, which consequently requires a higher level of suspension of disbelief from the recipient. The Bond genre is no exception; what is exceptional, however, is its capacity to create different levels of defamiliarization by coordinating multiple thematic narrative domains that require different degrees of suspension of disbelief, and thus structuring its message along a variety of semiotic codes.

Multi-Defamiliarization

As we observed earlier, the Bond novels introduce a very realistic note by making paperwork an integral part of the narration. Bond's world is not only about traveling, casinos, cars, guns and women, but includes offices, secretaries and administrative duties as well. The function of this somewhat mundane thematic area is not only to frame the narration within a realistic environment, which should theoretically ease the introduction of less believable events, but also to sharpen the contrast between normality (paperwork) and adventure (action). This dimension of the narration is already defamiliarizing by itself, for it allegedly reveals the cogs of a branch of the government, the Secret Service, that by definition is only supposed to be known from the inside; and so apparently innocuous occupations, such as examining and filing reports, become suggestive narrative motifs that serve the text's realistic intent. Dossiers and internal memoranda are integral parts of the narration, and the premises of James Bond's very first adventure, *Casino Royale*, are presented in the form of a report submitted to M by the head of Station S, which includes an appendix dedicated to the description of Le Chiffre — signed by an unmistakably bureaucratic entity appropriately named "Archivist."

Beyond this first level, which does not jeopardize the realistic intent of the narration but rather reinforces it, the Bond genre presents two more types of defamiliarization that correspond to the peculiar plot organization pointed out by Eco, and which results in conceding as much time to credible, albeit special and often pleasant activities rather than to adventurous events *per se*. We spend more time playing golf than assaulting Fort Knox in *Goldfinger* (novel), and discovering the beauties of Japan than confronting Blofeld in *You Only Live Twice* (novel). The short stories "The Hildebrand Rarity" and "Octopussy" are as much about the joys of snorkeling as about murder and betrayal, and the beginning of *Thunderball* (novel) which presents Bond's stay at Shrublands health clinic, resembles more an exposition of healthy living habits than a thrilling start for an adventure of international espionage. The menu selection at Blades in *Moonraker* (novel), and Bond's reminiscences of his experiences with French food in *On Her Majesty's Secret Service* (novel), are complacently described, although they connote an opposite universe to that of spy stories which is nonetheless still defamiliarizing, for it is signified by an activity that is not part of everyday life — in this case fine dining. The same can be said regarding skiing, scuba diving and elegant gambling, which, without being unfamiliar, remain outside of what we usually consider routine occupations. The third level of defamiliarization is the most obvious, for it corresponds to the main conflict opposing Bond to the Villain and represents the justification for the narration. However, as shown by Eco, the textual authority of Bond's novels is due to the representation of possible pleasures as much to that of heroic and much less believable feats; and in spite of being the most apparent, this level of defamiliarization is not necessarily the most determining.

The three levels of defamiliarization that we find in the Bond universe correspond to three narrative domains. The first one reveals the inner mechanisms of the Secret Service, eliciting our attention by informing us, at least in theory, of a part of reality that we are not supposed to know. The second suggests a world of pleasant, leisure-oriented activities, usually related to a higher standard of living. Finally, the third presents an epic confrontation between a lone but relentless Hero and a powerful Villain, along with its always reassuring triumphant resolution. These three levels of defamiliarization work in conjunction throughout the narration, and if one usually provides the dominant tone in accordance to a specific narrative moment, the others are never far behind, as illustrated by the following two quotes from the first chapter of *Moonraker*, precisely titled "Secret Paper Work":

> He [Bond] looked at his watch. Eleven o'clock. Mondays were hell. Two days of dockets and files to plough through. And week-ends were generally busy times abroad. Empty flats got burgled. People were photographed in compromising positions. Motor-car "accidents" looked better, got a more cursory handling, amidst the week-end slaughter on the roads. The weekly bags from Washington, Istanbul, and Tokyo would have come in and been sorted. They might hold something for him [6].
>
> Bond took out his black gunmetal cigarette-box and his black-oxidized Ronson lighter and put them on the desk beside him. He lit a cigarette, one of the Macedonian blend with the three gold rings round the butt that Morlands of Grosvenor Street made for him, then he settled himself forward in the padded swivel chair and began to read. It was the beginning of a typical routine day for Bond. It was only two or three times a year that an assignment came along requiring his particular abilities. For the rest of the year he had the duties of an easy-going senior civil servant—elastic office hours from around ten to six; lunch, generally in the canteen; evenings spent playing cards in the company of a few close friends, or at Crockford's; or making love, with rather cold passion, to one of three similarly disposed married women; week-ends playing golf for high stakes at one of the clubs near London. He took no holidays, but was generally given a fortnight's leave at the end of each assignment—in addition to any sick-leave that might be necessary. He earned £1500 a year, the salary of a Principal Officer in the Civil Service, and he had a thousand a year free of tax of his own [10–11].

The binary opposition between paperwork and action is already indicated by the title of the chapter, which already constitutes an antithesis by itself, since it points to two opposite semiotic code: Whereas "paperwork" refers us to a world of routine and subsequent boredom, the notion of "secret" elicits immediate diegetic interest and is easily identifiable as one of the most fundamental structural devices of Occidental narrations, from the Knights of the Round Table to Harry Potter, from detective stories to the fantastic genre. In spite of its apparent dreariness, Bond's paperwork environment is pregnant with adventurous possibilities suggested by the exotic origin of the "weekly bags" from Washington, Istanbul and Tokyo, which, although "Mondays are hell," might hold something for him. His cigarette box is both gunmetal and assorted to his brand name lighter, connoting his main work tool and his fashion consciousness, hence adding the other two levels of defamiliarization to that of Secret Paperwork: He may be at the office, but his cigarettes are custom made and his cigarette box is the color of his gun. The description of a "typical routine day for Bond," which expands into that of 007's life when he is not on a mission, emphasizes the apparent banality of a civil servant's life by mentioning trivial details such as his eight-hours-a-day schedule, his sick-time allotment, his exact salary and his tax arrangements. The use of semicolons suggest repetition, and words such as "senior civil servant" and "Principal Officer in the Civil Service" indicates banality, as does the simple idea of having lunch at the canteen. However, it also mentions high-stakes golf games, an occupation which seems more typical of idle playboys than of responsible senior civil servants, as well as regular if dispassionate sexual affairs with married women, again, an activity that we do not always associate with respectable government employees.

We can therefore detect many of the main semiotic elements that sustain the James Bond universe and that correspond to the three levels of defamiliarization described above amidst this apparently prosaic presentation of 007's routine. The higher and better life is suggested by the high stake golf games, the classy clubs on the outskirts of London and the free sexual gratification, while the adventure is referred to by the color of his cigarette case and by those "two or three times a year" when James Bond's "particular abilities" can be put to good use. Naturally, in order to remain exceptional, for they represent the ultimate level of defamiliarization, the missions only happen "two or three times a year," even if the adventures of James Bond are precisely about one of these "two or three times a year"— a couple of notable exceptions being *The Spy Who Loved Me* and *On Her Majesty's Secret Service*, in which the adventure is the result of chance rather than of a specific assignment. The two main attributes of 007 as described earlier (see Chapter 2) are equally connoted by his routine activities, for a high-stakes game of golf implies risks and therefore courage, and regular, casual sexual encounters indicate virility; the latter also reminds us of the secret agent's dual morality, for if gambling is generally accepted among well-bred gentlemen, adultery is not.

These three concomitant levels of defamiliarization each elicit a different degree of suspension of disbelief that carries a specific value from low to high: the office environment and the lunch at the canteen are highly credible, the high-stakes golf games and the habitual uncommitted sexual encounters definitely less, and the adventure not at all.

We find again these three levels of defamiliarization in the cinematographic Bond, albeit expressed under different forms — those more suited to the medium and its addressee. The imperatives of commercial action cinema naturally push forward spectacularity over credibility and increase the overall level of suspension of disbelief, and thus, in the films, Bond is often bordering the status of superhero, as chases and stunts are given a greater place in the narrative syntagm to comply with the exigencies of blockbuster distribution. He remains, however, an individual without superpowers who often relies on chance and ingenuity in order to defeat stronger adversaries, as illustrated, for instance, by his fights with Jaws in *The Spy Who Loved Me* (film) and *Moonraker* (film). For all the improbability of his feats, James Bond never leaves the realistic mode, and if the recipient is seduced into accepting the incredible events that create the last and more demanding level of defamiliarization, it is because he or she has already been progressively defamiliarized by the two prior levels. Although the explicit representation of the Paperwork/Action binary opposition has been mostly eliminated from the cinematographic Bond — we never see him in his office, reviewing files and answering the phone — the semiotic domain of the administration remains present, generally towards the beginning of the narrative syntagm in the traditional scene where M briefs Bond about the mission. Paperwork, or the administration of Order as it is represented by M/MI6, may also reappear briefly during the course of the adventure when Bond meets with M and his close staff in an unlikely place, such as in a shipwreck in *The Man with the Golden Gun*, inside an Egyptian tomb in *The Spy Who Loved Me*, in a Brazilian catholic mission in *Moonraker* or in a disused underground station in *Die Another Day*. This need to displace the administrative paradigm to an exotic, unpredictable location shows that the paperwork dimension no longer holds much interest on its own and must therefore be spiced with elements from the other two levels of defamiliarization. The cinematographic Bond appears dissociated from the purely administrative side of his occupation, which is represented mostly by secondary characters revolving around M, such as Miss Moneypenny and the different high-ranking officials with whom M confers occasionally in order to save the world.

If the character of Bond no longer participates directly in the first level of defamiliarization, which has mutated in the films from "Secret Paperwork" to "Imminent Crisis in the Free World," he is, on the other hand, involved from the beginning within the second level, that of pleasurable activity. In the micro-structurally significant opening sequences of the very first installment, *Dr. No*, 007 is shown impeccably dressed in a shiny tuxedo, winning at Baccarat in a fancy establishment and flirting with the equally elegant — and highly attractive — Sylvia Trench, who he will encounter in his flat after he returns from his meeting with M. The young lady, apparently wearing no more than one of Bond's own pajama tops, is playing golf in the living room and convinces him, without much effort, to delay his departure in order to allow for a sexual encounter. We know, through M's very first words when Bond enters his office, that it is the middle of the night — "It happens to be 3 A.M. When do you sleep, 007?" (0:10:33–0:10:36) — therefore Bond's routine life when not on a mission is already a reality of nightlife, casinos, tuxedos and fast love. The rejection of a fixed schedule is the negation of bureaucracy, which is precisely based upon a very rigid relationship between time and task, and a government employee without a fixed schedule is somewhat of a contradiction in terms. The filmic Bond is therefore relieved of the dull duties of his profession in order to represent from the very beginning the second level of defamiliarization — that of a pleasant, high-class oriented and a bit immoral lifestyle. In subsequent installments, especially during the Moore and Brosnan periods, Bond's agreeable off-duty routine has often been condensed into a single paradigm — that of the secret agent having sex when Headquarters requests his presence, which we can naturally relate to the typical ending of the traditional Bond movie. Once his mission is accomplished, 007 returns to his usual occupation by making love to the designated Bond girl, who functions as a natural intermediary between the third level of defamiliarization (i.e., the adventure *per se*) and the second (that is, a pleasant, sensual lifestyle, symbolized by sex with a young woman recently met in an exotic place).

Following the evolution of today's more realistic and darker action cinema, which responds to a more demanding addressee in terms of credibility, the recent rebooting of the series has done away with both scenes, as well as with the overly spectacular technological feats that contributed to heightening the degree of suspension of disbelief requested from the recipient in the late Brosnan installments. Still, we do find microchips, sports cars, high-priced resorts, sex and shamelessly advertised luxury watches in *Casino Royale* (film, 2006), which demonstrates that, in spite of valuable efforts to restore some credibility to the supposedly realistic universe of James Bond, the narration cannot simply dispense with the second level of defamiliarization. A James Bond adventure is not only one story — it is an entire conception of reality suggested by the constant reiteration of a single narrative syntagm that evokes more than it says and transcends its status of individual narration by virtue of sheer repetition.

James Bond Will Return

Any James Bond installment functions both as an independent narration and as part of a serial; one could read one James Bond novel or watch one James Bond film and appreciate its narrative authority without any prior knowledge of the Bond universe. It is also true that the slow degradation of Bond's mental state can only be appreciated if the novels are taken as a whole, and that the reading of each novel deepens our understanding of the characters. The Christmas meal at M's home in *On Her Majesty's Secret Service* (novel) and M's coldness when determining Bond's possible future in *The Man with the Golden Gun* (novel), introduce a new shade in Bond's psychological make-up, informing us further upon the nature of the relationship between Bond and his superior, and so on. Each installment is therefore susceptible to two different readings, functioning as both an individual entity and as part of a greater narrative syntagm composed all the James Bond narrative instances. Nonetheless, as the James Bond universe grew into a genre in itself, each installment acquired supplementary, inter-narrative semiotic weight.[20] The initial textual installment, *Casino Royale* (novel), already introduced all the ingredients for a serialized narration — that is, a hero and a to-be-continued super-structure along with the closed structure of an individual adventure. Chapman identifies a structural flaw in *Casino Royale* (novel), for the climax comes "two-thirds of the way into the book" (*Licence* 246), which results in two different plot structures that could be summed up within the oppositions Bond/Le Chiffre and Bond/Vesper. The binary conflict between protagonist and antagonist concludes with the elimination of the Villain and the foiling of his plans, while that relating to Bond and the Bond Girl ends with Vesper's suicide. Although the development of the secondary plot based upon the relationship between Bond and Vesper in the last chapters of the novel might seem, as Chapman points out, fairly anti-climactic, it introduces the notion of future continuity within the narration: The mission might be over, but the war for Order — that is, the reason for Bond to exist — remains, as suggested by his reaction after discovering Vesper's death:

> He saw her now only as a spy. Their love and his grief were relegated to the boxroom of his mind. Later, perhaps they would be dragged out, dispassionately examined, and then bitterly thrust back with other sentimental baggage he would rather forget. Now he could only think of her treachery to the Service and to her country and of the damage it had done. His professional mind was completely absorbed with the consequences — the covers which must have been blown over the years, the codes which the enemy must have broken, the secrets which must have leaked from the centre of the very section devoted to penetrating the Soviet Union.
>
> It was ghastly. God knew how the mess would be cleared up.... Well, it was not too late. Here was a target for him, right to hand. He would take on SMERSH and hunt it down [210–212].

The function of Vesper changes from object of desire to enemy accomplice, causing the secondary plot structure to dissolve into the main opposition between Order and Disorder and becoming yet another reason to pursue the struggle, for the damage that she has caused needs to be remedied. New battles await the secret agent, liberated from his affective chains, available for a new sentimental interest as the importance of the Order above any personal consideration is reinforced. The end of the secondary plot of *Casino Royale* can be conceived as the beginning of a new James Bond adventure, and the novel's last words indicate clearly that the champion of Order has reappropriated the entire narrative space:

> "This is 007 speaking. This is an open line. It's an emergency. Can you hear me? Pass this on at once. 3030 was a double, working for Redland. Yes, dammit, I said 'was.' The bitch is dead now" [212–213].

It is indeed not a coincidence that the text concludes focalizing the narration on Bond himself, and the harshness of his words confirm the supremacy of the Cause over any personal consideration, as well as his dedication to the Service.

The continuity found in the novels, and intrinsically related to Bond's psychological degradation after *On Her Majesty's Secret Service* (novel), is ignored in most of the films, which suggest rather than articulate the elements of the Story beyond the Plot. And so James Bond becomes a true popular hero for mass consumption, free from a problematic evolution and forever triumphing, and each of his adventures is but one episode of his never ending Story. Only the recent rebooting of the franchise, responding to a more discriminate audience in terms of suspension of disbelief, has reintroduced a similar type of continuity as that found in the novels, along with the effect it may have upon the hero's psyche. However, by now the damage has been done, inter-narratively speaking, and any true evolution of the James Bond character, aside from some added ruggedness that in the end only emulates the traits of the textual Bond, seems highly unlikely due to the structural harmony that transcends the semiotic value of each individual installment and makes it signify the entire story by reiteration. Each narrative instance of James Bond is a metonymy that contains the integrality of the James Bond universe, and the Story of James Bond includes an almost infinite amount of individual plots, based upon the combination in a set syntagm of the narrative paradigms corresponding to the three levels of defamiliarization enunciated earlier.

This overview of some of the main binary oppositions at work within the Bond universe has allowed us to identify several characteristic aspects of the Bond narration: the internalization of basic oppositions within the protagonist, the co-existence of different narrative conflicts, the ambivalence of moral absolutes, and the three levels of defamiliarization used to establish narrative authority. It has also led us to define the Bond narration as a genre in itself, a product of a precisely balanced combination of different paradigms from other popular genres, which signifies by metonymical reiteration and constantly refers to a pre-existing super-structure.

These considerations explain in part the enduring appeal of James Bond and its facility to adapt to new audiences: Violence, love, sex, independence, loyalty, and epic heroism, along with the pleasures of comfortable higher class living, the advantages of modern technology and the convenience of moral ambivalence, are sure values with which any recipient is susceptible to identify, regardless of his or her immediate context. However, there is a more universal thematic mechanism at the core of the Bond universe, for, as we shall see, any James Bond adventure is also a very precise syntagmatic organization of the most primal elements of our reality.

Chapter 4

Primal Forces

Natural Elements

By now, the natural elements — air, water, fire and earth — have become meaningful paradigms of the James Bond universe by acquiring specific functions within the narrative syntagm: Earth is signified by the agent's incessant journeys, Water and Air are the natural backdrops to his death-defying actions, and Fire concludes the plot by destroying the Villain's lair. The battle of the Hero against the Villain is also the triumph of man over natural elements, for James Bond must defeat physical probabilities throughout his adventure and assert his total control over the environment to reestablish the sacrosanct Order. The three first natural elements, Earth, Air and Water, can be seen as logical paradigmatic transitions from the second level of defamiliarization, that of the pleasant lifestyle, to the third, that of the actual adventure. Traveling, flying, rock climbing, scuba-diving, boating, skiing and snowboarding are pleasant, entertaining activities, which involve at least one natural element and remain within the second degree of suspension of disbelief. Holidays at sea or at a ski resort are indeed plausible scenarios which still establish narrative authority, for they suggest a certain level of risk and hence suggest not only leisurely escapism but the possibility of danger as well.[1] In this sense, the job of James Bond is assuredly any state employee's dream, for it consists in having from moderate to extreme fun while righteously serving the unquestionable cause of the Greater Good.

The correlation between both levels of defamiliarization is perfectly illustrated by Bond's escape from Piz Gloria in *On Her Majesty's Secret Service* (novel and film), where a ski descent, an activity which is generally associated with the pleasant, leisurely occupations of the higher class, becomes a decisive paradigm of the adventure itself. This particular scene has indeed been abundantly recycled in the films, notably in *The Spy Who*

Loved Me, For Your Eyes Only, A View to a Kill (pre-credits sequence) and *The World Is Not Enough*, which show 007 being chased by the Villain's henchmen during a ski descent.[2] Similarly, the barbarian practice of keelhauling, reenacted by Mr. Big and inflicted upon Bond and Solitaire in *Live and Let Die* (novel), which consists of dragging someone tied to a line along the keel of a ship, could be perceived as a cruel perversion of waterskiing — yet another fine occupation of the wealthier class. This particular scene was logically recycled in the film *For Your Eyes Only*, which demonstrates its efficiency as an independent paradigm of the Bond genre, susceptible to be sequenced within a different installment without losing its efficiency.

The element of Fire must be considered separately from the previous three, for it tends to be set exclusively within the third level of defamiliarization — that which concerns the conflict opposing James Bond to the Villain — and its connotations are not those of pleasant activities but rather of war and destruction. At a deeper semiotic level, we can still relate a campfire, a cozy chimney or the spectacle of fireworks to special activities that suggest situations of a defamiliarizing nature generally associated with free time and leisure. However, the function of Fire remains firmly defined both sequentially and semantically within the main narrative syntagm, for it denotes the conclusion of the main axis of conflict and signifies the inescapable punishment of those who dare to break the Order.

Beyond their status of recurring narrative motifs in the novels, the four natural elements have become mandatory paradigmatic fixtures on the screen, which has systematized their semiotic distribution through the narrative syntagm. So we can take for granted that 007 will defy and dominate the fundamental forces as he carries out the mission. The particularities of the cinematographic medium naturally magnify the tendency of the Bond narration to represent the hero's triumph over the elements, not only because they promote sheer spectacular authority but also because they favor a higher degree of suspension of disbelief. The rhythm of a cinematographic narration is imposed by its sending entity and implies a constant progression, while that of textual communication depends solely upon the recipient. A film can therefore push further the limits of credibility by lining up a quick succession of narrative paradigms which must be immediately accepted by the recipient in order for the transmission to go on, leaving little time for rational reduction. Once we have accepted to enter the world of James Bond, the rhythm imposed by the film, along with its sonic and visual stimuli, easily establishes a strong narrative authority that no longer depends solely upon the credibility of the message. Furthermore, assisted by the wonders of modern technology, the cinematographic narration can readily mimic the laws of reality in order to better pervert them and control the recipient's imagination — that is, suspend his or her disbelief— by directly showing an incredible reality rather than merely suggesting it.

By inserting the four natural elements, the universality of which echoes that implied by the 00 section number, within its narrative syntagm, the Bond universe is able to elicit a trans-cultural and a-chronological response, for it transcends the immediacy of any geopolitical context and establishes narrative authority at a level of tension identifiable to all. This completes the main conflict opposing Bond to the Villain and relates the second level of defamiliarization to the third one.

Dr. Crab

Each textual installment tends to emphasize one specific natural element as a dominating narrative motif. For instance, *Moonraker* and *Goldfinger* emphasize Air, while *Live and Let Die* and *Thunderball* revolve mainly around Water. However, the dominating function of one specific natural element does not preclude the presence of the others. For instance, the element of Water is also present in *Moonraker*, for Drax' facility is built on the coast. This contributes to the economy of the novel by providing a long sequence as well as its share of narrative tension, for it is during their walk on the beach that Gala and Bond escape an attempt on their lives (chapters 16 and 18).

Several natural elements can work in conjunction throughout the narrative syntagm, as shown by *Dr. No* and *You Only Live twice*, which emphasize Water and Air, as well as Earth, symbolized by Dr. No's island and Blofeld's "garden of death." Traveling, which is also related to Earth, is present in every single textual narration except in "The Property of a Lady," the only adventure of James Bond that happens in London; and with the notable exception of *Moonraker*, every mission takes 007 to a foreign land. Similarly, Fire is fairly omnipresent and tends to be related more or less directly to the conclusion of the main conflict in most narrations: Jack Spang dies in an helicopter crash at the end of *Diamonds Are Forever*, Sluggsy and Horror set the Dreamy Pines Motor Court on fire before being killed by 007 in *The Spy Who Loved Me*, Mr. Big's yacht is blown up in *Live and Let Die*, Blofeld's lairs are destroyed at the end of *On Her Majesty's Secret Service* and *You Only Live Twice*, and so on. Even the final duel between Bond and Scaramanga in the mangrove that concludes *The Man with the Golden Gun* can be associated with Fire through the metonymic value of gunfire. Nonetheless, and in spite of its frequency, the narrative function of Fire is not exactly systematized in the textual Bond, as shown by the short story "The Hildebrand Rarity" or the novel *From Russia with Love*, which emphasize Water and Earth respectively, and do not conclude on either an explosion or a gun fight.

However, as the Bond universe moved to the screen, the functions of the four natural Elements became further structured to the point of becoming indispensable paradigms of the narration, and the choice of *Dr. No* to be the first Bond novel adapted to cinema is from this point of view significant, for it represents them abundantly. Air is found at the beginning of the narrative syntagm and is directly related to the justification of 007's mission, for the investigation of Dr. No is decided after a plane carrying two representatives of the Audubon Society crashes on his island. Bond's own arrival by plane in Jamaica is described at length in chapter 4, as the action momentarily yields to the description of natural wonders:

> The sixty-eight tons deadweight of the Super-Constellation hurtled high above the green and brown chequerboard of Cuba and, with only another hundred miles to go, started its slow declining flight towards Jamaica. Bond watched the big green turtle-backed island grow on the horizon and the water below him turn from the dark blue of the Cuba Deep to the azure and milk of the inshore shoals. Then they were over the North Shore, over its rash of millionaire hotels, and crossing the high mountains of the interior. The scattered dice of small-holdings showed on the slopes and in clearings in the jungle, and the setting sun flashed gold on the bright worms of tumbling rivers and streams. "Xaymaca" the Arawak Indians had called it — "The Land of Hills and Rivers." Bond's heart lifted with the beauty of one of the most fertile islands in the world. The other side of the mountains was in deep violet shadow. Lights were already twinkling in the foothills and spangling the streets of Kingston, but, beyond, the far arm of the harbour and the airport were still touched with the sun against which the Port Royal lighthouse blinked ineffectually. Now the Constellation was getting its nose down into a wide sweep beyond the harbour. There was a slight thump as the tricycle landing gear extended under the aircraft and locked into position, and a shrill hydraulic whine as the brake flaps slid out of the trailing edge of the wings. Slowly the great aircraft turned in again towards the land and for a moment the setting sun poured gold into the cabin. Then, the plane had dipped below the level of the Blue Mountains and was skimming down towards the single north-south runway" [41–423].[3]

The place given to this description in the economy of the text emphasizes the importance of the four natural elements in the narration, including air, since it is presented from the plane. Dr. No's island is associated with

4. Primal Forces

aerial wildlife, for it became known initially as a bird sanctuary, established by the Audubon Society as a natural colony to protect an endangered species, namely, the Roseate Spoonbill. The notion of an island itself symbolizes not only Earth but also Water, for it constitutes the most elementary opposition between both elements and provides an ample reserve of narrative motifs in direct relation to the context, such as the arrival of Bond by boat, the exploration of the beach, the apparition of Honeychile Rider emerging from the sea, and the battles against spiders and squids.

The island is also metonymically related to one of the main terms of the basic conflict — that is, the Villain — for Dr. No defines himself as the Enemy through the reality that he has created for himself and from which he intends to disrupt the Order. Being the unquestioned master of a microstructural society, he represents a valid threat since his very existence demonstrates the possibility of an alternate Order, which is naturally inadmissible. The lair of Dr. No reflects the dual semiotic value of the island in relationship to the natural elements, for it is both land and sea. Consequently, the first climactic confrontation between Bond and Dr. No takes place in a hybrid space that combines Earth and Water:

> What was this? An aquarium? Bond looked upwards. A yard below the ceiling, small waves were lapping at the glass. Above the waves was a strip of greyer blue-black, dotted with sparks of light. The outlines of Orion were the clue. This was not an aquarium. This was the sea itself and the night sky. The whole of one side of the room was made of armoured glass. They were under the sea, looking straight into its heart, twenty feet down [202].

Dr. No's lair is characterized by the land and the sea, and the Evil Doctor himself could be considered an amphibious sea creature, an arthropod *crustacea*, such as a crab or a lobster, for not only is his lair underneath the sea, but he has "steel-pincers" in lieu of hands, which assimilates him to both the name of his island, Crab Key, and the torture he has designed for Honeychile, for she is to be eaten alive by black crabs.

Dr. No can also to be associated with Fire, for he uses a flame-throwing swamp buggy disguised as a fire-spitting dragon in order to keep intruders off his island, the importance of which in the development of the narrative syntagm cannot be underestimated, since it is the direct cause of the death of Bond's ally, Quarrel, and the capture of Bond and Honeychile by Dr. No's men. Hence, fire deepens the level of tension and increases that of narrative authority; and, needless to say, there will be a copious exchange of gunfire when Bond and Honeychile escape at the end of the novel.

Dr. No and his island are therefore intricately related to the four elements; however, this is not to say that the latter are partial to the Villain, for they are treated in a rather ambivalent fashion and turn indifferently against both protagonist and antagonist, adding a pervasive level of tension that functions as an unspoken narrative backdrop to the main conflict. Naturally, the end result of this implicit struggle favors the forces of Order, and thus we eventually find out that black crabs are not particularly fond of flesh, which explains why Honeychile has been spared by the sea and its creatures; or that the reef that was supposed to wound Bond and Solitaire while being dragged by Mr. Big's yacht in *Live and Let Die* eventually saves their lives by protecting them from the shock-wave of the explosion when the limpet mine Bond placed on the hull of the ship detonates. However, this end result is presented as mostly due to 007's mental and physical strengths, and to his determination, rather than to any sympathetic collaboration on the part of the elements: The hero must defeat not only the direct threat to the Order that of the Villain incarnates, but also the latent chaos of nature that surrounds his actions. The natural elements are therefore neither good nor bad, and we are indeed very far from any type of anthropomorphic representation; what they provide, besides the assurance that the Hero can order nature as well as society, is narrative tension and spectacularity at their most universal levels, for anyone can identify with what we perceive as the most fundamental and primal forces of our reality. Furthermore, they allow the Bond universe to acquire a mythological resonance by implicitly referring us to the most ancient myths of the Occidental *Imaginary*,[4] in which the hero fights the elements and its monstrous creatures. Bond's battle against the sharks and the barracudas in *Live and Let Die* (novel), and against the giant squid in *Dr. No* (novel), should indeed remind us of Perseus beheading Medusa or slaying the Ketos.

Casino to Casino

If *Dr. No* appeared to be an ideal choice for a first cinematographic adaptation of the Bond universe, it is in part because it conferred a much greater role to the natural elements than the initial *Casino Royale*, which happens mainly indoors and uses the narrative motifs of the natural elements in a very subdued manner. The action does take place in Royales-Les-Eaux, a seaside resort; however, besides its function as a context belonging to the second level of defamiliarization, that of the high life, the sea has no active part in the development of the main narrative syntagm and only becomes significant after Bond's convalescence, when Le Chiffre is dead and the adventure concluded, as an ideal setting for a romance novel rather than for a spy story. We can appreciate the importance that the representation of the natural elements and the challenges they imply have acquired within the Bond narrative syntagm when we compare the novel to its recent screen adaptation, which has been seen as a rebirth of the franchise, oriented towards a more faithful representation of Fleming's novels, darker and more realistic.[5] *Casino Royale* (film, 2006) has indeed kept the main elements of Fleming's original story, and the paradigmatic changes, if connotatively significant (such as Texas hold'em in lieu of baccarat or a black Felix Leiter), do not alter the development of the narrative syntagm. However, in direct response to what the Bond genre has become beyond Fleming, the film has added an abundance of motifs directly related to the natural elements: the chase from crane to crane in Madagascar, Bond emerging from the sea under the eyes of Dimitrio's wife in the Bahamas (very much like Honeychile/Honey in *Dr. No* [novel and film] or like Jinx in *Die Another Day*), Le Chiffre's scheming to sabotage an airplane in Miami, and, of course, the grand finale in Venice, which involves both Fire and Water as an entire building collapses into the Grand Canal after a copious exchange of gun fire between Bond and the Villains. The very last scene, set against the backdrop of lake Como, directly relates Fire and Water to the Bond universe, as Bond shoots Vesper's contact in the leg with a remarkably oversized gun before uttering his most self-describing trademark phrase: "The name is Bond ... James Bond."

As we see, a long game of cards in between four walls and limited traveling to the French seaside resort of Royale-Les-Eaux simply no longer suffice to sustain the narrative authority of the Bond narration as we conceive it today, and the presence of the four elements, which relate the second and third levels of defamiliarization, have become active paradigms— that is, semiotically significant and indispensable parts of the Bond universe. The last film of the series to date,[6] *Quantum of Solace*, which, contrarily to *Casino Royale*, has nothing to do with the short story that bears the same title, further illustrates the pervasiveness of the natural elements within the narration by directly associating Water with the primary conflict, for the Villain's main objective, which would inevitably disrupt the Order, is to secure the control of the entire Bolivian water supply. The Earth is abundantly represented by the Bolivian desert and signifies the death of the Villain, symbolically condemned by Bond to die of thirst in the middle of a wasteland after having wanted to own Water. In the pure Bond tradition inaugurated in the very first installment, *Casino Royale* (novel), Greene does not die of thirst but is assassinated by his own accomplices from the Quantum organization, just as Le Chiffre is eliminated by a SMERSH operative; nonetheless, Greene's body is still found in the middle of the Bolivian desert, intrinsically tying Earth to his death, and Bond's plan turns the primal forces of nature into active narrative paradigms, as Earth replaces the gun and the desert becomes the bullet.

The progression of the main conflict in *Quantum of Solace* (film) is itself outlined by the use of Air, Water, Earth and Fire as decisive narrative motifs, for it is after they *parachute* into a *cavern* from their *plane* of *fire* that Bond and Camille discover the *underground dam* built by Greene in order to secure the monopoly of *water*, hence linking the four elements at a crucial point in the development of the narrative syntagm. The desire to do away with the over-the-top special effects that characterized most of the Brosnan installments has not altered the fundamental function of the natural elements in the narration but only their appearance, and so, for instance, we can easily oppose the wilderness of the desert to the artificiality of the ice palace conceived by Graves in *Die Another Day*. However, both still remain metonymically representative of a specific element, Earth and Water respectively, and both fulfill the same function, i.e., suggesting another conflict, as timeless as it is universal — that of the human versus the indifference of nature as it manifests itself through its primal forces.

The World Is Just Enough

The collective and fragmented sending entity of the cinematographic Bond message, as described in Chapter 2, does not represent a cohesive critical point of view. Therefore, beyond the simple identification of fashionable paradigms and their insertion within the Bond narrative syntagm (a move which tends to be exclusively determined according to the projection of a hypothetical box office success), the actual makers of the James Bond films are more simple operators than true creators. As established earlier, the Bond genre is not exactly a "mobile" or "floating" signifier, as some critics claim, but a fairly rigid semiotic structure that tolerates a vast albeit finite, amount of paradigmatic variations and very few syntagmatic alterations. Russia can merge into SPECTRE which in turn can morph into Quantum. Mr. Big, Goldfinger or Dr. No can become Carver, Graves or Greene. Nonetheless, all occupy an identical function in a set narrative syntagm that admits no real deviation. The control that the sending entity (namely, the production team) has over the general organization and thematic orientation of any installment is mostly cosmetic, for the appeal of any Bond movie resides as much, if not more, in what the audience recognizes rather than on the element of surprise,[7] which limits remarkably the possibilities for real authorship. We expect to see the same story dressed differently and to receive the same narrative syntagm expressed through new but identifiable paradigms, semantically related to those used in the previous installment. Whether Bond goes to Kingston or to Bangkok, and then on to Hong Kong or Honolulu, is irrelevant as long as he goes somewhere "special." Whether the Bond girl is a blonde or a brunette, white or non-white, does not matter as long as she corresponds to a desirable stereotype, and so on.

The laws of promotion and marketing oblige the members of the production team to assure the audience that any given installment contains the usual narrative motifs, distributed according to the three levels of defamiliarization enunciated earlier, and to simultaneously claim some type of originality, since no one is easily lured into watching the same film over and over again. Hence, the highly publicized different directions taken by the Bond narration over the years are in reality limited to only two tendencies: a hard Bond, allegedly closer to the textual Bond — Connery, Dalton, Craig — and a soft Bond, as incarnated mostly by Moore but also by Brosnan. If the attempt to return to a darker, more serious Bond failed in the case of Dalton but seems to prove successful in that of Craig, it is due to the turn towards grittiness taken by today's action cinema and not so much to the "originality" of Craig's interpretation; for in the highly structured narrative universe of the Bond genre, the story mostly tells itself, and the actual contribution of the production team is confined to non-determining, usually market-conscious elements. 007 quit smoking when smoking was no longer associated with glamour, his Aston Martin became a BMW, and his Rolex a Seiko and then an Omega to comply with the new, ferocious practices of product placement; however, these changes did not modify his narrative function in any way. Even the very few paradigmatic changes that seem to have affected the narrative syntagm at a deeper level, such as the evolution of female roles, respond to contextual rather than aesthetic motivations and do not alter the relationships between the other preexisting paradigms, nor the overall evolution of the narrative syntagm; they are simply updates in response to a changing market and to a more politically conscious audience. Consequently, the characters of Anya Amasova (agent triple X from *The Spy Who Loved Me*, film), Pam Bouvier (*Licence to Kill*), Wai Lin (*Tomorrow Never Dies*), Jinx (*Die Another Day*) and Camille Montes (*Quantum of Solace*) would seem to indicate a progression towards a stronger female counterpart. Anya Amasova suggests an already strong character, though still subjected to the authority of a male superior, and Camille Montes embodies an independent woman with her own agenda. While Wai Lin and Jinx represent an update of Anya Amasova, all three being secret agents in their own right working for the just cause (that is, the Order administered by the establishment), Camille Montes can be seen as a revised version of Pam Bouvier, for both of them are free women in pursuit of their personal goals. Nonetheless, all of them except Pam Bouvier will be saved from certain death by Bond, demonstrating that their apparent strength does not suffice to defeat the enemy, and that they remain all potential victims of Disorder without the virile intervention of 007. Furthermore, this evolution of the female character can hardly be considered a real departure from the narrative matrix created by Fleming, for the figure of a strong, independent woman is already very much present in the textual Bond, as exemplified by Vivienne Michel in *The Spy Who Loved Me* and by Tracy from *On Her Majesty's Secret Service*. The feminization of M, which might pass as a daring pro-feminist move, has in actuality only exacerbated the parenting tendencies that the original M already presented; thus, rather than contributing to a true feminization of authority, M's sex change has turned him/her into a real parent. As seen in Chapter 2, M functions semiotically as a Mother figure, for (s)he literally gives birth to 007 by charging him with a mission. Hence, rather than a rupture, the feminization of M constitutes a confirmation of an already existing tendency of the Bond narration. As a genre rather than a simple formula, the Bond universe already includes all its functional paradigms, and the innovations brought forth by the designated production team consist, most of all, in emphasizing different elements from an already established pool of possibilities.

A proof of the Bond genre's narrative independence from its collective sending entity is the interchangeability of said entity's members, acting — as well as directing-wise. The authorship of any adventure of James Bond has become diluted and yields to the intentionality of the narration itself, which precedes and supersedes that of any individual associated with the project of producing another iteration of the narrative structure: The production team does not create a James Bond installment as much as it is created by it, professionally and commercially. In our Society of Spectacle,[8] where, contrary to the past, the characters are less important than the actors that interpret them,[9] James Bond remains a notable exception, able to turn the confidential fame of one Daniel Craig into international stardom.[10] Similarly, the subsequent directors working for the Bond franchise have been more or less consciously conditioned by the laws of the Bond universe, and each film bears both narrative and visual traces of previous installments. For instance, we see Jinx and Bond himself emerging from the sea in *Die Another Day* and *Casino Royale*, respectively, just as the very first Bond girl on film, Honey Rider (Ursula Andress), did in *Dr. No*, and the discovery of Strawberry Fields' dead body covered in crude oil in *Quan-

tum of Solace is a reenactment of *Goldfinger*'s well-known scene where Bond finds Jill Masterson dead, covered in gold paint. These are not metafictitious elements but mere narrative and visual staples which do not call the attention of the addressee to the creative process nor to the artificiality of the narrative universe by playing with its conventions, but rather reassert them through mere repetition. We can oppose these narrative reiterations to the truly meta-narrative moments we encounter in *On Her Majesty's Secret Service*, such as Bond addressing the audience at the end of the title sequence or the soundtracks of past films playing while he cleans his office, for they do not transcend the limits of the narrative syntagm but rather provide recognizable markers that contribute to its authority by merging an individual installment within a greater and unquestionable diegetic tradition. The vision of agent Fields laying dead and naked in an identical position to that of Jill Masterson in *Goldfinger* does not challenge the narrative conventions of the Bond genre but rather reinforces them; it is a mere paradigmatic repetition that does not create any type of distance vis-à-vis the fictitious universe and is perfectly integrated to the narrative syntagm at hand — namely, *Quantum of Solace*. This particular example illustrates as well the dependence of directors and writers alike upon the Bond tradition, which seems to render the notion of subjective contribution impossible; the message itself determines the options of the sending entity, which naturally all but disappears behind the authority of the preexisting narrative structure.[11] The mitigated reception of *On Her Majesty's Secret Service* indicates clearly that the Bond genre does not tolerate any type of narrative distance that might endanger the different degrees of suspension of disbelief on which it is based.

The members of any designated Bond production team are understandably reluctant to recognize that their room for maneuver is mostly a response to necessary commercial updates, and so when *Quantum of Solace*'s director Mark Forster decided to center the narration on the four natural elements, as reported by Anne Thompson,[12] he may not have been aware that he was merely following the exigencies of the genre, nor that he was far from being the first one to do so. *Quantum of Solace*'s originality might consist in using the control of water as the Chaotic Function (i.e., the concrete means appropriated by the Villain to create Disorder); however, this supposes a simple paradigmatic change, which in the end might not appear all that significant. The traditional chaotic agent of the Bond universe tends to be related to Fire, appearing in the form of either a bomb, a rocket, a missile, or a laser beam; therefore, in this case, one natural element — Water — has simply replaced the other.

The four natural elements are unquestionably fundamental paradigms of the Bond genre, and *Casino Royale* (novel), albeit micro-structurally representative of most James Bond traits, is the proverbial exception that confirms the rule. In the long run, the four natural elements, served by the spectacular priorities of the cinematographic medium, have imposed themselves as recurrent paradigms of the Bond universe as much as casinos and gambling. They can even suggest the entire Bond universe in the pre-title sequence, as they do in the first installment from the Brosnan period, *GoldenEye* (1995), directed by Martin Campbell, which shows 007 riding a motorcycle on the snow, jumping off a cliff to catch a falling airplane and eventually flying away as the Russian facility that he has come to sabotage blows up. *GoldenEye* is to be considered a new beginning for the series, marked by a hiatus of several years and by the arrival of Brosnan in the role of 007; and it is therefore significant that the producers chose to emphasize the four natural elements as active narrative paradigms from the very start of the film in order to secure a narrative authority that could have suffered from Bond's extended absence.

The narrative structure of the installment appropriately titled *The World Is Not Enough* is particularly representative of the important narrative function of the four natural elements in the Bond universe, and its long pre-title scene(s) include Air, Earth, Fire and Water, as Bond jumps from a balcony, chases a mysterious sniper from Bilbao to London, and ends up free-falling from an exploding hot-air balloon after a long boat chase on the Thames. Throughout the film the four natural elements are intrinsically related to the development of the plot and take the form of various narrative motifs, which include an avalanche, a submarine, underground installations, flying snowmobiles and, for good measure, a crucial meeting in a cave were the Villain, Renard, handles burning rocks with his bare hands. The main syntagm concludes with the underwater explosion of Renard's stolen submarine, hence combining two natural elements as logical opposites to resolve narrative tension: The Villain dies in the explosion, i.e., is killed by Fire, while Bond and his designated female counterpart, Christmas Jones, escape through Water.

By integrating the four natural elements within the narrative syntagm as functional paradigms, the Bond genre has become an elementary force in itself, self-generating and authoritative, which imposes its laws and paradigms upon the collective sending entity and only allows authorial contributions insofar as they represent a reorganization of preexisting motifs. By now, the laws of the Bond genre are as unquestionable as those of Nature itself.

Motifs and Motivations

Such an overwhelming representation of the four natural elements implies a finite amount of narrative motifs that must be reiterated periodically in the filmic installments, such as cars, planes, submarines, helicopters, and boats, but also parachutes (*The Spy Who Love Me, Moonraker*), ski runs or cable cars (*On Her Majesty's Secret Service, Moonraker*). All are related to one or several natural elements that the hero must dominate in order to fulfill his mission, suggesting a direct equivalence between administrative and natural orders. James Bond is more than ever the agent of the Greater Status Quo, able to tame men as well as natural forces.

Considered from the point of view of their structural role, each of the four elements acquires a specific semiotic weight in direct relationship with the narrative syntagm. MI6's codename, "Universal Exports," connotes both Earth and Air, for it implies space as well as displacement, and suggests a hold upon the world through the logics of modern capitalistic movement. In the development of the story, Earth and Air become paradigmatic supports for the most primal narrative tension — that created by sheer action, and naturally magnified by the process of spectacularization: defying gravity remains one of 007's favorite activities[13] and his ability to travel edges on the gift of ubiquity. James Bond, as a trustworthy representative figure of Universal Exports, exports himself universally and effortlessly, dominating Air, Earth, Water and Fire through breathtaking action scenes perfectly justified within the narrative syntagm, which is the reason why no action scene in any Bond installment, regardless of how farfetched it may appear, ever seems out of place nor even contrived. The very semiotic structure of the Bond genre calls for concrete demonstrations of Bond's ability to impose Order and stability over chaos in any situation.

If Fire can be associated with the resolution of the main conflict and usually signifies the Villain's punishment through the destruction of his lair, Water tends to be related to the epilogue, which, far from being a simple conclusion, participates in the continuity of the series, for it indicates that the adventures of James Bond carry on beyond the narrative limits of any given installment — let's remember that the adventures of James Bond are not only about epic endeavors and heroic battles but also about playing golf, gambling, skiing and having casual sex. During the epilogue, the third level of defamiliarization — the epic conflict — yields to the second one, that of pleasure-oriented activity, as the triumphing hero enjoys the sexual reward of his victory, the proverbial *repos du guerrier* ("the rest of the warrior"), while waiting for his next battle. And this comes within a natural element that we tend to associate with free time, pleasure and fun, as well as with sexuality — Water. The beach and the sea, a bath, a Jacuzzi, a boat ride, scuba-diving, all belong to the semantic field of Water and connote pleasant activities which can be directly related to the most accessible level of defamiliarization, socially recognized and available to all — that is, vacations.

The semiotic correlation between sexual gratification and water is already present in the first textual installment of the series, *Casino Royale*, as Vesper and Bond enjoy each other's company on the beach after Bond's convalescence and before Vesper's suicide. The very same paradigms — Bond, the girl, the sea and free time — are reorganized in the second novel of the series, *Live and Let Die*, albeit in a promising rather than tragic manner, consolidating the notion that sexual gratification is the due reward for the warrior after battle. Both *Casino Royale* and *Live and Let Die* are open narrative structures, for they each suggest the possibility of a continuation; however, whereas the conclusion of *Casino Royale* promises new battles between Good and Evil, that of *Live and Let Die* suggests a restful, sexually pleasant interlude. While the conclusion of the first installment alludes to the third and most demanding level of defamiliarization — that which requires the highest degree of suspension of disbelief for it tells of the mysterious and constant international secret wars between the agents of Order and the foul manifestations of Disorder — the end of *Live and Let Die* refers to the second level, that of desirable but possible activities, and is hence more "credible" than that of *Casino Royale*: a sexual encounter is probably easier to come by than a super-villain organization set on taking over the world. As the narrative syntagm evolves throughout the novels and especially on the screen, this particular paradigm acquires two functions: Not only does it provide a positive resolution of the syntagm without closing the structure, but it also makes the overall installment more believable, hence asserting its narrative authority by eliciting a lesser degree of suspension of disbelief. And so, many subsequent installments will retain the same three elements — Bond, Girl and Water — and eliminate the return to the third level of defamiliarization found in *Casino Royale* after Vesper's suicide. In sheer structural terms, the conclusion of *Live and Let Die* is indeed identical to that of *Casino Royale*, minus the Bond girl's tragic ending, which causes the narrative syntagm to return to the terms of the main conflict rather than remaining at a more credible level of defamiliarization.

Although not as systematically as in the films, Water and sexual promises are found at the end of several textual installments, such as *Goldfinger*, as Bond and Pussy Galore are about to make love on the boat that rescued them; and in the last installment of the series, *The Man with the Golden Gun*, as Mary Goodnight is attempting to convince Bond to spend a few days at her villa and specifies that it "overlooks the Kingston Harbour." Water is also intrinsically associated with the development of the relationship between Bond and Honeychile after the resolution of the main narrative conflict in *Dr. No*, as she bathes him after they escape from Dr. No's island; and to that between Bond and Kissy Suzuki in *You Only Live Twice*, which is amply documented in a fairly explicit manner after the main conflict has concluded with the death of Blofeld and the destruction of his lair.

The association between Water and imminent sexual pleasure functioning as a closure to the narrative syntagm, which has become a true cliché of the cinematographic Bond, can therefore easily be traced back to the textual Bond. It should be observed, however, that the element of Water plays a more semiotically complex role in the novels than in the films, for its value as narrative function fluctuates beyond that of simple backdrop used either to enhance the tension produced by the action or to signify the sexually charged provisional conclusion of any given installment. In "Octopussy" for instance, far from connoting the well-deserved sexual rest of the warrior, Water and its semantic field become one term of the binary opposition on which the narration is grounded and signify death rather than love, as well as the definitive closure of the narrative syntagm. Informed by Bond that he shall be arrested for murder within a few hours, Dexter Smythe attempts to finish his experiment, which consists of feeding a scorpion fish to the octopus that he has adopted and affectionately named "Octopussy" in order to determine if the octopus is immune to the scorpion fish venom. Somewhat shook up by Bond's recent visit and the trouble that will ensue, Smythe lets himself be stung by the scorpion fish and will eventually be attacked and killed by his own pet octopus. Bond may have been the one who started the process that leads to Major Dexter Smythe's demise; however, as illustrated by the very title of the story, the determining conflict at the core of the narrative syntagm is based upon the opposition between Dexter Smythe and the element Water, metonymically represented by his struggle with the scorpion fish and the octopus. This particular sequence reminds us of James Bond swimming through shark and barracuda-infested water to place a mine on the hull of Mr. Big's yacht in *Live and Let Die* (novel) or defeating a giant squid in *Dr. No* (novel), and hence illustrates the superiority of the Hero, who dominates the natural elements rather than being dominated by them, over a guilt-ridden, morally corrupt double, for Major Dexter Smythe used to be an honest representative figure of the Order. Although, as noted before, we cannot say that the Bond genre exhibits an anthropomorphic conception of nature and the natural elements, we can, however, discern a certain intentionality in the organization of the paradigms related to the aggression of nature's agents, for they eventually always demonstrate the righteous invulnerability of the Hero and often participate more or less directly in the punishment of the Villain, as they do in "Octopussy." For instance, in *Dr. No* (novel) the Villain dies under a mountain of guano, a substance metonymically related to both Earth — as a growing aid — and Air, for it comes from birds. In *Goldfinger* (novel), the depressurization of the plane's cabin causes Oddjob to be sucked out the window, turning Air and Earth into Bond's allies. The text specifies that Bond is not exactly certain of what may happen when he cuts through the window; however, the result of the direct intervention of sheer natural elements in the struggle works very much in his favor, allowing him to get rid of a formidable opponent whom he could not have defeated in regular combat.

The adaptation of a narrative structure by a collective entity for a would-be universal addressee, a process subjected to very rigid marketing laws, necessarily implies a simplification of its organization as well as a certain fossilization of its main operative paradigms, and thus the motif of Water is overwhelmingly represented in the films as part of the concluding, sexually promising sequence. It is found at the end of the very first installment, *Dr. No*, which shows Bond and Honey Rider on a rescue boat in the middle of the ocean preparing to make love after Bond lets go of the cable that is towing them, a scene which can be considered microstructurally representative of most Bond film conclusions (notable exceptions being the ill-fated and hardly influential adaptation of *On Her Majesty's Secret Service* and the two installments of the recent rebooting). The Water motif related to sexuality contributes to the continuity of the series, for we usually find Bond in or about to have an intimate rapport with a woman at the beginning of the narrative syntagm, when he receives the call from headquarters. Hence, sex naturally links one installment to the next; only the girl changes, to add a supplementary touch of defamiliarization. Life as usual for Bond is indeed as interesting and pleasant as when he is on a mission, and normality appears just as entertaining as the exception.[14]

Water takes different forms as semiotic complement of the conclusive sexual paradigm of any given installment and can be suggested by a shower taken with the Bond girl, as in *A View to a Kill*, or by a passionate kiss in a swimming pool, as at the end of *Licence to Kill*. In a more subdued manner, Water associated with post-mission sex is represented by the canals of Venice at the end of *From Russia with Love*, which simply re-adapts the paradigms found at the conclusion of *Dr. No* along the register of sophisticated tourism by opposition to that of adventurous holiday. The final scene of *The Man with the Golden Gun*, as well as that of *Octopussy*, suggests yet another modality of grand tourism — namely, the boat cruise, as Bond and the designated Bond girl (Mary Goodnight and Octopussy respectively), sail away and prepare to make love.

Naturally, Water, as well as Fire, in spite of having fairly well-defined functions within the narrative syntagm, participates fully in the narrative tension, just as Air and Earth does, and contribute to turn the Bond genre into a universally appealing narrative syntagm that represents the constant struggle of Human vs. Nature through collectively identifiable paradigms, while at the same time telling yet again how Good and Order always triumph over Evil and Disorder.

On 007's Time

This review of the role of the primal forces in the James Bond universe would not be complete without a mention of Time, which, just like the four natural elements, represents a fundamental determination of human consciousness logically associated with space and displacement, two recurring motifs of the Bond genre. James Bond not only triumphs over the obstacles created by Earth, Air, Water and Fire, but defeats Time as well by mastering it in the logic of the narrative syntagm, and his timeless struggle between good and evil is very severely timed.

The very first textual installment, *Casino Royale*, shows Bond saved *in extremis* by the intervention of a SMERSH agent who dispatches Le Chiffre when the latter is about to destroy the very semiotic essence of James Bond — that is, to finish castrating him ("Say good-bye to it, Bond," 141) — and this privileged relationship with time is one of the constant characteristics of the Bond narrative universe. The Order that the Hero restores is hence not only territorial (that is, spatial) but also temporal, and acquires therefore a historical depth; by triumphing over the forces of evil, by dominating the natural elements and mastering time, James Bond becomes a would-be architect of History, allowing the syntagm to establish yet another level of narrative authority. The incorporation of various elements from the historical context into the narration, a characteristic of the Bond universe amply documented, corresponds at a structural level to Bond's ability to master the moment: When he saves Fort Knox at the last moment in *Goldfinger* (novel and film), 007 is making History — that is, appropriating reality to reorganize it according to the parameters of the

Order. Just as the narrative syntagm evolves to reflect changing cultural, political and cinematographic trends, and remains in synchronicity with History, Bond himself is always in perfect synchronicity with the narrative moment regardless of the circumstances. The function of the complicated schemes designed by the Villain in order to kill Bond, yet another constant paradigm in the Bond universe, is naturally to provide the Hero with enough time to escape. In the Bond genre, the World, the Villain and, of course, the receiver are all on 007's time.

James Bond's perfect timing is not the product of careful planning but rather the result of his improvisational skills served by chance, and betrays the same type of intentionality observed above in regard to the treatment of natural elements within the economy of the narration. Time, like Earth, Air, Water and Fire, introduced as essentially objective values by the logic of the narration, always turn in favor of the Hero, becoming an improbable ally in his attempt to foil the Villain's plans. The resolution of the main conflict in *Live and Let Die* (novel) is in this sense particularly significant, for Bond and Solitaire's torture is scheduled to begin at six, while the mine that Bond has placed on the hull of the ship is set to detonate at exactly three past six. Mr. Big's chronological projection therefore completes and facilitates Bond's design, and Time, seemingly presented as an indifferent notion within the narration, directly contributes to the Hero's victory, for it determines the death of Mr. Big and the survival of Bond and Solitaire.

Although the addition of a supplementary level of narrative tension towards the resolution of the syntagm is hardly a novel idea, the originality of the Bond genre consists in presenting from the very beginning the narrative acceleration that we generally associate with a climactic conclusion. The narrative syntagm is initiated by the crisis itself, and although we sense a progression in the main conflict, the fundamental tension between Bond and the Villain is present from the start as the main axis of the narration. The first encounter between Bond and the Villain, be it with Goldfinger in the eponymous novel and film, Drax in *Moonraker* (novel and film), Grant in *From Russia with Love* (novel and film), Blofeld in *On Her Majesty's Secret Service* (novel and film) or Scaramanga in *The Man with the Golden Gun* (novel), already represents an extreme tension that could perfectly suggest that of a final confrontation. However, in the spy genre as defined by 007, where exposure and secrecy work together to produce maximum narrative authority, this initial confrontation between Bond and the Villain can be resolved temporarily without endangering the overall narrative tension generated by the basic binary opposition between both parties.

Narrative Countdown

Contrary to the typical norms of tension administration in action narration, the Bond genre presents a narrative acceleration from the start of the syntagm, an effect which has been magnified on the screen by introducing the end of a previous mission, usually followed by a spectacular chase involving a struggle against one or several natural elements, in the pre-credit sequence. Although the recent rebooting of the series attempts to do away with some motifs that have lost their suggestive power due to sheer repetition and have become therefore unable to produce a defamiliarizing effect, such as the visit to the Q branch or the usual after-mission sexual reward, the race against time remains a functional paradigm in both *Casino Royale* and *Quantum of Solace*. In *Casino Royale*, Le Chiffre's initial scheme depends exclusively on Time, for it is based on financial speculation (namely, short-selling), and Le Chiffre himself is living on borrowed time after Bond prevents the bombing of the airliner that was supposed to trick the market. In *Quantum of Solace*, as in the vast majority of the Bond adventures, both textual and cinematographic, Greene's plan must be stopped within a certain time to prevent Disorder from taking hold; therefore, the narrative clock has started ticking from the beginning of the syntagm. If *Casino Royale* benefits from the original novel, which appears less paradigmatically structured than many of its sequels, *Quantum of Solace*, on the contrary, exhibits the typical Bond structure as it has been fashioned over the years by a fragmented sending entity and reduces Time to its most elementary yet fundamental function — that of a narrative countdown at work from the very beginning of the adventure. Despite the efforts of the production team to add a different, less commercial dimension to the film, *Quantum of Solace* remains determined by the limits of the preexisting narrative structure collectively elaborated upon in film after film within the exchange between sender and receiver, with all its cultural and financial implications, and is, ironically, much more of a typical Bond film than the Fleming-inspired *Casino Royale*. The pre-title sequence, which presents the originality of picking up the narration exactly where the previous installment ended, is in actuality only exploiting further the notion of continuity suggested in the previous installments. Furthermore, it consists exclusively of a chase, a paradigm that we have become accustomed to see in the pre-title sequence of any Bond Film. In *Casino Royale*, SMERSH remains in the background of the narration, and its narrative function is somewhat paradoxical, for one of his agents actually saves Bond's life: The SMERSH agent simply does not have the order to kill Bond and therefore cannot do it, a fine tribute to Communist sense of discipline. This tripartite binary opposition involving Bond/Le Chiffre, Le Chiffre/SMERSH and SMERSH/Bond is more complex than the typical binary opposition between Bond and the Villain that we find in *Quantum of Solace*, which closely follows the most identifiable Bond narrative structure: Quantum has replaced SMERSH and SPECTRE, and if Greene is indeed eliminated by his own allies (a common practice among Bond Villains) for having betrayed the secrets of his organization, he is still part of Quantum, unlike Le Chiffre, who could be seen as an independent contractor. The reduction of the diegetic axis to a pure binary opposition increases the narrative countdown effect, and so the action in *Quantum of Solace* moves much faster than in *Casino Royale*, as narrative authority is mainly supported by Bond's race against Time to foil the Villain's designs rather than by the complexity of a tripartite conflict. The original pre-title sequence of *Quantum of Solace* represents in reality a perfect micro-structure of the Bond genre in its most simple expression: a multifaceted chase where time is always of the essence.

The Watch and the Bomb

Two semantically interrelated motifs, the watch and the bomb, abundantly represented and under a variety of forms throughout the novels as well as the films, clearly illustrate the relationship between Time and the Bond universe at the level of the narrative syntagm. We are informed in *Live and Let Die* (novel) as well as in *On Her Majesty's Secret Service* (novel) that Bond sports a Rolex, just as we are informed in *Casino Royale* (film, 2006) that it is actually an Omega. Product placement might explain the change of brands but not the presence of the watch itself, which is to be considered as a semiotically charged paradigm.[15] In the Bond universe the watch has three main functions related to three levels of defamiliarization enunciated earlier. It suggests first of all the scheduled Order of the administration that Bond is in charge of protecting. Secret paperwork, just as any paperwork, runs on a specific schedule, and the watch is not only an indispensable tool for any devoted employee, it is also the rule by which he or she conceives time in relationship to the Order. It is as well a status symbol associated with the higher class, that which precisely partakes in the pleasant activities that compose the second level of defamiliarization, such as playing golf or driving fine cars. An expensive watch is the unmistakable sign of James Bond's social position, that of a gentleman, as well as a metonymy of his impeccable sense of timing. Finally, it has become on the screen an integral part of the secret agent's arsenal, saving his life on various occasions, hence acquiring the value of an active paradigm at the third level of defamiliarization, that which tells the story of the eternal and epic battle between Good and Evil. Throughout the different installments, Bond's watch is alternatively a miniature rotating saw (*Live and Let Die*), a teletype receiver (*The Spy Who Loved Me*), an explosive device (*Moonraker, Tomorrow Never Dies, Die Another Day*), a digital two-way transmitter-receiver (*For Your Eyes Only*), a universal direction finder (*Octopussy*), a built-in laser beam (*GoldenEye, Die Another Day*) and a grappling hook (*The World Is Not Enough*). Bond's personal time piece evokes therefore his professional status, his pleasant lifestyle and his sacred mission, and constitutes a meaningful paradigm which relates all levels of defamiliarization — that related to an official schedule, that created by the display of the finer things in life, and that provoked by the basic epic conflict between Order and Disorder. As the most obvious metonymy of time, the watch establishes a direct connection between Time and the hero that adds a dimension of modernity and currency to the traditional opposition between Good vs. Evil by locking it within a very precise, temporal reference — an everlasting present contained in the narrative leitmotif of 007's Rolex, with or without the added gadgetry. The watch, as a symbol of precision and as the means to control time, represents perfectly the main properties and priorities of the Order as embodied by the precise machinery of MI6 and its ontological need to control reality, both spatially and chronologically: The fight against time, just as that against the dragon, is as traditional as can be, but the chronograph has greatly improved.

The motif of the bomb, already onomastically significant (as indicated in Chapter 2), is intrinsically related to that of the watch, for both are determined by Time. In the Bond universe, bombs are usually time bombs, which means that their function depends exclusively on timing, and this correlation directly affects the evolution of the narrative syntagm: Whether Bond is placing the bomb (*Live and Let Die*, novel; "Quantum of Solace," short story) or defusing it (*Goldfinger*, film; *The Spy Who Loved Me*, film), the heroic secret agent is risking his life and owes his survival to his perfect timing. The defusing of the time bomb left in Fort Knox by Goldfinger (*Goldfinger*, film) is particularly revealing of the intentionality of Time in the Bond genre in relationship to the time bomb motif. After killing Oddjob, thanks to his wits and determination, Bond desperately fumbles about with the bomb mechanism, unable to stop the countdown, and is about to pull out a handful of cables picked at random when the hand of a U.S. atomic specialist stops him and expertly pulls the correct switch; the bomb's clock, which has been ticking throughout the fight between Bond and Oddjob, and has contributed in a large part to the narrative authority of the scene by adding a supplementary level of tension, is shown stopped seven seconds before detonation — which naturally reads "007" on the dial (1:40:32–1:40:45): Time is hence the Hero's ally both diegetically and symbolically. At the narrative level, Bond's desperate decision to yank a few cables at random from the atomic bomb seems imprudent at best, and we can thus suppose that once again he has been saved by chance just as he was in his very first adventure, *Casino Royale*. From a symbolic point of view, the presence of his code number on the bomb's clock once it has been defused — that is when the Order is no longer directly threatened — suggests the appropriation of the narrative countdown by the Hero as well as his undeniable victory in the ever-present race against Time.

The death of Mr. Big in *Live and Let Die* (novel) is from this point of view, highly symbolic, for it presents the villain's defeat in relationship to his loss of control over Time:

> Both arms stopped flailing the water and the head went under and came up again. A cloud of blood welled up and darkened the sea. Two six-foot thin brown shadows backed out of the cloud and then dashed back into it. The body in the water jerked sideways. Half of The Big Man's left arm came out of the water. It had no hand, no wrist, no wrist watch [272].

The bomb placed by Bond on the hull of Mr. Big's yacht has robbed the villain of his life as well as his time, symbolized by the reference to his wristwatch, and once again secured Time and Order. Eco considers this very passage as representative of the "*école du regard*," considering the detail of the wristwatch as narratively superfluous: "The absence of the watch on the wrist bitten off by the shark is not just an example of macabre sarcasm; it is an emphasis on the essential by the inessential, typical of the *école du regard*" (*Reader* 165). However, when we consider the semiotic distribution of Time throughout the narrative syntagm, especially in reference to its resolution, the detail of Mr. Big's watch acquires a very specific function by symbolically completing the Villain's loss of control over time and the reappropriation of the latter by Bond in the name of the Order; it is indeed a macabre and perhaps sarcastic detail, but it is also semiotically *essential* for it participates in the overall harmony of the narration.

The time bomb motif can itself be perceived as a metonymy of the crisis that puts the Order in jeopardy and that must be defused by its heroic champion, James Bond 007. The crisis appears from the very start of the narrative syntagm and usually involves an exploding device, whether literal, such as a bomb or a missile, or metaphorical, such as a submarine or a laser beam. Therefore, in the Bond genre, the bomb — the Chaotic Factor — starts ticking from the start, and the diegetic progression becomes a narrative countdown.

4. Primal Forces

The race against time is a pervasive paradigm of the Bond genre, and not only because it constitutes a mean to establish narrative authority through a very traditional suspense effect, but also because the constraint of Time is a fundamental component of the character. The 00s have a very limited life expectancy, therefore their very existence is on the clock:

> It was his ambition to have as little as possible in his banking account when he was killed, as, when he was depressed, he knew he would be, before the statutory age of forty-five. Eight years to go before he was automatically taken off the 00 list and given a staff job at Headquarters. At least eight tough assignments. Probably sixteen. Perhaps twenty-four. Too many [*Moonraker* 11].

The short life expectancy of 00-agents is explicitly mentioned as well by Bond himself in *Casino Royale* (film, 2006) after M expresses regrets for having promoted him so early to the 00-section:

> M: I knew it was too early to promote you.
>
> BOND: Well, I understand double-00s have a very short life expectancy, so your mistake will be short-lived [*Casino Royale*, 2007, 0:23:07– 0:23:17].

These 00s are precisely the defining attribute of James Bond and relate form to content in a highly coherent and semiotically functional manner. Bond is therefore living on borrowed time, and his belonging to the 00-section, which defines him both on the professional front and from the point of view of his function within the narrative syntagm, is already in itself a race against time that adds yet another level of urgency to the narrative countdown. It is the first time that the short life expectancy of 007 is so explicitly stated on the screen, as if the rebooting of the series needed to reinstate this particular paradigm in order to establish a higher degree of narrative authority by emphasizing urgency at a fundamental level — that of Bond's existence.

Of course, this particular race against certain death, along with those against time and Bond's battles against the natural elements, is meant to be won by the Hero. Indeed, by now Bond has more than largely surpassed the limits of his alleged life expectancy, narratively as well as culturally. Just as Bond masters the natural elements and Time in each of his adventures, he defeats the stark projections regarding his life expectancy, which simply become one more obstacle to overcome, one more shinning example of his undeniable superiority, and, consequently, a demonstration of the triumphing righteousness of Order over the evils of Disorder.

By attributing defined paradigmatic values to primal forces, such as the four natural elements and Time, the Bond genre elicits an equally primal attention from the addressee who identifies spontaneously (we may even say at the reptilian level) with the universal struggles at play in the narrative universe, beyond political and cultural divides. The constant fight against the Natural Elements and their capacity to produce Disorder (i.e., death and destruction) is very much part of the human psyche at large, regardless of color or creed, and is as eternal as it is current.[16] However, in order for the Bond genre to be unique and establish narrative authority, these preternal conflicts and their predictable resolutions have to be presented according to specific aesthetic rules, hence exhibiting some type of artistic merit that deserves close attention.

Chapter 5

Bondian Art

Artless Bond

Although the borders between low-brow and high-brow culture — that is between art and non-art — are currently being seriously challenged, the objective evaluation of the possible artistic qualities to be found in popular cultural artifacts has not yet become systematic, for scholars naturally tend to shy away from the type of canonical judgments that have deprived popular culture of academic consideration for so long. Consequently, the task of establishing the aesthetic merits of any popular artifact does not appear as important as, for instance, that of analyzing its possible ideological content or its sociological implications. However, and regardless of its ultimate political implications, a work of art must logically exhibit artistic qualities in order to be considered as such, whether it is deemed to belong to culture or only to "popular culture." If popular culture artifacts should not indeed be summarily dismissed on the basis of their anti-canonicity, they should, on the other hand, be able to stand some type of aesthetic scrutiny.[1]

Due to his long standing as a popular hero, James Bond is an emblematic example of the canonical ambiguity that surrounds many popular figures — not only Sherlock Holmes and Maigret, but also Luke Skywalker and Wolverine — and thus the question of his artistic qualities (or absence thereof) is a crucial one. It is indeed significant that scholars often feel the need to express their own personal appreciation for the adventures of James Bond so as to compensate with the expression of a personal taste for the lack of academic prestige generally associated with their object of study. Answering to the quickly evolving tastes of their projected recipient — namely, students within the academic world — popular culture studies have only recently begun to acquire scholarly legitimacy, which might explain why anyone involved in this discipline feels the need to somewhat justify his or her endeavor. We are indeed still in the process of elaborating a functional canon of popular culture — that is, to define canonical properties to an entire corpus of study which is usually defined as primordially anti-canonical.

Are the semiotic correlations between form and content described in the previous chapters and their capacity to induce narrative authority through separate levels of defamiliarization enough to claim the status of true art for James Bond? Or are we just simply in the presence of an extremely subtle and highly balanced narrative machine, the only goal of which is to produce mindless entertainment in the form of spectacular escapism by favoring identification?

For starters, Bond himself does not seem to care much for art. He may even be perceived as an extension of a decidedly utilitarian way of life, which excludes by definition any type of artistic manifestation or enjoyment. As early as 1965, Furio Colombo, although recognizing in the textual James Bond the varnish of a proper primary education, denies him any type of artistic sensitivity: "We never find him with a book in his hands or in his suitcase, looking at a painting or making a reservation at the theater, not even for one line."[2] This evaluation is perhaps a bit severe, for, if it is true that the textual Bond is never caught admiring a painting or enjoying a piece of music, he does, however, occasionally read, especially during traveling, as he does in *From Russia with Love* and in *Diamonds Are Forever*, or on a stake-out, as in "The Living Daylights," where 007 kills time reading a German thriller he has bought of his own free will "during his wanderings." We can also remember that 007 exhibits some knowledge of classical painting in *Dr. No* when he sees Honeychile appearing on the beach: "The whole scene, the empty beach, the green and blue sea, the naked girl with the strands of fair hair, reminded Bond of something. He searched his mind. Yes, she was Botticelli's Venus, seen from behind" [105].

Nonetheless, these moments of artistic reminiscences are few and far between, and, along with Colombo's observation, the fact remains that, in general terms, the textual Bond does not indulge in the contemplation and appreciation of art at large. His cinematographic counterpart is no more sensitive to artistic manifestations, and if we find lavish, luxurious backgrounds throughout the films that often include works of art, such as paintings or sculptures, they are usually associated with the Villain as part of his natural environment, as in *The Man with the Golden Gun*, *Moonraker*, *A View to a Kill* and *Die Another Day*. In *From Russia with Love*, we meet Kronsteen, the Villain with the plan — he is the one who imagines how to ruin James Bond's reputation — at a chess tournament that takes place in a sumptuous Venetian palace; in *Casino Royale* (film), the meeting between Vespa and Mr. White takes place in between classical statues in an old Venetian palace, which, naturally, will be destroyed as a direct consequence of Bond's intervention. Even the latest installment to date, *Quantum of Solace*, implicitly associates criminality with the fine arts by setting Greene's meeting with his accomplice at the opera during a performance of *Tosca*. If anyone displays openly a certain affinity towards art in the Bond universe, it tends to be the Villain, who shows some undeniable creativity in his mischievous plans as well as in the conception of his lair: Stromberg's Atlantis (*The Spy Who Loved Me*, film), which is reminiscent of Dr. No's underwater refuge (*Dr. No*, novel), or Graves' ice palace (*Die Another Day*, film) are original, striking constructions that are not deprived of some artistic flair. Blofeld's "garden of death" (*You Only Live Twice*, novel) in particular has a somber poetry to it which corresponds aesthetically, as well as functionally, to two traditional paradigms of Romanticism — namely, the anthropomorphic conception of nature and suicide: the garden becomes a concrete expression of human emotions of despair and desperation, and its function is precisely that of facilitating the means to kill oneself. From Goethe's *The Sorrows of Young Werther* to Chateaubriand's *Atala*, suicide is indeed one of the accepted resolutions to the romantic conflict, and Blofeld's imaginative "garden of death" is hence both original and within a well-established artistic tradition, as well as totally opposed to the fundamental values purported by Bond and MI6.

In comparison, the few glimpses that the films offer into Bond's personal environment do not reveal any special preoccupation with art nor creativity. Quite to the contrary, Bond's home, as it appears in *Dr. No* when Bond returns from his meeting with M and encounters Sylvia Trench practicing her putting in his living room, or in *Live and Let Die* when M and Ms. Moneypenny come to seek him at home in the middle of the night, seems comfortable albeit very traditionally arranged, and is somewhat reminiscent of the style and design of M's office, as if Bond's personal space was nothing more than a metonymical complement of his superior's environment. The scarcity of the representations of Bond's flat is, of course, due to the narrative function of the character: 007 must travel the globe and naturally associate with the luxurious but soulless atmosphere of fancy hotels, casinos and resorts. The Villain's lair, on the other hand, is a direct extension of himself and of his machiavelic plans, and we therefore find it abundantly represented throughout the narration. Whether in his own personal environment or in the outside, the Villain often finds himself surrounded by artistic luxury.

Naturally, since it tends to be connected to the antagonist — be it Russia, Scaramanga, Drax, Zorin or Graves — any artsy environment tends to be submitted to harsh treatment, just like the lair of the Villain is eventually destroyed at the end of the narrative syntagm. For instance, as he flees from Chang, the first official Villain's henchman in *Moonraker* (film), Bond willingly leads the fight into the antique glass museum, which, considering that he is being chased by a masked samurai who intends to slice him with his sword, suggests a certain disregard for the preservation of historical works of art. Throughout the fight (0.33.40–0–34–41), Bond actively participates in the systematic destruction of a wide variety of antique glass artworks, ranging from the sixteenth to the nineteenth centuries, which have been introduced earlier in the film by a tour guide as all handmade and signed unique pieces. Bond even threatens his adversary with the most valuable piece of the entire collection — a vase from the fifteenth century — before the alarm forces him to put it back in place. Needless to say, the aforementioned irreplaceable artifact will be shattered a few seconds later by his enemy's counterattack, following the fate of most of the collection. This particular fight concludes with the fall of Bond's opponent upon a *bel canto* performance, head first into the grand piano, as a final counterpoint that underlines the futility of art in general, the integrity of which appears superfluous when compared to that of Bond's and of his mission. During the sword cockfight that opposes 007 to Graves in *Die Another Day*, several antiques and works of art that decorates the prestigious sword club where the fight takes place are joyfully ruined, and although Graves appears to be the most destructive of the two, slashing, for instance, a classical painting, 007 does not appear in the least concerned with sparing the historically and culturally significant artifacts that surround him.

Music is not better considered than priceless glass antiques if we are to judge by its representation in the short story "The Living Daylights," as well as in its eponymous film. Although the art of music occupies a definite narrative space in both instances, mainly due to the fact that the designated Bond girl doubles as an assassin and a classical cello player, its function is that of a simple backdrop rather than a theme or a motif. The only significant musical paradigm emphasized by the narration is the cello, which appears separated from its original artistic connotations in the short story as well as in the film, and recycled within an artless Bondian universe. In the short story the cello becomes the subject of a sexually-oriented rant related to the cello player, with which the agent occupies himself while on stakeout:

> How old would she be? Early twenties? Say twenty-three? With that poise and insouciance, the hint of authority in her long easy stride, she would come of good racy stock — one of the old Prussian families probably

or from similar remnants in Poland or even Russia. Why in hell did she have to choose the cello? There was something almost indecent in the idea of this bulbous, ungainly instrument between her splayed thighs. Of course Suggia had managed to look elegant, and so did that girl Amaryllis somebody. But they should invent a way for women to play the damned thing sidesaddle [110].

For the informed reader, Bond's apparent disinterest regarding the last name of "Amaryllis somebody" could be interpreted as a sign of modesty, or at least as a wink on the part of the historical author, Ian Fleming himself, since renown cellist Amaryllis Fleming was none other than his half-sister.[3] However, beyond this immediate level of response, which is most likely limited to Fleming's generation and naturally transcends the narration by basing textual authority upon a biographical and historical frame of reference rather than upon the plot, Bond's considerations revolve around the most external aspects of cello playing — to the detriment of music itself — by focusing on the sensual connotations of the player's position rather than on the art.

In the film, the cello is further separated from its intended artistic function and fully integrated into the action, as 007 escapes from KGB agents with Cara Milovi using her cello case as a sled and the cello itself — allegedly a one-of-a-kind Stradivarius — as both a tiller and a shield (0.47.28–0.48.33). During Cara's performance at the end of the film, the bullet holes left on her instrument are prominently featured in close-up shots, eclipsing the art of music by that of Bondian survival.

In the end, the only critical judgment about music ever voiced by James Bond seems to be his well-known quip about the Beatles in the film *Goldfinger*, which illustrates perfectly his musical aptitudes:

> My dear girl, there are some things that just aren't done, such as drinking Dom Pérignon '53 above the temperature of 38 degrees Fahrenheit. That's just as bad as listening to the Beatles without earmuffs! [*Goldfinger* 0.15.10–0.15.21].

Whether it is Bach or the Beatles, music, just as the other arts, is not a significant paradigm in the James Bond universe but rather a simple narrative complement that is used either as a backdrop to the action or for character development.

Paradoxically, the general rejection of art that pervades the James Bond universe, rather than being simply, as Colombo suggests,[4] an extension of a purely utilitarian consciousness, can be considered as its first artistic dimension, for it strengthens the overall semiotic coherence of the narration. Order by definition excludes art, just as administrative language rejects semiotic violence; therefore its most distinguished defender, agent

007, cannot be sensitive to the artistic manifestations that surround him. Creativity and imagination are necessarily found on the other side, that of the Villain, and although the schemes designed by his evil mind have the same object — substituting the Order with his own vision of reality — they materialize in as many ways as this particular paradigm will allow. If the first two installments of the recent rebooting, *Casino Royale* and *Quantum of Solace*, have done away with the secret lair of the Villain, which could be considered as an explicit sign of his creativity, they still point to the innovative projects of a mysterious organization, "Quantum of Solace"; and both plots culminate with the destruction of an original construction, traditionally artistic in the case of *Casino Royale*— a Venetian house — and decidedly artsy, or at least ecologically ground-breaking, in that of *Quantum of Solace*. This distribution of the creative and artistic intents is intrinsically related to the genesis of the narrative syntagm itself, for Bond, as an embodiment of MI6 and the Order it represents, reacts rather than instigates and protects rather than innovates: His relationship to creativity is hence limited to the technological devices he has at his disposal, traditionally associated with the Q branch, and to his capacity of improvisation when in harm's way.

James Bond's apparent disinterest in art is therefore logically related to the overall narrative structure and could be considered as an artistic merit in its own right, for it serves aesthetic cohesion by favoring semiotic harmony. The fact that 007 himself does not care about art does not imply that there is no art in Bond — it is already in itself an artistic move that does not exclude creativity or art from the narrative universe but associates it with the antagonist rather than with the protagonist.

Art at the Movies

Any consideration of the possible artistic qualities of the Bond narration are immediately subjected to the common opposition between literature and cinema, and it has become commonplace to affirm the superiority of the earlier over the latter. Burgess' well-known summation — "It is time for aficionados of the films to get back to the books and admire their qualities as literature" (5) — is a perfect illustration of this still-canonically-informed attitude that tends to unquestionably situate literature higher than cinema on the cultural scale. However, such a judgment implicitly confines James Bond to his historical context and does not acknowledge his uncanny ability to adapt without altering his essential nature: If James Bond is alive and well today, it is indeed on the screen rather than on the page. In his appreciation of Fleming's novels, Burgess does not take into account the structural peculiarities of the Bond narration, which have allowed it to survive not only the death of its author but also several successive generations of senders and recipients, as well as radical geo-political and socio-cultural changes. For Burgess, "Bond belongs to history and these are historical novels" (3), and the attempts to adapt the literary Bond to the screen have become increasingly disappointing:

> The films, which grew more and more gimmicky and less and less psychologically interesting, are grotesquely parodic of the novel, and the cinema version of *Casino Royale* [1967] is a disgraceful distortion of a fine taut story which owes nothing at all to lurid fantasy" [5].[5]

To many, Burgess' negative view of the Bond film might seem a bit excessive, and the example of *Casino Royale* (film, 1967) is, of course, particularly unconvincing, for it was conceived as a parody to begin with. Furthermore, it was produced in fairly chaotic conditions, as a succession of screenplay writers, actors and directors did not seem to agree upon the correct manner to make fun of 007, which resulted in a somewhat incoherent narrative structure.

Burgess' insistence on separating the literary from the cinematic Bond does not take into account the close ties between the historical author, Ian Fleming, and the cinematic medium, the traces of which can be found in the novels as well as on the screen from the very beginning. As pointed out by Chapman, the first novel to be adapted on the screen, *Dr. No*, started off precisely as a screenplay (*Licence* 56). The remarkable success of Bond's transition from the page to the screen can in part be explained precisely by the "cinematographic," resolutely modern stylistic tendencies that we find in Fleming's novels, and to neglect the very much alive cinematic Bond in favor of the quickly aging textual Bond seems an overtly canonical and slightly fossilized position.

If Eco's lack of interest in the films might seem understandable in 1965, Burgess' position, expressed in 1988, appears a bit more controversial, since by then 007 had already become a filmic hero as well as a literary one. The narrative structure of the films is indeed dependent upon that of the novels and represents an evolution rather than a recreation, for it either preserves or clones the most significant paradigms of the original text and sequences them in the same order. It could be said that, in essence, all the possible important variations of the Bond narration are already present in Fleming's text at a micro-structural level, and each concretization downplays, magnifies, ignores or exaggerates the elements that, according to the production team, fit the preferences of the audience at any given moment. If the loyalty of the adaptation to any given novel does not guarantee its success, as in the case of *On Her Majesty's Secret Service*, neither does an excessive freedom vis-à-vis the original narrative intent, as demonstrated by the two last Brosnan installments, which, although achieving comfortable financial gain, failed to convince many critics and fans due to their exceedingly spectacular quality and led the production team to reboot the series with a very close adaptation to the original first novel of the series.

As shown by *Casino Royale* (film, 2006), the literary Bond has never really left the set, for, notwithstanding a few paradigmatic alterations that do not affect the logic of the narrative syntagm (such as Baccarat becoming Texas hold'em, Royale-les-Eaux turning into Montenegro, an added-on spectacular ending or the intervention of an African guerrilla group), the film remains close to the original novel. The production team's decision of rebooting the film franchise with a close adaptation of the first novel of the series and its consequent success clearly demonstrate the authority the textual Bond holds over the entire narrative universe, regardless of the medium. Even though the films have tended to increasingly stray from the novels as to the composition of their narrative syntagm, which has acquired a structural coherence of its own beyond Fleming's creation, the linguistic umbilical cord with the textual Bond has never been truly severed, as shown by the relationship between the texts and the films over the last five decades.

While the first four features—*Dr. No*, *From Russia with Love*, *Goldfinger* and *Thunderball*—followed the novels' plots more or less closely, the fifth, *You Only Live Twice*, whose script was entrusted to Roald Dahl, only retained a few of the original novel's main paradigms, such as Japan and Kissy Suzuki, and can be considered as the first real departure from the textual Bond and the birth of the autonomous narrative structure that supersedes both the original author and the production team. The narrative syntagm of *You Only Live Twice* is a mixture of those of *Dr. No* and *Thunderball*, and thus creates a second-generation narrative structure based upon the elements of two previous interpretations, as the Bond genre begins to self-generate, feeding upon itself. Roald Dahl's declarations regarding the Bond formula as it was presented to him by the franchise producers are highly indicative of the production team's state of mind, or at least of Roald Dahl's own vision of the Bond narrative structure:

> So you put in three girls. No more and no less. Girl number one is pro–Bond. She stays around roughly through the first reel of the picture. Then she is bumped off by the enemy, preferably in Bond's arms.... Girl number two is anti–Bond. She works for the enemy and stays around throughout the middle third of the picture.... Girl number

three is violently pro–Bond. She occupies the final third of the picture and she must on no account be killed.⁶

Although we will probably never know which part of the above statement is accurate and which part is due to Dahl's usual humorous disposition, the fact remains that the script of *You Only Live Twice* is the first of the series to generate a narrative syntagm within the Bond genre and without Ian Fleming, implying therefore a conception of the Bond universe as an autonomous narrative system that could be structured independently from its direct origin, even though its materialization in this particular instance proved somewhat problematic.

Box-office-wise, *You Only Live Twice* did not fare nearly as well as its predecessor, *Thunderball,* and its critical reception was far from enthusiastic. Some scenes, such as the pre-credit sequence, which shows an American spacecraft being swallowed by a much bigger ship in a motion that evokes a fish feeding, or the chase that involves Bond's autogyro, "Little Nellie," seem almost parodic, betraying the true nature of the film — that is, an adaptation of an adaptation. From a structural point of view, it could be argued that Dahl, a writer himself, attempted to appropriate the Bond narrative structure by adding a supplementary humoristic dimension to the original Bond universe and thus disrupting the coherence of its primary semiotic organization, which resulted in an unsatisfying installment.

Most likely preoccupied by the franchise's apparent loss of popularity, the production team then returned to the "real" Bond for the following installment, *On Her Majesty's Secret Service,* which adapted Fleming's novel scrupulously. As we know, the public and critical receptions of *On Her Majesty's Secret Service* were even more mitigated than those of *You Only Live Twice,* and it is to this day one of the most problematic Bond films. An equilibrium between the original texts and the Bond cinematographic clichés was reached with *Diamonds Are Forever* and perfected throughout the long tenure of Roger Moore. Different plot elements from various novels and short stories were adapted and sequenced in a fairly regular narrative syntagm, which responded directly to the cinematic trends of the moment: *Live and Let Die* was released at the height of the blaxploitation film wave, *The Man with the Golden Gun* followed the rise of kung-fu cinema, *Moonraker* surfed on the *Stars Wars* fad, and so on. *Live and Let Die* is microstructurally significant, for it meant the launching of a new Bond actor, and is highly indicative of the particular strategy adopted by the production team, which proved particularly enduring since, to date, Moore's tenure as Bond is still the longest. *Live and Let Die* set the model for the remaining six films featuring him as James Bond by successfully merging the most obvious paradigms of blaxploitation films, including settings and language, with the basic narrative structure and main motifs of the first Bond cinematographic installment, *Dr. No*, such as Mr. Big's island or the crab-like pincer that his main henchman, Tee Hee Johnson, parades in lieu of a right arm, which is indeed reminiscent of Dr. No's prosthesis. Although Dalton's short tenure was presented as some type of return to a tougher, more serious 007, closer to the textual than to the cinematographic Bond, both *The Living Daylights* and *Licence to Kill* applied essentially the same composition principle as their immediate predecessors and recycled some elements from different novels and short stories into a straightforward narrative syntagm corresponding to the basic structure described in Chapter 3. If Timothy Dalton's interpretation was indeed closer to the textual Bond, especially in *Licence to Kill*, and gave both films an overall darker tone, the fundamental narrative structure remained the same.

The Brosnan period, which meant the return of James Bond to the screen after several years of absence, strayed completely from Fleming's novels, as if the disappearance of the Soviet Bloc legitimized a further degree of independence vis-à-vis the textual Bond, a position symbolized by the chosen titles (*GoldenEye*, *Tomorrow Never Dies*, *The World Is Not Enough* and *Die Another Day*) that, following the trend originated by Dalton's last film, *Licence to Kill*, did not correspond to those of Fleming's novels. Just as in the case of *You Only Live Twice*, which represents the prototype of a Bond structure generated independently from an original Fleming text, the later films from the Brosnan period tend to emphasize gadgetry and technological feats. The result was to substitute a missing narrative tension with spectacularly authoritative scenes, especially in *Die Another Day*, which may have seemed to many as over the top in terms of spectacularity and underwhelming plotwise. With its multiple, non-metafictitious references to previous films and to the Bond universe in general, including Graves' Union Jack parachute (*The Spy Who Loved Me*), diamond smuggling (*Diamonds Are Forever*), the avalanche (*On Her Majesty's Secret Service*), the solar power beam as the Chaotic Factor (*The Man with the Golden Gun*) and a brief glimpse of the book from American ornithologist James Bond, *A Field Guide to the Birds of the West Indies*, *Die Another Day* resembles more a paradigmatic collage than a truly coherent narrative syntagm. By openly introducing so many elements from previous cinematographic installments without granting them a truly meta-fictitious status, which would go against the logics of the Bond genre,[7] the narrative universe of *Die Another Day* appears to be the imitation of an imitation, an empty narrative structure which simply goes through the motions.

The decision to reboot the series with a very faithful adaptation of

Casino Royale, and the very positive public and critical receptions the film received, suggest that the uneasiness created by the apparent artificiality of *Die Another Day* might have been due in part to its extreme degree of independence from Fleming's text, and so the re-initialization of the series shows a deliberate intention to return to the textual source, with the occasional addenda of spectacular action scenes in order to keep up with the action tradition of the cinematographic Bond universe. As if to subliminally emphasize its connections to the textual Bond, *Casino Royale* incorporates a paradigm from the novel *Moonraker*— namely, Le Chiffre's eye condition, which is reminiscent of that of Hugo Drax. In *Moonraker*, half of Drax's face is more or less paralyzed due to his accident during the war, and his right eye appears "painfully bloodshot"; while in *Casino Royale*, Le Chiffre suffers from a lachrymal conduct dysfunction that causes him to cry blood from one eye.

The title of the latest installment to date,[8] *Quantum of Solace*, is in itself very significant of this unspoken umbilical cord which relates the films to the novels, and clearly reveals a need to cling on to Fleming's words in order to claim narrative legitimacy, regardless of their actual referential value. If the use of the original titles seemed perfectly justified in the cases of *From Russia with Love*, *Goldfinger* and *Thunderball* for it naturally aimed to benefit from the novels' popularity, it appeared a bit more contrived during the following decades concerning *The Spy Who Loved Me*, *Moonraker*, *Octopussy* and *A View to a Kill*; by then, the audience had changed, and a vast portion of the public was no longer familiar with Fleming's texts, which had no longer anything to do with the films in terms of plots. The choice of a title such as *Quantum of Solace* in 2008 is more puzzling still, for by now the vast majority of the audience has not read nor intends to read the original story, which, furthermore, is not even remotely related to the film. Fleming's original words have therefore acquired a symbolic value beyond their actual meaning and signify in function of the original sender rather than according to what they actually express. The main value of Fleming's words is as much in the words themselves as in the fact that they are Fleming's.

The above analysis of the constant and uneven negotiation between the original textual Bond and his cinematographic counterpart indicates that, regardless of how much independence the narrative structure might have acquired over the years, there is still a certain mystique regarding Fleming's specific words, and that a complete separation between the spirit of the novels and the films tend to generate unsatisfying, semiotically weak installments, such as *You Only Live Twice* and *Die Another Day*.[9] The titles have functioned as semiotic anchors that legitimize any given installment, regardless of the liberties it might take vis-à-vis the original text, and have been either Fleming's or variations upon the semantic field of the James Bond universe, with the exceptions of *Tomorrow Never Dies* and *Die Another Day*. The first film not to be named after a Fleming novel was *Licence to Kill*, which directly refers to one of James Bond's most well-known official qualities that could even stand as a functional semiotic micro-structure of the Bond universe. *The World Is Not Enough* is the motto Bond decides to adopt in *On Her Majesty's Secret Service* (novel) and can be seen, as well, as the metaphorical description of both the character and his adventures, underlining the undying appetite of 007 for action. And as to *GoldenEye*, it applies to Ian Fleming himself, for it was the name of his estate in Jamaica as well as that of an operation in which he participated while working for British Naval Intelligence. Although neither *Tomorrow Never Dies* nor *Die Another Day* refer directly to a specific element of the Bond narration, as do *Licence to Kill* or *The World Is Not Enough*, they are still related to the Bond tradition, albeit in a more indirect manner, by echoing the lexical fields of *Live and Let Die* as well as of the "other" Bond film, *Never Say Never Again*. The only title that appears to be unrelated to the James Bond onomastic tradition is precisely that of the upcoming film, *Skyfall*, still to be released as I write these lines, and which, as rumor has it, should represent some type of narrative departure from the first two previous installments of the recent rebooting, *Casino Royale* and *Quantum of Solace*, as well as from Ian Fleming's text altogether. It should be observed, however, that the last installment to date, *Quantum of Solace*, already meant a departure from Fleming's text, having preserved no more than the title of the original short story, and having turned a psychological concept, the "quantum of solace," into a secret organization, Quantum, a worthy successor to SPECTRE. A fairly loyal adaptation, as is *Casino Royale*, can therefore spawn a sequel totally unrelated to Fleming's text without threatening the coherence of the series, demonstrating once again the Bond narration's capacity to self-generate. By now, the caption "X as Ian Fleming's James Bond 007" should suffice to introduce the Bond universe and to lure audiences everywhere. We can also observe that the main connotations of the title *Skyfall* belong to the semiotic code of the Bond narration, for they are related to one of 007's main attributes — namely, his ability to defy gravity. From *You Only Live Twice* to *GoldenEye*, we have already seen Bond literally "falling from the sky" in many of his cinematographic adventures and expect him to defy gravity in the next one. *Skyfall* also suggests some type of ominous, global threat, yet another fundamental staple of the Bond narration. Whether consciously or not, the production team therefore chose an "unrelated"[10] title that alludes directly to one of the main qualities of the hero, to the spectacularity of the narration, and to one of the terms of the most fundamental binary opposition upon which the plot is built. Given the highly structured nature of the Bond narration and the apparent autonomy it has acquired over the years, this openly-stated departure from the Fleming tradition may not be such a departure after all and will most likely result in yet one more adapting move of the Bond narration to the current market without altering its fundamental mechanisms.

The history of the cinematographic adaptations of the James Bond narration can thus be seen as a constant negotiation between an essential textual Bond narration and its possible interpretations within the wider context of current cinematic trends. For all its variations, and in spite of straying considerably at times from the original, the cinematic Bond is still bound to its literary origins in terms of narrative structures and semiotic harmonies. If it is a given that most of the literary qualities of Fleming's text are lost when 007 becomes a filmic hero, this does not necessarily imply that the narrative merits of the original semiotic structure disappear altogether: descriptions, similes and images are naturally untranslatable to the screen; however, characters, situations and conflicts, as well as the most fundamental textual signs, remain at the core of the narration and function in the same manner as in the novels. The art of Bond does not depend exclusively upon the fine writing skills of Ian Fleming but also upon the suggestive power of his words, which has inspired two-and-a-half generations of screenwriters. To defend the novels to the detriment of their cinematographic adaptations is to ignore that the James Bond narration has transcended its original medium remarkably well, to the point of becoming a cinematic hero rather than a literary one, a level of adaptation that was never reached by, for instance, such a widely accepted figure as Sherlock Holmes. The artistic dimensions of the Bond narration are therefore not limited to the written realm, and if there is indeed art in Bond, we must be able to find it on the page as well as on the screen.

Original Bond

When we consider the traditional paradigms the Bond narration administers in its semiotic structure, such as the fearless knight, the captive princess or the evil king, and the nature of the conflict it presents as well as its resolution (that is, Good vs. Evil in its Order vs. Disorder modality), the James Bond narration is far from original, which might lead one to dismiss its manifestations, either textual or cinematographic, as artistically insignificant, for originality, along with aesthetic merits and polysemy, remains perhaps the most fundamental feature of any artistic endeavor. Not only are the narrative motifs and themes blatantly traditional, their successive arrangements appear repetitive as well and offer little in terms of character development. Throughout his long trajectory, James Bond has remained more or less his usual self, minus a few adjustments along the way that have made him suitable for the new century, oscillating between a tougher and a softer version of himself, the first being incarnated by Connery, Dalton and Craig, and the second by Lazenby, Moore and, in a lesser measure, Brosnan, who presented a more ambivalent Bond, alternatively tough and soft. The slow degradation of 007's mental condition apparent in the novels after *On Her Majesty's Secret Service*, which could be seen as some type of character development, has not survived on the screen, and although Bond's latest incarnation appears less one-dimensional in terms of psychological depth and emotions, he still gets the job done as efficiently as his predecessors. We must therefore search for the originality of the Bond narration in the form rather than in the content; after all, it is telling a story we have all heard before and in many different ways.

Eco identifies a wide variety of cultural and literary sources within the Bond narration, some of them quite erudite, from Judith Gauthier to Joris Karl Huysmans, reaching the conclusion that Fleming's text is a collage, a "patchwork" of different literary styles and genres, which range from science fiction to the French *nouveau roman*, blending "narrative elements with an unstable montage" (*Reader* 168). Such a position relies naturally on specific conceptions of genres and styles and can hence be debated upon the same bases. In order to see any "science fiction" in James Bond, one must adopt a very wide definition of the genre that considers the presence of the technological paradigm or the exaggeration as generically determining and does not take into account its original intent: Not only does science fiction imply a different chronological context, but it could even be conceived as an openly dystopian genre, which would allow us to distinguish it from an offspring of the adventure narration (namely, space opera). Still, even *Moonraker* (novel and film), doubtlessly the Bond installment which contains the most elements commonly associated with the genre of science fiction, especially in its cinematographic version, does not correspond to the parameters of space opera as exemplified by *Star Wars* or *Dune*. Neither science fiction nor space opera intend to represent our world or our time, while the James Bond narration is always happening here and now, and its capacity to adapt to current trends and events is precisely one of its narrative characteristics, which makes its semiotic intent radically different from that of space opera or science fiction. Similarly, to compare Fleming's descriptions to those we find in Robbe-Grillet's novels[11] is to make abstraction of their narrative context: Whereas Robbe-Grillet's descriptions only lead to more descriptions, Fleming's lead to action, and we are informed of such textual intent from the beginning of the transmission, for the Bond narration usually starts *in medias res*. What Eco describes as *nouveau roman* style — this propensity to fill the textual space with seemingly insignificant details — can also be seen as fundamental to the creation of a plausible narrative frame in which, naturally, very implausible things will happen. This mode could be described as hyper-realism and has a similar function in the Bond narrative as it does in Fantastic fiction — namely, to create a very monosemic narrative background that apparently presents no particularities at all but, on the contrary, seems almost boring, that is, deprived of real narrative authority, in order to favor the tension created by the supernatural threat (in the case of the Fantastic) or by the Villain's menace (in the Bond narration). Notwithstanding Eco's keen stylistic appreciation, it can be argued that the use of hyperrealism in the Bond narration is a fully integrated part of its narrative tension mechanism, and that its textual purpose is hence the exact opposite to that which it fulfills in the *nouveau roman* universe. A *nouveau roman* rejects from the beginning the possibility of evading this hyper-reality, which becomes the only possible narrative universe; this is a far cry from any James Bond adventure, where those hyper-realistic elements, beside often pointing to the second level of defamiliarization by connoting a higher life (that is, not being so hyper-realistic after all), are mostly functional because they ease the introduction of the unbelievable in a supposedly realistic narrative universe. Just as in the case of the typical fantastic narration, the hyper-realistic mode allows for the most immediate and automatic identification of the recipient with the narrated universe and requires little suspension of disbelief, which allows an increased narrative tension when the unbelievable — be it supernatural or not — is introduced into the narration. However, whereas in the Fantastic, hyper-realism is used as a pervasive narrative mode to emphasize the collision between two radically different and semantically opposed semiotic codes (reality and the supernatural), in the Bond narration, hyper-realism only functions in a fragmentary manner, contributing to the overall narrative universe rather than determining it.

Taken as a whole, the structure of the adventures of James Bond could indeed correspond roughly to that of any other adventure narration; however, said structure is infinitely wide and could describe the adventures of Sinbad the Sailor as well those of the three musketeers, the Hobbit or Mad

Max. If the Bond narration is indeed a sub-genre of the very inclusive adventure genre, it exhibits enough particular traits to exist as a category in itself, which has become the model for countless imitations, especially in its cinematographic form.

No literary text is born in a vacuum, and Fleming's 007 is understandably also the product of many narrative and literary influences, among which one could mention French author Maurice Leblanc's popular Arsène Lupin, *Gentleman Cambrioleur* (Gentleman Burglar), who is, along with Raffles, the great absent from Eco's brilliant display of scholarship, and whose elegance associated with the lifestyle of a thief could indeed remind us of the binary opposition found in the Bond narration between the thug and the gentleman. As pointed out in Yeffet's *James Bond in the 21st Century* (158), the sixties Bond film trailers introduced 007 as a "Gentleman Secret Agent," thus reminding us of Arsène Lupin's professional description. Both characters do share a similar taste for elegance, suave manners and the capacity for violent action outside or beyond the law; however, their narrative functions are opposed, for while Bond is in charge of protecting the Order, Lupin is busy disrupting it. Besides being an art lover and expert collector, Arsène Lupin is an outlaw who does not operate within a larger, superseding and legitimizing structure as MI6, and is truly an independent protagonist rather than the extension of a preexisting and socially sanctioned structure.[12]

If there is no doubt that we can find traces of a variety of popular literary themes and motifs in the Bond universe, this does not necessarily condemn its originality, for the Bond narration becomes original as soon as it transcends its numerous influences and structures them within a coherent, independent narrative entity. Just as secret agent Bond can usurp any identity and still remain James Bond, the Bond narration can, with all impunity, appropriate pre-fabricated themes and motifs without losing its proprietary cohesiveness. Rather than a "patchwork" or a "collage," the Bond narration is a fusion of a variety of influences which stands on its own, as demonstrated by its status of reference in today's cultural landscape. In our collective consciousness, James Bond remains the Original Spy, a narrative model as well as a household name, and this might be due in part to the fact that the James Bond narration is not as monosemic as it appears.

Polysemic Bond

The James Bond narration offers different levels of narrative tension which do not interfere with one another but rather complete the overall harmony of the story and allow for the coexistence of several semiotic narrative codes that can be received in a variety of ways. Within the all-encompassing conflict between Good and Evil, we have at least a love story, a travel log, a political commentary, a sport exhibition and a higher lifestyle catalog. Narrative authority is distributed among different poles of interest, all more or less explicitly incarnated in the character of James Bond, who himself personifies many significant binary oppositions and therefore escapes the confines of a stock figure; his cruelty, for instance, often mentioned in the texts and suggested in the films, is not a trait that we would expect from any modern adaptation of the fearless knight, a stock, one-dimensional character with whom Bond is often compared; and neither are smoking, drinking or lusting after adulterous relationships. If Bond is indeed fearless, he is not irreproachable, which makes him less predictable and more complex than one would expect from a typical popular hero. His self-indulgence towards trivial commodities and casual sexual encounters go against the typical make up of any traditional hero involved in saving the world from the forces of evil, and his receptivity to pleasure contrasts sharply with his heroic sense of duty throughout his adventures. Heroes may have weaknesses: 007 has vices that he chooses to cultivate. Complying with the expectations of a more health-conscious audience, and notwithstanding a few relapses (such as the cigar he lights before he meets Jinx in *Die Another Day*), 007 more or less quit smoking by the end of the cold war; however, his drinking, his appreciation of luxury and his appetite for women remain defining features of his character, which are fully integrated into the struggle between Good and Evil. It is precisely his knowledge of evil and his facility to adopt a villainous attitude that makes 007 such a valuable and efficient protector of the Order; therefore his anti-heroic qualities are paradoxically related to his ability to act heroically. It is either by cunning or by force, using means that we more generally associate with evil than with righteousness, that Bond infiltrates the Villain's organization in the same way the Villain would infiltrate MI6 (as actually happens at the beginning of *Quantum of Solace* [film]) when Mitchell reveals himself as a mole and facilitates the escape of Mr. White). In order to accomplish his mission, James Bond must break the very rules that he enforces, thus implicitly calling into question the validity of the system of values upon which they are founded. In the name of his loyalty to the Order, 007 must be disloyal and disorderly, thus underlining the relative value of both loyalty and the Order, and introducing a fundamental ambiguity at the core of the narrative universe. 007 as a heroic character is therefore more ambivalent than it appears at first sight, and his adventures are not simply an adaptation of the Epic mode to modern times but rather a perversion of its most fundamental element — the hero — and of its narrative hierarchy.

By incorporating different semiotic codes within the major conflict that opposes Good to Evil, the Bond narration overcomes the limitations of the adventure genre and tolerates excursions into other narrative realms. In *On Her Majesty's Secret Service* (novel), we are treated to a rather lengthy gastronomical introduction before the action (that is in theory the story) actually begins. The short stories "Quantum of Solace," "Octopussy" and "007 in New York" practically do away with the spy part as the narrative authority shifts from the typical structure of the adventure narration to a much more elusive universe of personal conflicts, which can be as serious as spousal disaster ("Quantum of Solace") and deadly ambition ("Octopussy"), or as silly as frustrated consumer expectations ("007 in New York"). The films have naturally magnified many signs which do not belong to the semiotic code of the spy narration, broadening the appeal of a straight thriller to that of a more complex structure that exhibits different centers of narrative authority, such as good living, fashion and style, but also sex and even humor. For Eco, these type of digressions do not always complement the narration, their function being mainly to facilitate the identification of the receiver with the narrative universe by representing not only actions that can be easily recognized by anyone — such as driving — but also objects that belong to everyday life, such as a pack of cigarettes. Eco points out two particular instances of what he considers superfluous digressions — the description of a scorpion at the beginning of *Diamonds Are Forever* and that of Grant laying by the pool in the first pages of *From Russia with Love* — which appear unrelated to the actual narrative syntagm (that is, the James Bond adventure *per se*):

> It is also "purposeless" to introduce diamond smuggling in South Africa in *Diamonds Are Forever* by opening with the description of a scorpion as though seen through a magnifying glass, enlarged to the size of some prehistoric monster.... And more even typical of this technique of the aimless glance is the beginning of *From Russia with Love* where we have a whole page of virtuosity exercised upon the body ... of a man lying by the side of a swimming pool.... The fact that lying on the ground he seems dead has no relevance to the narrative that follows.... Fleming abounds in such passages of high technical skills with a relish for the inessential and which the narrative mechanisms of the plot not only does not require but actually rejects [*Reader* 166].

Eco contrasts this technique with that of a typical popular narration, which often interrupts the narration at a crucial point in order to create supplementary tension by introducing what he calls encyclopedic information — that is, a meticulous description of a relevant element to the action that delays the resolution of the conflict, a device abundantly found in the works of pioneering popular writers such as Emilio Salgari and Jules Verne. Although Eco's distinction between two very different narrative levels at the core of the textual Bond — that which tells of a life and death adventure, and that which tells of a game of golf or of baccarat — is indeed most accurate, their mutual exclusion can, however, be debated, for we can perceive some type of semiotic coherence between the two aforementioned scenes and the narrative syntagms to which they belong. The description of Grant at the beginning of *From Russia with Love* as a corpse surrounded by objects suggests that he is both an object and a metonymy of death. Much more so than James Bond as described by Ian Fleming himself, Grant is a "blunt instrument," a soulless mercenary with no real conscience of his own, stashed in a villa waiting to be used by his owners. The relationship between him and death is quickly established by the narration, for, as we discover his past, we learn that he is possessed by the urge to kill "around the time of the full moon," which is the reason why SMERSH has recruited him in the first place. His incontrollable need to kill, what he refers to himself as "The Feelings," has substituted any other compulsion, and he is totally deprived of sexual desire. Hence, he is incapable of giving life and only apt to give death. This relationship between Grant and death is strengthened throughout the story, as he assassinates Darko Kerim, the head of the British station in Turkey and Bond's closest ally, along with an MGB agent. His encounter with Bond is the closest that 007 comes to death in this particular installment, if we except the undeveloped cliffhanger ending, which leaves 007 crashing to the floor after having been stabbed by Rosa Klebb's shoe-blade. The struggle between Grant and Bond is, to the contrary, fully developed and represents the moment when 007 confronts death most explicitly. Grant is hence death and deadly, as well as deeply dehumanized to the point of reification — that is, symbolically dead. The manner in which he is presented at the beginning of the text can easily be seen as a symbolic microstructure of both his nature and his narrative function: He is an object surrounded by other objects.

The filmic adaptation of *From Russia with Love* retains the scene where Grant is laying on the grass, and although the soulless killer does not appear quite as dead as he does in the novel, he is still presented as an automaton whose eyes only open briefly with the arrival of the masseuse and who only comes to life upon one order from his handler. The scene where Rosa Klebb hits him in the stomach with brass knuckles without him flinching, which we find in both the novel and the movie (albeit slightly displaced in the action),[13] suggests a certain dead-like quality, for it underlines an inhuman resistance to pain. Grant's insensitivity and composure make him appear more robotic than human and more of an object than a subject. On an onomastic level, the name "Red Grant" functions according to the character, for "Red" naturally connotes blood and danger, and Red Grant is the one in charge of "granting" death to James Bond.

The lengthy description of a scorpion at the beginning of *Diamonds Are Forever* (novel) — rightfully compared by Eco to the opening credits of a film — is micro-structurally significant, for not only does the scorpion belong to the same environment as the Spangled Mob, the desert, but it represents the same type of ruthless and deadly predatory behavior as that exhibited by Jack Spang and his associates. The scorpion can be seen as a symbolical link between the geographical origin of the diamonds, Africa, and the Spangled Mob, whose headquarters are located in Nevada, as well as a metaphor for the primary antagonist forces in the narration. This symbolism is emphasized by the text, which reintroduces the scorpion in the last chapter, first at the beginning — "There was now no scorpion living in the roots of the great horn bush which stood at the junction of the Three African states" (277) — and a few pages later, right before Jack Spang commits his last murder by killing the smuggler who brings him the diamonds: "Like the scorpion, a month earlier, he [the smuggler] sensed the raised stone above him" (284). This reinforces the connotation of the arthropod-like relationship between the different actors of the conflict: the smuggler crushes the scorpion in the first chapter and becomes in turn the victim of Jack Spang in the last chapter, as if all parties involved, Spangled Mob, smugglers and scorpions, acted, lived and died according to the primary laws of nature. At a more general level, and considering Fleming's narrative as a whole, we can identify the scorpion as one of the staples of the Bond universe, metonymically related to the crabs of Dr. No's island, to the prosthetic claws of the good doctor himself, and to the scorpions of Blofeld's garden of death.

In the film, the association between the scorpion and the Villain is much more direct, as Mr. Wint and Mr. Kidd, after observing a scorpion and referring to it as a "master," use it as a weapon to commit their first murder. The scorpion has thus become an extension of the Villain and still functions at least partially as an opening sequence, since it represents the means by which the two main antagonists of Bond in this particular installment, Wint and Kidd, commit their first murder. The fact that the scorpion survived as a significant paradigm when the narration was adapted to the screen seems to indicate that its presence is indeed not superfluous but rather part of an overall semiotic harmony.

For Eco, the textual Bond universe can only be received by the enlightened reader as a game, the outcome of which is already known to us, and that sustains our attention by the variations it introduces between one installment and the next. We know the characters and how the story ends, therefore textual authority is established through means of repetition rather than of invention (*Reader* 160). There is indeed a game at the core of the Bond narration, as we will see shortly; however, the narrative authority of the Bond novels, as well as that of the films, also relies upon their capacity to produce a coherent structure that includes different types of narrative messages which are, in theory, mutually exclusive. And so heroism is juxtaposed with self-indulgence, fashionable elegance with dirty, life-threatening fights, and exotic landscapes with highly localized interest, allowing the recipient to focus his or her interest on the action as much as on the scenery or on the ties. In *Live and Let Die* (film), we see 007 being fitted for suits and selecting several ties in his hotel room before asking Felix Leiter about Mr. Big's headquarters in New Orleans — the restaurant "Fillet of Soul"—while he has him sign the bill for a sumptuous room service cart, which we see in the background tended by a respectful African American groom in full luxury hotel regalia; the narrative universe hence merges effortlessly the mission and the tailoring, duty and room service, the essential and the superficial, causing the collapse of traditional narrative priorities. By treating the choice of a tie or the correct temperature for champagne with the same interest as his mission to save the world, the Bond universe transgresses the usual narrative hierarchy and allows for a constant interplay between parallel poles of narrative authority, which depend, as seen earlier, upon different levels of defamiliarization. What has constituted until very recently (with one exception) the traditional, openly anti-climactic ending of any James Bond cinematographic adventure is a good illustration of this structural particularity, for it challenges accepted notions of narrative tension. Until the recent rebooting of the series, and if we except *On Her Majesty's Secret Service*, the conclusion of any James Bond film is not only predictable but also essentially unrelated to the specific narrative syntagm of that particular installment: 007 ends up with the girl, who is as interchangeable as the ending itself, a sequence that represents a sort of generic epilogue rather than a real conclusion, and is, nonetheless, within the logic of the Bond universe, just as satisfying in terms of closure. We are not concluding a specific adventure as much as leaving temporarily an entire narrative universe, which precedes us and that will always return. Once the Villain is dead and his lair has been destroyed, the narrative authority based upon the main conflict that opposes Bond to Evil no longer operates; however, our interest is still sustained, in this case by sexual tension, which, curiously, suggests an unexpected openness in an apparently very tightly closed structure (indeed, we are only treated to the start of the sexual encounter between 007 and the designated Bond girl, and never to its ending).

By incorporating symbols that work in semiotic harmony with the main narrative conflict, hence reinforcing the overall coherence of the narration, and by openly rejecting traditional narrative priorities, the adventures of a James Bond narration transcend the monosemic tendencies we commonly associate with minor, popular genres. Any Bond installment, whether written or cinematographic, is susceptible to be enjoyed for different reasons — that is, received and interpreted according to different parameters. Each adventure of 007 is not merely a simple narrative syntagm based upon the oldest conflict in the world but an entire universe where guns, scorpions and ties are equally significant, and where Bond's tuxedo can be as meaningful as his license to kill.

Pretty Bond

The different correlations between form and content that we have observed so far, which range from the simply connotative, such as those concerning 007's license number and name, to the symbolic, such as those regarding the watch or the scorpion, should already be considered as aesthetic merits, for the semiotic harmonies they establish are not easily found in a genre for the masses such as the spy narration and therefore contribute to elevate the Bond narration to a higher aesthetic ground than one would expect from a popular artifact. Fleming's text is in this sense truly literary, both linguistically and narratively, for its style as well as its organization escape the preexisting limits of the genre by exhibiting a constant alternation between different stylistic registers and narrative priorities. This is clearly illustrated by the following passage from *On Her Majesty's Secret Service*, which takes place the night before 007 flies to Zurich in order to meet with Bleuville-Blofeld under the guise of Sir Hilary Bray:

> The taxi was waiting. It was seven o'clock. As the taxi got under way, Bond made his plan for the evening. He would first do an extremely careful packing job of his single suitcase, the one that had no tricks to it, have two double vodkas and tonics with a dash of Angostura, eat a large dish of May's specialty — scrambled eggs fines herbes — have two more vodkas and tonics, and then, slightly drunk, go to bed with half a grain of seconal.
>
> Encouraged by the prospect of this cozy self-anaesthesia, Bond brusquely kicked his problems under the carpet of his consciousness [97].

Whereas the three first sentences of the paragraph, short and to the point, denote an action story, the style of which admits the repetition of the word "taxi," the fourth one, considerably longer, refers to a radically different narrative universe, unrelated to the mission but equally important, perhaps even more if we are to judge by the stylistic economy of the sequence, which dedicates more words and a more complex structure to Bond's musings about his plans for the evening than to the action itself. The last sentence refers us to yet another narrative domain, that of the psychological introspection, for it concludes the chapter with a metaphorical construction, inviting the recipient to meditate upon the value of mind-altering substances — vodka and seconal — to elude the reality principle. Neither this type of preoccupation nor the manner in which it is expressed correspond to the typical popular action narration, making Fleming's text aesthetically more interesting than the average spy story, for it is capable of fusing different centers of attention, stylistically and diegetically, without disrupting the overall narrative coherence.

The implicit artistic preoccupation for originality and aesthetic quality that we find in the novels has influenced their filmic adaptations, which have always strived to reproduce in one way or another the artistic dimensions of the text. We find in the very first installment, *Dr. No*, a similar juxtaposition of the different semiotic codes described above, both in form and content, as early as the opening credits,[14] which move from an abstract animated background composed of moving colored dots to a cartoon-like scene of shadow dancing to the silhouette of the three beggars who will materialize as real actors in a real setting as the narration begins. These visual shifts are completed by the soundtrack which plays first the Bond theme during the moving dots sequence, then a percussion-based piece during the shadow dancing, and finally the song "Three Blind Mice" when the three beggars appear. Therefore, from the very beginning of its filmic existence, the Bond narration puts forward several semiotic codes, along with different visual and musical textures, emulating the coexistence of the different narrative universes we find in the novels. The film introduces three radical changes of scenery, as we go from the assassination of Strangways and his secretary in Jamaica to the MI6 information center in London before moving on to the elegant *Le Cercle les Ambassadeurs*, where Bond is flirting with Sylvia Trench while winning against her at baccarat, hence establishing three very different diegetic moods. Whereas the views of Jamaica suggests poverty and underdevelopment, those of London and of MI6 headquarters indicate extreme urbanization and advanced technology; and while the atmosphere at the MI6 information center is one of work and functionality, that of *Le Cercle* is of leisure and entertainment. In sheer formal terms, the ground shots of the Jamaican landscape contrast with the view of London City and the rows of computers at MI6's information headquarters contrast with the oval-shaped table at which 007 is playing baccarat. In spite of their disparities, these three narrative domains are naturally integrated within the plot, the link between rural Jamaica and MI6's main cybernetic nerve being the radio-transmitter that Strangway's secretary uncovers from behind a fake bookshelf before being assassinated.

Just as *Casino Royale* can be considered a micro-structure of the entire Bond universe, for it contains all its characteristic paradigms, *Dr. No* presents all the main features of the filmic Bond while attempting to restitute the artistic intent of the novels within cinematic parameters. According to Chapman, its success is precisely due to the aesthetic efforts of the production team:

> But if *Dr. No* harks back to the glories of Britain's imperial past, why was the film received as something so fresh and new? The answer lies not in the narrative ideology of the film, but in its visual style. *Dr. No* established the look of the Bond films with its glossy surface and highly detailed *mise-en-scène*.... Everything in *Dr. No* emphasizes color, from the pop-art title sequence — a kaleidoscope of brightly colored dots which flash on and off in rapid succession, suggesting that the film is going to be fast, fun and frenetic — to the high definition Technicolor cinematography which creates a travel brochure image of Jamaica, all sunshine and bright primary colors [*Licence* 62–63].

Chapman points out in particular the meticulous care that went into the realization of the different sets, from the fancy gambling club *Les Ambassadeurs* to Dr. No's disquieting underwater lair (*Licence* 63), which can be considered as visual supports to the endless interplay between the different narrative domains that animate the Bond universe, already foreshadowed — albeit in a more abstract manner — during the opening credits.

Onomastically, the title of *Dr. No* has a similar weight to that of the first installment of the textual Bond, for it points to one of the terms of the primary conflict at the heart of the Bond narration — that is, the rejection of the Order — just as *Casino Royale* connotes two fundamental paradigms of the Bond narration, Order and Gambling. The title *Dr. No* expresses the existence of evil as pure negation through the basic opposition Yes/No, which presupposes the existence of a primordial conflict and suggests the most basic binary movement of the Bond narration: Bond is affirmation while the Villain represents negation.[15] The vaguely threatening "doctor" adds to the menace by reminding us of other evil doctors well anchored in our collective perception of popular narrative, such as Dr.

Frankenstein and, of course, Dr. Fu Manchu, while underlining the existence of a dangerous knowledge. Before the narration even begins, the receptor is aware that Dr. No is no good but intellectually prepared — hence, more ominous yet. Indeed, the crisis that Bond must resolve is always of an extreme gravity and as crucial as the resolution of the simple linguistic opposition Yes/No.[16]

Dr. No also introduces deception, a characteristic pole of narrative tension in the spy genre in general, which is associated to James Bond by definition and to the Villain in practically every installment, from Drax (*Moonraker*, novel) to Greene (*Quantum of Solace*, film). In the universe of 007, nothing is what is seems, and so an abstract cartoon can turn into shadow dancers just as easily as three blind beggars can become professional hit men or a bookshelf uncover a radio-transmitter. This shifting nature of some key elements in the narration — usually Bond himself, women, villains and landscapes — is found across most levels of the transmission and can be related to the facility with which the Bond universe has adapted to modern times: James Bond shifts identities as a profession, the geopolitical terms of the basic opposition upon which the conflict is based in any given installment shift according to current historical and cultural contexts, and the narration shifts codes as well as priorities in order to establish multiple centers of narrative authority, which sustain tension not only within the different narrative levels but also among the levels themselves. Since meaning is created essentially through binary oppositions, a narrative structure such as Bond's, which thrives upon a wide range of oppositions both in form and content, benefits from an internal dynamic semiotic impulse, which goes a long way in explaining its remarkable resilience and surprising currency. Significantly enough in regard to the artistic qualities of the Bond narration, we find a similar narrative phenomenon in a highly canonical novel such as Cervantes' *Don Quixote*, where the interplay between the different levels of opposition allows for a variety of interpretations.[17]

Besides exhibiting onomastic microstructural qualities similar in nature to those found in *Casino Royale* (novel) and responding to the aesthetic concerns of the novels with the palette of cinematic language (from the artfulness of the credits to the immediate and continuous fusion of several narrative domains recreated through very carefully produced sets), the first cinematographic installment of the Bond narration adds an entire new artistic dimension to the Bond narration: music. 007 may not care much for music, but music does care about 007, and the soundtracks of the films greatly contribute to their aesthetic value by completing the semiotic harmony of the cinematic Bond. The very first sound we hear in *Dr.*

No is the white noise of a radio transmitter, connoting the world of secret communications as well as establishing a peculiar contact with the receptor, who is precisely about to receive a transmission. During the gun barrel sequence we hear a minimalist, unresolved chimes melody that merges with the beginning of the Bond theme, as if the later was resolving the uncertainty produced by the preceding abstract melody, just as 007 turning around and shooting at the barrel eliminates the virtual threat. The Bond theme itself works as a musical counterpoint to the narrative diversity that characterizes the Bond narration, as well as Bond himself, by integrating a rock-sounding guitar within a be-bop/swing arrangement, thus blending two musical genres with separate connotations. The swing/jazz orchestration suggests a fairly conservative mood that clashes with the rock guitar riff in the same way that Bond's elegant demeanor contrasts with his occupation; metaphorically speaking, this dirty-sounding rock guitar that crops up amidst a respectable swing orchestration is the musical equivalent of the gun that 007 hides under his tuxedo. The versions used in the last two installments of the series, *Casino Royale* and *Quantum of Solace*, further emphasize this fusion of genres by adding strings as well as drums, magnifying the contrasting effect while preserving the balance between respectability and independence.

Besides an enduring and particularly suited theme, the Bond soundtrack has also shown its capacity to accommodate any musical addition, just as the Bond narrative structure can absorb different cinematic trends. And so the opening credits of each Bond film after *Dr. No* have benefited from a variety of musical styles represented by popular artists, ranging from Shirley Basset, Tom Jones and Nancy Sinatra to Duran Duran, Madonna and Alicia Keys, which successfully coexist within a more formal, classical score. Some of the greatest names in pop music have become associated with the Bond universe, such as Paul McCartney, who, showing no resentment for 007's apparent disdain towards his former band, composed and performed the song "Live and Let Die" for the eponymous film.[18] The soundtrack can even invigorate an otherwise weak, somewhat contrived installment, as it does in the case of *A View to a Kill*, where the energy of Duran Duran's performance carried by Simon Lebon's clear and youthful vocals during the opening credits, and suggested throughout the film by the soundtrack orchestration, compensates in part for the weariness of a visibly aging Moore-Bond. "A View to a Kill" (song) is credited to John Barry, Bond's longtime soundtrack composer, and to the five original members of Duran Duran,[19] which demonstrates the capacity of the Bond structure to update its soundtrack just as effortlessly as it updates its narrative paradigms. We naturally associate the sound of Bond with John Barry's composition and orchestration styles, so the success of his collaboration with a contemporary rock band[20] denotes the openness and flexibility of the musical possibilities inherent in the Bond universe.

Needless to say, the criteria used to evaluate the aesthetic qualities — the beauty — of any artifact necessarily responds to more subjective than objective parameters: If we never deemed the Beatles to be artists, chances are that we would not consider McCartney's song as an added artistic quality to the film *Live and Let Die*. This debate naturally exceeds the scope of this essay; nevertheless, it can pointed out that the entire medium of cinema itself has long suffered from scholarly indifference and is still to achieve the same canonical recognition as literature. As implicitly suggested by Burgess' position, the cinematographic manifestations of the Bond narration are not in principle worthy of academic attention, hence all the efforts that might have gone into the creation of the cinematographic Bond could not be considered artistic. Such a position is, of course, hardly tenable, especially when one considers the aesthetic characteristics we have encountered in the filmic Bond — variety of narrative domain, semiotic harmony and symbolism — which could very well be considered as artistic qualities. In the end, to deny any art to the cinematic Bond belongs to the same canonical and exclusive attitude which has often dismissed the literary Bond as pure pulp fiction. The semiotic richness of the narration, its many levels of internal correlations and correspondences, confer on the Bond universe a depth that should suffice to defend its status as a work of art. However, if this were not enough, the Bond narrative structure also presents a very peculiar characteristic, which, according to the original formalists, was the mark of the great works of art, for it produced the ultimate defamiliarization: the ability of the artifact to lay its own devices bare — in other words, self-consciousness.

Bond's Game

Gaming and gambling are omnipresent throughout the Bond universe, not only as simple tropes, such as cards and casinos, but also as distinctive features of 007's character and behavior; James Bond takes chances, whether playing at baccarat or with his life, and relies on opportunity and improvisation — that is, upon unpredictability — as much as on timing and planning. As pointed out earlier, it is significant that the first Bond installment happens to be entitled *Casino Royale*, and just as significant that the production team selected this particular title to reboot the series after a long absence, for it still stands as a remarkable microstructure of the entire

Bond universe, in form and content as well as symbolically. But the Bond narration also establishes a game with the recipient which is based upon its own subversion, for it continuously bares its own devices without interfering with narrative authority. This constant double entendre does not quite correspond to the chess game–like interaction that, according to Eco, a Bond novel establishes with the reader, and which indeed resembles that elicited by a typical detective story, the outcome of which is already known to us.[21] The Bond narration not only plays on the level described by Eco, it also gambles upon the very nature of its intended reception.

From a linguistic point of view, and we have observed earlier the type of mystique Fleming's words seem to hold over the production team of most James Bond installments, the text itself bares the traces of its own subversion by blending two different semio-narrative codes, which could be described as direct and self-conscious narrations. While on the one hand the text conveys the overall notion that the narrated universe is to be taken seriously, as a monosemic referent, on the other, some of its most significant elements denote a self-consciousness that contrasts sharply with the dominant would-be realistic tone. The most representative of such elements tend to be onomastic, as exemplified by the names chosen for the female characters: Pussy Galore, Solitaire, Tiffany Case, and Mary Goodnight are all names intrinsically related to the narrative syntagm in which they appear (Pussy Galore loves women, Solitaire reads tarot cards, Tiffany Case is involved with diamond contraband and Mary Goodnight exemplifies the *repos du guerrier*). Perhaps not as systematically, but nonetheless just as significantly, the names and nicknames of the Villains also tend to complete the narrative referent: Le Chiffre is an accountant, Dr. No opposes the Occidental world, Mr. Big is the "big boss" of the New York Black underworld, Auric Goldfinger is obsessed with gold and Scaramanga was psychologically scarred into becoming a professional hit man. If we are willing to accept a higher degree of latency between the sign and its connotations, we can as well associate the most enduring Villain of them all, Blofeld, with his narrative function, for his pervasive ambition is indeed to *blow* up the *field*—i.e., destroy the Order by holding the world hostage with either nuclear or chemical weapons. Similarly, we can establish a direct correlation between the all–American Spangled mob from *Diamonds Are Forever* and the U.S. flag—that is, the "Star Spangled Banner." The choice of names for female characters seems to indicate that the historical author Ian Fleming was onomastically very conscious, strengthening the thesis that the sign "James Bond 007" has always been more than the name of a distinguished ornithologist and a simple random section number; the issue is not so much whether Ian Fleming was conscious or not of the semiotic implications of his choice, but rather the fact that he appeared to be sensitive, as a literary author, to the semiotic weight of proper names.

This onomastic consciousness has been loyally adapted by the subsequent senders of the Bond genre and has become a staple of the narrative universe, in some cases to the point of interfering with the original texts, such as in *Moonraker* (film), where the name of the female protagonist from the novel, Gala Brand, has been replaced by the much more suggestive Holly Goodhead, so as to reproduce the semiotic effect of Pussy Galore's name through the use of the same lexical field. The characters of Plenty O'Toole from *Diamonds Are Forever* (film), and of Xenia Onatopp from *GoldenEye* follow the same pattern: Plenty O'Toole indeed appears to exhibit all the tools of her trade in fine order, and the name of Xenia Onatopp clearly indicates her favorite sexual position, as exemplified when she makes love to Admiral Chuck Farrell before squeezing him to death in a leg lock (0:22:19–0:23:13). This tendency has survived the recent and successful attempt to adapt the James Bond narration to the realistic trend of contemporary action cinema, for although the main female protagonist of the latest installment to date, *Quantum of Solace*, has a regular name, Camille Montes, the MI6 operative sent in by M to escort Bond back to headquarters is named Strawberry Fields, an obvious reference to the Beatles' song, as well as a fairly evocative name for a young, attractive woman. The main Villain himself is named Dominic Greene, which explicitly underlines his cover as president of an alleged environmentalist foundation, as well as his ambition to control a main natural resource semiotically associated with his last name — that is, water.

These self-referential elements, which elicit the attention of the recipient upon the construction of the narrative universe, naturally subvert the openly realistic ambition of the narration itself, introducing a dimension of self-parody that might explain in part why the actual "serious" parodies of the James Bond films started to appear as early as the mid-sixties,[22] and why, paradoxically, they have not endangered the reception of the original. By not taking itself completely seriously, without, however, surrendering its realistic pretensions, the Bond narration creates a balance between direct and self-conscious communicative attitudes, and makes any parodic intent redundant since the parody is already suggested in the original.[23]

One of the closing paragraphs of *Diamonds Are Forever* is a clear example of this delicate balance between seriousness and irony, for it opposes the tone of the message to its immediate referent without giving preference to either of them:

> The job M had given him had only been to find out about them [the Spangled Mob]. But, one by one, they had tried to kill him and his

friends. Violence had been their first resort, not their last. Violence and cruelty were their only weapons. The two men in the Chevrolet in Las Vegas who had shot at him and hit Ernie Cureo. The two men in the Jaguar who had bludgeoned Ernie and had been the first to draw guns when it came to the fight. Seraffimo Spang, who had started to torture him to death and had then tried to shoot them or smash them down on the railway track. Wint and Kidd, who had given Tingaling Bell the treatment, and then Bond, and then Tiffany Case. And, of the seven, he had killed five — not because he liked it, but because somebody had had to. And he had had luck and three good friends, Felix and Ernie and Tiffany. And the bad men had died. And now here came the last of the bad men, the man who had ordered his death, and Tiffany's, the man who, according to M, had built up the traffic in diamonds, organized the pipeline and run it ruthlessly and efficiently through the years [280].

This recount of the action, which takes place as Bond is waiting for Jack Spang in order to close the diamond smuggling pipeline, is cold and ruthless in its content; however, its apparent stylistic nonchalance, which allows it to begin four consecutive sentences with the word "and," and to repeat twice the expression "bad men," results in an overall resentful tone that suggests an almost childish insistence which, curiously, does not interfere with the serious, decidedly grown-up crimes it describes. The mention of M at the beginning of the paragraph denotes the universe of the mission, with all its administrative weight, while the development of Bond's indirect monologue puts the accent on rather personal concerns, as 007 rationalizes his murders to himself in a tone that is almost reminiscent of an adolescent justifying his pranks. The passage that describes the shooting down of Jack Spang's helicopter follows the same principle by alternating warfare-dedicated vocabulary with a simple onomatopoeia:

> The Corporal delicately twisted the two levers.
> "Boompa."
> The tracer curved away high over the rising machine. Bond reached forward and pulled the selector lever to "Auto Fire." The movement of his hand was reluctant. Now it would be certain death. He was going to have to do it again.
> "Boompa-boompa-boompa-boompa-boompa."
> The red fire sprayed across the sky. Still the helicopter went on rising towards the moon, and now it was turning away to the north.
> "Boompa-boompa."
> There was a flash of yellow light near the tail rotor and the distant bang of an explosion.
> "Got him," said the officer. He picked up a pair of night-glasses. "Tail rotor's gone," he said [285–286].

Specific technical words such as "tracer," "selector lever" and "tail rotor" contrast with the abundant "Boompas," which considerably offsets the otherwise serious tone of the narration with the addition of an almost comic-book note.

The dual semio-narrative mode found in Fleming's text is represented throughout the films by stunts and special effects which allow 007 to effectively defy gravity without ever leaving a realistic, highly contextualized environment that is easily identifiable by the recipient, both culturally and geo-politically. It is also contained within the gun barrel sequence, which is arguably one of the most, if not *the* most, fundamental trademark of the cinematic Bond, as well as being its very first manifestation (for it is our very first glimpse into the universe of 007 in *Dr. No* and has been the opening image of most installments). By incorporating a drawn element, the gun barrel itself, this sequence is both bloody and cartoonish, and hence suggests the two coexistent tones of the Bond narration: deadly serious but in a cartoon-like manner. In the recent *Casino Royale* (film), the gun barrel sequence is integrated within the narration and functions precisely as a transition between the black-and-white, grainy realism of the pre-credits sequence and the computerized animation of the credits, becoming the effective link between two theoretically mutually exclusive semiotic codes. The gun barrel sequence exhibits as well a high level of self-consciousness, for it calls attention upon its own construction by presenting an angle of vision that is simply impossible to achieve in our reality, that which corresponds to the reception of the Bondian universe. As pointed out by Chapman, the gun barrel sequence "foregrounds" the action by underlining the motif of looking, which is essential to the spy narration (*Licence* 63). The filmic adventures of Bond naturally flatter our voyeuristic tendencies, for they consist mainly in turning secrets into spectacle by constantly playing upon the exposition of deceptions and lies. Hence the gun barrel sequence is a symbolic introduction to one of the dominant themes of the narration; it also denotes constant and invisible danger, as well as sudden, unpredictable death, two other major themes of the narrative universe. From a formal point of view, it corresponds to the representation of its dual narrative mode and is therefore micro-structurally significant on two levels, for not only does it suggest the essence of the narration — a spy is indeed a professional voyeur — but it also represents the situation of the recipient of the transmission who is about to become him or herself a voyeur.[24]

The possibilities offered by the cartoon side of Bond are naturally exploited in the opening credits, another well-established staple of the cinematic Bond, which we expect to be visually arresting as well as enthusiastically anti-realistic. Both the opening credits and the film tell the same story, but in the same two opposite manners that we have found fused in the gun barrel sequence. Whereas the film tells the story in a pseudo-realistic mode, in spite of the fairy tale–like narrative syntagm, the opening credits organize the main paradigms of the narration — usually girls and guns — in a non-linear, metaphorical manner, the polysemic qualities of which allow for a synthesis of the Bond universe. The opening credits of *GoldenEye*, which represent the end of the Soviet Union by showing the fall of its most obvious symbols (such as the red star and the hammer and sickle), clearly illustrates the integration of two diegetic modes within one narration, for they constitute a logical articulation between the pre-credit sequence and the film itself: the pre-credits sequence opposes Bond to Russian soldiers, and the film starts nine years later, after the Soviet Union has collapsed.[25] The two narrative modes at play in the Bond universe are suggested by this radical opposition between the opening credits and the film itself, and are further emphasized by the pre-credit sequence, which responds to the rules of a would-be realistic representation of the world but is directly linked to the unrealistic gun barrel scene, when not generated by it. The white dot opens just like the lens of a camera to reveal Bond in action, concluding the previous mission, hence reinforcing the continuity of the narration and strengthening the relationship between the realistic and the unbelievable.

The Bond narration creates a similar duality in the recipient, who, in order to accept the transmission (that is, the narrative authority of the Bond universe), has to adopt a double mode of perception and conceive the message as both serious and ironic, geo-politically relevant and marvelously fairy tale–like. However, far from being "unstable," this balance between seriousness and irony remains carefully balanced in order to remain narratively authoritative.

In *Octopussy* (film), Vijay, Bond's contact in India, plays the James Bond movie theme on his snake-charming flute, thus calling attention to the artificiality of the narrative universe, a self-conscious move which seems somewhat out of place in the universe of 007, most likely because the narration is already as self-conscious as its own nature allows it to be before becoming its own parody. One of the most obvious examples of this narrative self-consciousness inherent in the original universe of James Bond is, of course, the choice of names — Dr. No, Goldfinger, Pussy Galore, Miss Goodnight, etc. — which cause the narration to call attention to its construction rather than its content. A similar type of meta-narration is attempted in *On Her Majesty's Secret Service* (film), as George Lazenby faces the camera at the end of the title sequence and states, "This never happened to the other fellow" (0:06:31–0:06:33), or when he cleans his office as the soundtrack underlines the inter-narrative value of each object that he manipulates by playing the main themes of the past film to which it refers. Although these excursions into a more postmodern-conscious cinema are not deprived of interest, they simply do not work well with the type of direct communication that the James Bond narration naturally elicits, and it is not a coincidence that *On Her Majesty's Secret Service* remains one of the most problematic of all canonical Bond films.

Whether during the Moore tenure, which tended to privilege charm over raw violence, or in its present incarnation, as a ruthless killer with definitely less of a sense of humor, James Bond, as both a character and the metonymy of an entire narrative universe, retains its capacity to express realistic death in an unrealistic manner, eliciting simultaneously the reception of two very different narrative modes and therefore covering a wide range of human emotions and preoccupations. For all his softness and ironic detachment, Moore-Bond is still a cold-blooded killer, and in spite of all their technological exaggerations, installments such as *Tomorrow Never Dies* or *Die Another Day* still call for a direct, non-ironic response from the recipient by incorporating direct references to his or her historical context. The opposite is true as well, and all the valuable efforts of Timothy Dalton or Daniel Craig to create a realistic, darker, "serious" Bond will not hide the fact that 007 will always be the central character of a modern fairy tale narrative syntagm that may seem to many anything but "serious." By blending serious matters and impossible feats, just like the gun barrel scene merges cartoon and blood, the adventures of James Bond force us to take our childishness seriously. After all, the mission of saving the world with a license to kill is not child's play. But it can still be fun.

The Fun in Bond

The humoristic side of the Bond universe, best exemplified in the films by agent 007's famous tension-breaking quips after he has escaped from a perilous situation, can be seen as one more manifestation of the narration's self-consciousness, which, contrary to common belief, can also be found in the textual Bond, albeit perhaps in a more subtle manner. In *Goldfinger* (novel), for instance, Bond meets Auric Goldfinger and sizes him up without indulgence:

> Bond always mistrusted short men. They grew up from childhood with an inferiority complex. All their lives they would strive to be big — bigger than the others who had teased them as a child. Napoleon had been

short, and Hitler. It was the short men that caused all the trouble in the world [37].

These tongue-in-cheek considerations are all the more amusing because they appear quite out of place and rather unexpected coming from a government employee of the "blunt instrument" variety. The literary Bond is by nature a rather serious individual, which accentuates the ironic charge of his conclusions regarding short people; it is a joke, but it is delivered seriously. The same could be said about Bond's reflections regarding another passenger on his flight to New York in *Diamonds Are Forever*:

> It was one of the two American businessmen, the fat one, lying slumped down with his safety belt still fastened round his stomach. His face was green and sweating. He held a briefcase clutched across his chest and Bond could read the name on the visiting card inserted in the leather label tag. It said Mr. W. Winter and below, in neat red ink capitals, was written MY BLOOD GROUP is F. Poor brute, thought Bond. He's terrified. He knows the plane is going to crash. He just hopes the men who pull him out of the wreckage will give him the right blood transfusion.... He won't even dare to go to the lavatory for fear he'll put his foot through the floor of the plane when he stands up [60].

These observations are made in a matter-of-fact tone, which fits the rather dispassionate outlook Bond has on life and emphasizes the sarcasm of their content, particularly the bit about the lavatory, which is a narrative motif that belongs to comedy rather than to the spy narration. The narrative focus remains the smuggling of the diamonds; however, narrative authority is suddenly elicited by the ironic description of a fearful traveler with stomach trouble and his improbable chances to make it to the bathroom on time.

Even the very respectable M can himself be caught in a silly situation, as shown in *The Man with the Golden Gun* when he instinctively puts his heterosexuality to the test following a ludicrous affirmation that he has found in C.C.'s report regarding the psychological make-up of Scaramanga:

> I have also noted, from a "profile" of this man in *Time* magazine, one fact which supports my thesis that Scaramanga may be sexually abnormal. In listing his accomplishments, *Time* notes, but does not comment upon, the fact that this man cannot whistle. Now it may only be myth, and it is certainly not medical science, but there is a popular theory that a man who cannot whistle has homosexual tendencies. (At this point, the reader may care to experiment and, from his self-knowledge, help to prove or disprove this item of folklore!— C.C.) (M. hadn't whistled since he was a boy. Unconsciously his mouth pursed and a clear note was emitted. He uttered an impatient "tchah!" and continued with his reading.) [36–37].

We naturally do not expect the cold-blooded and skeptical head of MI6 to take the bizarre notion that links the inability to whistle with latent homosexuality seriously, let alone try it on himself, and the contrast between his dignified position and his unconscious reaction creates an ironic distance vis-à-vis the character as well as the text.

In the films, the funny side of Bond has been more or less emphasized according to periods and installments, reaching almost the point of self-parody in some instances, as at the end of Moore or Brosnan's tenures, which prompted in both cases the subsequent introduction of a more serious Bond — Dalton and Craig — to remind us that James Bond 007 is actually a fearless killing machine and not some elegant comedian who happens to be lucky. In reality, Bond is both, and we can almost tolerate Jaws as long as 007 risks his life fighting him and kills a few other villains along the way. In the end, the overall tone of the Bond narration is that of a self-pastiche, an imitation conscious of being an imitation of itself, which tells a serious story without taking it entirely seriously. Unlike the typical pastiche, which imitates a given model while explicitly revealing its nature as an imitation, the Bond narration only refers to itself, and its ironic, self-conscious dimension allows it to be resistant to parody. In spite of Austin Powers, there is still a James Bond, simply because James Bond is already making fun of himself — only with more style. By now, and notwithstanding Daniel Craig's admirable efforts, the predictability of the narrative syntagm, as well as of its main paradigms, have become such a determining factor in the reception of any installment that Bond will always be somewhat fun, even when he tries hard not to smile and when his most amusing joke is to abandon the villain in the middle of the desert with a can of motor oil.

This paradoxical fusion of semio-narrative domains and modes that establishes several centers of authority by eliciting a wide variety of responses, which we could probably call Bondian art, has proven to be remarkably flexible in terms of both media and international reception, just as the Bond narrative syntagm has shown its constant capacity to alter its paradigms in function of the geo-political and cultural contexts. Borrowing Juri Lotman's concept from his seminal article "On the Semiosphere," we can describe the Bond universe as a narrative semiosphere composed of different semiotic interdependent codes which not only elicit different types of responses by generating several poles of narrative authority, but also create tension (that is, meaning) from within by opposing each other throughout the narrative syntagm. Whereas detective fiction establishes oppositions between its different materializations, from the classical sleuth to the hard-boiled detective and all their respective variations, each eliciting a separate response, the Bond narration generates internal oppositions, both narrative and semiotic, which elicit different sets of decoding moves and hence constitutes an entire narrative semiosphere by itself.

There is a Bondian narrative grammar, with its proprietary lexicon (the paradigms we associate with the Bond universe) and its own syntax (the rules by which these paradigms are sequenced). Each installment corresponds to a possible utterance of a narrative matrix susceptible to generating a virtually unlimited amount of performances, which, just as any narrative language — detective fiction being the most obvious example — has adapted and evolved along with its environment. If the Bond narration has been able to survive so many contextual changes over the years, it is mainly because it is rich enough, as a narrative semiosphere, to self-generate narrative competency. Just like detective fiction has adapted to a variety of stylistic, mediatic and cultural changes, the Bond genre has demonstrated its capacity to evolve along with its context through a constant dialogue with the receiver, being complex enough, thanks to its dual narrative mode and its three concomitant levels of defamiliarization, to produce an infinite amount of reiterations.

The narrative qualities of Fleming's text have thus transcended their literary form as well as the confines of their historical and national origins, allowing James Bond to become an international popular hero, having been easily translated and, indeed, *universally exported*. As we shall see now, the ideology purported by the Bond genre presents similar universal ambitions, for it does not necessarily correspond to a specific political position but rather addresses, in a strangely subversive manner, fundamental moral issues of a collective nature.

Chapter 6

Bonding the New World Order

"I dislike Bond. I'm not sure that Bond is a spy. I think it's a great mistake if one's talking about espionage literature to include Bond in this category at all. It seems to me he's more some kind of international gangster with, as it is said, a licence to kill." — John Le Carré[1]

Textual Bonding

If in historical and political terms James Bond embodies MI6, her Majesty and the Motherland, which quickly become assimilated to the Western "free world" as it is configured by structures such as NATO, he also purports, at a fundamental level, a specific ideology that is not related to any specific geo-political configuration, and this explains why the Bond genre has been able to survive, among other major changes, the fall of the Soviet bloc and the evolution of the Sino-Occidental relations. The ideology that the Bond genre promotes is more of an ethical system than the materialization of a particular political tendency, and corresponds to universal human concerns rather than to any particular geo-political context. In this sense, it is more of a philosophical statement than a political stand.

The first level of ideology produced by the Bond genre is that of commitment, which manifests itself at the most elementary level of linguistic fidelity. In a remarkable semiotic fusion between form and content, the notion of commitment informs every aspect of the Bond narrative, as well as its transmission, and the sender as well as the receiver seem to be irremediably committed to Ian Fleming's text. We find, at the core of the Bond phenomena, an undying loyalty to the original signs, a deep allegiance to the words of Fleming, regardless of their commercial impact or marketing value, as shown by the choice of title for *Quantum of Solace*, which could not elicit any type of predetermined reaction among a public who, for the most part, is unaware of Fleming's texts. However, Ian Fleming as author of James Bond has been absorbed by the Bond genre to the point of becoming a reference inherent in the narration, and the communicative process has assimilated both author and hero into one entity at the heart of the Bond universe. There is indeed a "legend" of Ian Fleming, narratively exploited in the film *The Secret Life of Ian Fleming*, where the character of Fleming is played by Sean Connery's son, Jason, illustrating the intricate relationship existing between Fleming, his novels and their cinematographic adaptations. It is a well-known fact that Fleming gave Bond Scottish origins to match Connery's as a sign of appreciation for his interpretation of the character. Bond, therefore, started existing very early at both textual and cinematographic levels, and a dialectical relationship was established from the beginning between novels and films, as well as between Bond and Connery. Any Bond iteration is conceived in function of an idea of Fleming, however accurate it may or may not be, and this loyalty to his words echoes that of Bond himself towards the Order, as well as that of the recipient vis-à-vis the Bond genre. As we identify with the Bond universe, we internalize its main moral trait, commitment, which is the condition *sine qua non* for the existence of any ideology in the first place, as well as a philosophical positioning in its own right.

Suggested Politics

Fleming's titles stand as significant microstructures of the Bond universe and suggest its ideological tendencies at a semiotic rather than semantic level, for they only acquire their value when interpreted within the context of the entire Bond genre. For instance, the title *Live and Let Die* is the subversion of a common idiom, and thus turns an expression of collective wisdom, in this case fraternal and positive, into its exact opposite, suggesting a materialistic epistemological outlook, individualistic and lucid, vaguely reminiscent of those of Hobbes as well as of de Sade, and in perfect harmony with the content of the typical Bond adventure, which tends to present its fair share of egotism, totalitarianism, torture and murder. Without the presence of 007 as the guarantor of the Order, the world would quickly turn into the dystopian, barbarian reality feared by Hobbes and celebrated by de Sade.[2]

The same materialistic notion is conveyed by the use of the seme "gold" in both *Goldfinger* and *The Man with the Golden Gun*, which can naturally be associated with the other precious element mentioned in the titles of Fleming's novels — namely, the diamonds from *Diamonds Are Forever*. Both "gold" and "diamonds" correspond to the second level of defamiliarization characteristic of the Bond universe, that which refers to the occupations and pleasures of the higher class and connotes the materialistic phenomenological consciousness of the modern capitalistic World Order. *From Russia with Love* as well as *The Spy Who Loved Me* present contradictions in terms by associating the notion of love with that of conflict — "Russia" being the archenemy of the Order that Bond embodies, and "spy" suggesting the undercover wars of the Secret Services. Both titles creates a tension between collective duty and personal desire, the resolution of which is not as clear-cut as it may appear, for, in the Bond universe, individual gratification, generally of a sexual nature, does not necessarily yield to the greater Reasons of State but rather negotiates with it. Albeit apparently innocuous, the title of *On Her Majesty's Secret Service* describes Bond's professional activity as well as the limits of the power structure that justifies his actions, an essentially concrete and secular entity which reflects the anti-metaphysical stand expressed throughout the Bond universe. Although the concept of royalty conveys an undeniable metaphysical dimension, the notion of "secret service" refers unquestionably to the down-to-earth reality of an administrative office, which, in spite of its connotations of adventure and mystery, leaves little room for divine providence: Faith does not need secret agents.

These ideological tendencies — namely, individualism, materialism and secularism — are constantly represented in the Bond narrations and are to be conceived beyond the specific geo-political context of any given installment, for they have proven their capacity to effortlessly adapt to the major changes that have altered the order of the world over the last six decades. More than a political position defined by a specific context, the ideology of the Bond genre applies to human nature and social organization at large from a strictly pragmatic point of view that excludes the possibility of religious beliefs from the start. James Bond might incarnate an unquestionable righteousness; however, the ethical system that conditions his actions and reactions is based exclusively upon his relationship to physical reality and implies the rejection of any metaphysical dimension.

Jesus 007

James Bond evolves in a world without god or religion, and although he appears to correspond to the archaic archetype of the traditional, morally irreproachable hero — strong, witty, courageous and incorruptible — he does not benefit from the same metaphysical backing as, for instance, a knight, a figure to whom he is often compared when it comes to his narrative function. Just as a knight errant does, James Bond travels the world, visits "strange" (i.e., exotic) lands, and encounters monsters that he defeats and damsels in distress whom he saves from certain death in virtually every one of his adventures. Following the rules of ancient courtship, he earns the love of the damsel through his physical feats and the righteousness of his sword, and what was until very recently the final scene of the typical Bond narrative syntagm, a pleasant sexual encounter with the designated Bond girl, can be seen as an updated version of the knight's reunion with his lady after the good work is done. However, Bond answers to M rather than to the king, and M answers to the Prime Minister rather than to God; therefore, the Cause defended by the agent of Order is represented by administrative elements that may fill the same narrative functions as King and God but carry an entirely different semiotic weight. King and God are absolute values that are not susceptible to being reduced to rational terms, whereas M, as well as the Prime Minister — and Bond himself, for that matter — are cogs of an administrative superstructure exclusively dependent upon social organization. Since M is named directly or indirectly by the Prime Minister, who is himself elected by the people, we are very far from inherited and faith-based authoritative privileges. As one "blunt instrument" of the system, and a representative figure of its values, Bond is indeed an exceptional soldier, but knight he is not, which might explain why the Lady, the love of whom he has won with his righteous Walther PPK, changes with every installment.

In *Ian Fleming's Seven Deadlier Sins and 007's Moral Compass*, Benjamin Pratt argues that the Bond novels are in actuality religious parables that must be read and interpreted according to the Holy Scriptures. Pratt bases his interpretation upon one particular translation of the opening line from the "Letter of James" ("James, a bond servant..." in *James*, 1.1), and on a little known collection of essays by diverse authors coordinated by Fleming, published originally in the *Sunday Times* and collected in a volume in 1962, *The Seven Deadly Sins*. Notwithstanding its originality and undeniable ingenuity, such an approach presents two major problems. First, it attributes to the author an intentionality which is not demonstrated by the texts and which precedes the interpretation itself; we are indeed searching for what we have already found, and the polysemic nature of literature creates enough latency between signifier and signified to allow the imposition of a preexisting interpretive frame onto the text. If Bond is so religiously oriented, we should probably be able to find narrative motifs and themes that reflect such preoccupation in the novels at a primal structural level and without the need to apply a metaphorical, somewhat contrived reading. The exclusion of the cinematographic Bond from the analysis, an understandable move given its premises, does not help either when it comes to proposing a comprehensive reading of the Bond universe, for it limits the Bond phenomenon to one specific moment in time and discards its uncanny ability to adapt and survive as a semiotically valid structure through major historical and cultural changes, which is perhaps one of its most remarkable features. To neglect the dialectical relationship between the textual and the cinematographic Bond may seem at this point a rather reductive view of the Bond universe. Secondly, and perhaps more importantly, Fleming's idea behind *The Seven Deadly Sins* is precisely to replace the original sins as established by the church (pride, envy, anger, sloth, covetousness, gluttony and lust) with new ones (avarice, cruelty, snobbery, hypocrisy, self-righteousness, moral cowardice and malice). Consequently, to interpret this correction of a list approved by the Christian institutions as a gesture of dedication to the divine message of the Gospel requires a great leap of faith: any religious institution is grounded upon the very notion of absolute self-righteousness, and religious practices have demonstrated abundantly their capacity for cruelty as well as for hypocrisy. Therefore, Fleming's new list, far from showing the faithful acceptance of Christian principles, demonstrates, on the contrary, the need to reform our system of moral values according to secular priorities. It corresponds much more to the necessities of the Social Contract as conceived by Rousseau or Hobbes than to the abstract ethical system suggested by the Scriptures. As to the name of James Bond coming from a specific translation of the "Letter of James," the hypothesis seems a bit far-fetched and quite uneconomical, and not only in regard to a distinguished ornithologist named James Bond, but also vis-à-vis the protagonist of Agatha Christy's story mentioned in Chapter 2. There are indeed at least two much more plausible scenarios when it comes to the inception of 007's name that appear less speculative than the one proposed by Pratt.

There are no traces of religious intent to be found anywhere in the Bond universe, and the only narrative motif related to religion or religious practices in its narrative syntagm is that of superstition, generally associated with non-white culture and ignorance, such as in *Dr. No*, where the population nearby is convinced that Crab Island is haunted by a fire-spitting dragon, or in *Live and Let Die*, where the Villain is a voodoo leader who uses a storytelling card reader, Solitaire. Those types of beliefs are not only opposed to those of the official religion, but they are also useless against Bond, thus demonstrating the superiority of pragmatism and reason over irrational beliefs. In the filmic adaptation of *Live and Let Die*, which, as previously pointed out, merges several paradigms from the original novel into the basic Bond narrative syntagm, the voodoo motif is developed in order to create spectacular rather than narrative authority and has a similar function to that of Dr. No's dragon-like fire-spitting Swamp buggy: a simple trick thought to frightened uneducated minds. If Bond, as we have seen, does exhibit the qualities of an Epic hero, his epic unfolds within a fundamentally human dimension, where gods and religions are simple tricks, and the Order that he represents and imposes is that of secular society. When we do find some traces of the Christian religion as secondary narrative paradigms, they are usually perverted by their very function, as illustrated by the words that precede the very first assassination ever committed in the Bond cinematic universe. At the beginning of *Dr. No*, Strangways gives alms to the first of the three false blind beggars who are about to murder him and is rewarded with a "Bless you, man, thank you." Strangway's charitable gesture, as well as the thanks of the killer, are indeed within the Christian tradition, which appears as nothing but a cover when a few seconds later Strangways is repeatedly shot in the back while opening the door of his car. In *Diamonds Are Forever* (film), the scene where Mr. Wint and Mr. Kidd surrender the diamonds to Mrs. Whistler is bristling with religious signs: Mrs. Whistler is presented as a missionary-style schoolteacher who teaches with a cross in the background; Mr. Wint quotes the scriptures as he hands her the diamonds — "Ask and you shall receive"; and Mrs. Whistler receives and hides the diamonds in a hollowed bible. This particular copy of the Good Book is leatherbound and has the appearance of a 19th century edition, which confers upon it a supplementary degree of respectability. As the camera closes in, we see the words "HOLY BIBLE" in golden letters on the side of the book, and Mrs. Whistler — who looks exactly as a missionary schoolteacher ought to look — executes a small finger-drumming on the cover (0.13.25–0.13–30), underlining its hollowness and its function as repository for the stolen diamonds. Since we have just seen Mr. Wint and Mr. Kidd murder the corrupt dentist and the helicopter pilot in order to secure the diamonds, the word of God is hence directly associated with theft and murder, as well as with human bonding, and is emptied of its content not only figuratively, for the scriptures are associated with blood-soaked diamonds, but literally as well, since the pages of this fine, respectable copy of the Holy Bible have been carved out in order to provide the perfect hiding place for the product of highly unholy activities. The incineration of the false Bond represents a transgression of a most solemn religious rite, and its very context — that is, the Slumber Funeral home — facilitates the representation of religious signs, such as crosses, an altar and religiously-infused music.

In *Moonraker*, the catholic mission where 007 reunites with M and Q is but a cover for an MI6 base in Brazil, where operatives dressed as monks practice martial arts and inventive ways to assassinate. Here again the paradigms directly associated with a materialization of Western official religion are subverted, and, in the same way as a fine, older edition of the good book can be used to stash dirty diamonds, a house of prayer and meditations can be put to good use as an undercover training base for the secret services. On the side of the villains, as well on that of the good guys, religious practices are most of all ingenious ways to dissimulate agendas which have nothing to do either with religion nor with the law of God. The religious paradigm functions as a cover, be it a blessing for receiving charity, a missionary teacher, an incineration ceremony or the Bible itself.

It is understood that James Bond does fulfill the narrative function of a savior with a tendency for self-sacrifice, symbolized by his commitment to the double-00 section, which translates into his apparent readiness to die for a Cause that appears unquestionable and absolute. However, and notwithstanding the utter importance of his mission that confers upon him and his superiors (as well as the structure of which they are active parts) a certain halo of sainthood — they are, after all, in charge of saving the World — or the varied connotations of the first name "James," which can be related to St. James as well as to King James, the cause that Bond represents and defends is an irremediably secular one: 007 is the savior of the Social Contract, and God is not included in the transaction. The New World Order James Bond must save is grounded in capitalistic imperatives, where the consumption of goods (envy, gluttony and covetousness) is encouraged, for it favors production and distribution; where rebellion (anger) is justified; where patriotism (pride) is a quality; and where having sex (lust) is no longer a bad thing. Consequently, 007's adventures are punctuated with acts that might appear sinful according to the accepted standards of Christian morality as it has been assimilated by collective consciousness.

The Crimes of James Bond

For all his undeniable righteousness, which is an intrinsic trait of his narrative function, James Bond is licensed to commit a variety of crimes — that is to transgress the rules of morality as understood by the majority — and hence suggests a new, decidedly modern moral order. The crimes of 007 range from simple cons to cold-blooded murders and about everything in between. Lying and manipulating, as well as snooping and stealing, are included in his job description and are integral parts of his activity, as well as hurting and killing, which could be considered the ultimate consequences of his commitment to the 00-section. He is allowed, of course, to break the rules, as well as all kinds of things, in the process, a tendency that has been magnified on the screen, for it naturally feeds the spectacular factor,[3] as exemplified by the function of the car paradigm within the narrative syntagm. If Bond is a fairly careful, albeit daring, "rally class" driver in the novels, occasionally concerned about the noise of his engine, as he is at the beginning of *On Her Majesty's Secret Service*, his cinematographic counterpart has, on the other hand, adopted a nonchalant disdain for equipment, and we expect him to wreck at least a couple of pieces of heavy machinery throughout his adventure. This facility to total cars serves a cathartic function by allowing the addressee to vicariously set him or herself free from the constant preoccupation that the ownership and maintenance of a car implies in real life, not to mention the omnipresent threat of a possible accident. By being such a reckless driver on the screen, Bond not only displays the ever-present power of his 00s, but he also allows us to escape from the hold that machinery has taken over us in real life. The fancy, sporty car — one of the most significant paradigms of the Bond universe, along with tuxedos, casinos and women — not only serves the second and third level of defamiliarization by implying both high-class living and intense action, it also represents the means to break the rules, a tendency which has becomes increasingly important in the narrative syntagm as it has moved from the novels to the screen. Indeed, we could hardly conceive of a Bond film without a healthy serving of traffic violations and deadly car accidents. Following the evolution of collective perception, Bond's treatment of his vehicle has evolved considerably in order to retain its capacity to induce defamiliarization, and although its basic functions have remained the same (mainly chasing or escaping), it has become in the films one of the most obvious representations of Bond's disregard for the rules.

In the novels, Bond tends to favor classical vehicles, which are culturally as well as narratively authoritative, for not only are they reminiscent of a certain British grandeur incarnated by the prestigious Rolls-Royce firm, but they have as well a past of their own. Bond's pampered Bentley, which he drives "hard and well and with an almost sensual pleasure" is "one of the last of the 4½-litre Bentleys with the supercharger by Amherst Villiers" (*Casino Royale* 35–36), a fairly unique and valuable vehicle that already represents by itself a factor of defamiliarization without the need for any added gadgetry.[4] After it is destroyed in *Moonraker*, Bond procures another Bentley, equally noteworthy:

6. Bonding the New World Order

> Bond had the most selfish car in England. It was a Mark II Continental Bentley that some rich idiot had married to a telegraph pole on the Great West Road. Bond had bought the bits for £1500 and Rolls had straightened the bend in the chassis and fitted new clockwork—-the Mark IV engine with 9.5 compression. Then Bond had gone to Mulliners with £3000, which was half his total capital, and they had sawn off the old cramped sports saloon body and had fitted a trim, rather square convertible two-seater affair, power-operated, with only two large armed bucket seats in black leather. The rest of the blunt end was all knife-edged, rather ugly, trunk. The car was painted in rough, not gloss, battleship gray and the upholstery was black morocco. She went like a bird and a bomb and Bond loved her more than all the women at present in his life rolled, if that were feasible, together [*Thunderball* 86].

The relationship the textual Bond has with his car is more of a personal affair than in the films, as demonstrated by the last sentence of the above quote: Bond loves his car, treats it and drives it expertly, and does not seem all that eager to break both the rules of traffic or the car itself. However, we do find in *On Her Majesty's Secret Service* a hint of both the upgrades and the accidents to come, as well as an indication of Bond's disregard for safety and mechanical integrity, as he chases Tracy's Lancia at excessive speed and at the risk of seriously damaging his vehicle, which reveals in passing an interesting peculiarity:

> Against the solemn warnings of Rolls-Royce, he [Bond] had had fitted, by his pet expert at the Headquarters' motor pool, an Arnott supercharger controlled by a magnetic clutch. Rolls-Royce had said the crankshaft bearings wouldn't take the extra load and, when he confessed to them what he had done, they regretfully but firmly withdrew their guarantees and washed their hands of their bastardized child [17].

The textual Bond has therefore already in him this preference towards performance to the detriment of equipment that so infuriates Q in the films, for he blatantly disregards specific recommendations of the respectable Rolls-Royce house, just as the filmic Bond jokes about Q's solemn warnings regarding the return of the equipment in "pristine condition." Both the Rolls-Royce firm and Q are representative figures of the establishment, naturally commanding, if nothing else because of their seniority; and Bond is disobeying in both cases an allegedly unquestionable authority. The reference to the "bastardized child" is indeed reminiscent of Q's paternalistic — and useless — admonitions.

But if the description of a car by itself, along with the occasional modification and the sporadic accident, were enough to maintain or even constitute a pole of narrative authority in the fifties, this was no longer the case in the sixties and beyond, as the car became a common staple of everyday life in the Occidental world and hence lost much of its capacity to induce defamiliarization. Bond's car was then turned into a spectacular vehicle, usually headed for an early demise, in order to respond to the demands of the action genre. By the same token, this displayed both the inventiveness and the technological capacities of the agents of Order, for the car ceased to be a personal affair and became a tool provided by MI6, just like the Walther PPK that Bond was issued in the first filmic installment.[5] Besides participating in different levels of familiarization, as well as suggesting distinctive ideological trademarks of the Bond universe, such as undying courage, status symbol and the triumph of technology, Bond's use and abuse of vehicles in the films also reminds us of how seriously the Bond universe takes our childishness: The car serves 007's mission, often saving his life — but it is also a shinny new toy that will be destroyed without regrets and to the great displeasure of a father figure, Q.

Nonetheless, Bond only wrecks cars, boats, planes — and furniture for that matter — in order to escape from the Villain's henchmen, to apprehend a suspect or to beat the Villain at his own game; therefore, it could be argued that this first degree of criminality is somewhat justified by his occupation and falls under the category of the exceptional measures an officer of the law is permitted to take while in service.

Cheating, conning and manipulating are, on the other hand, undeniably immoral actions, which, in spite of coming with the territory in the Secret Service trade, could still produce some type of ethical tension since they theoretically contradict the values for which the Hero stands. Such tension is altogether absent from the Bond universe, and the positive treatment of reprehensible behavior at the heart of the narration pushes forward the notion of pragmatism as a pivotal concept of the ethical system that it represents. Cheating becomes acceptable when it is performed by the Guardian of the Order, as illustrated at the beginning of *Moonraker* (novel) when Bond doctors a deck of cards in order to trick Drax, who has endangered the reputation of Blades by cheating at bridge and must be made aware that such impropriety is unacceptable without, however, creating a scandal. Rather than simple card doctoring, Bond's con is actually a frame which involves the complicity of M and the club's authorities, and includes pretending to be drunk in order to lower his opponent's defenses. It is, therefore, a complete act of manipulation that 007 accomplishes, and not without a certain satisfaction:

> It was all right. The trap was set.
> He almost felt Drax stiffen as the big man thumbed through his cards, and then, unbelieving, thumbed them through again. Bond knew

that Drax had an incredibly good hand. Ten certain tricks, the ace, king of diamonds, the four top honours in spades, the four top honours in hearts, and the king, knave, nine of clubs. Bond had dealt them to him — in the Secretary's room before dinner. Bond waited, wondering how Drax would react to the huge hand. He took an almost cruel interest in watching the greedy fish come to the lure [80].

Naturally, Bond is only acting to restore Order, even if this particular assignment is off-duty; he is only cheating a cheater and his conduct is therefore justified in the name of a greater good. Still, his expertise and enjoyment in committing this crime, for which he has been duly trained by the Secret Service,[6] reveal a very pragmatic view of moral values — one cheerfully endorsed by Bond and tacitly encouraged by the system itself, as represented by M and by the chairman of Blades, Lord Basildon. We find the same narrative paradigm applied to a game of golf in *Goldfinger* (novel and film), where the unsavory Auric Goldfinger is taught a lesson in fair play by being cheated after he has himself cheated several times on the course, demonstrating once again that Bond can behave immorally in perfectly good conscience. The film adaptation, although relatively close to the novel, introduces a small change of roles between Bond and his caddy, Hawker, so as to further underline Bond's ability to cheat. Whereas in the novel, Hawker is the one who decides spontaneously to hide Goldfinger's ball under his bag of clubs and then takes care of the substitution, in the film, it is Bond who accomplishes both acts, being the one who thought of the con in the first place, as well as the one in charge of its most delicate part (exchanging Goldfinger's ball with the one he found on the course). Just as he did with Drax in *Moonraker*, Bond puts on an act, missing his final shot on purpose and feigning surprise as he "innocently" discovers that Goldfinger has been playing with the wrong ball throughout the last hole.

In the novels, both Drax and Goldfinger will attempt to express their anger when they realize that they have been cheated; however, in both instances they will be cut off before they can finish pronouncing the word "cheater," as if the text itself was reluctant to admit that Bond's conduct — or that of his caddy in the case of *Goldfinger* (novel) — corresponds in actuality to that of a cheater. In a pragmatic conception of morality that by definition cannot admit any absolute value, Bond is allowed to cheat once the Order has been broken without becoming himself a cheater, rather, he becomes the instrument of a well-deserved punishment. By breaking the rules of bridge or of golf, Drax and Goldfinger directly challenge the Order according to how either game is structured — that is, the Social Contract based on the acceptance and the respect of a set of agreed upon conventions. Consequently, their actions constitute an immediate threat, one more serious than it may appear at first sight: the threat created by the Chaotic Factor, even at such a mundane level as within a simple game of golf, not only affects the objective fairness of the exchange (that is, the game in itself) but our epistemological certainties as well, for it directly defies our understanding of reality. Simply put, if one doesn't follow the rules of golf, then anything can happen on the course, and a rationally pre-structured phenomenon such as a game of golf becomes suddenly incomprehensible. The threat of Disorder is also the highjacking of comprehensible reality, and Bond is thus considered to be the protector of our epistemological achievements. Establishing yet one more level of semiotic correspondence, Drax's breach of the Social Contract, which, just as in the case of Goldfinger, is to be considered a microstructure of his greater evil design, concerns precisely a game of cards based on the fulfillment of a contract according to specific rules of engagement, the original name of which happens to be "contract bridge."

Whether Bond can adopt the immoral conduct of the Villain without himself becoming his own negation depends exclusively upon the rejection of absolute moral values and upon the adoption of a pragmatic ideology, cold and lucid, for which, more than ever, the end — the preservation of the Order at all costs — justifies the means, whatever they may be. The immoral behavior of Bond becomes a socially positive act within the logic of the narration, for it is geared towards the protection of social and epistemological integrity; in the end, the evil crimes of Bond are for the Common Good.

Naturally, this applies to hurting, torturing and murdering, and we find a similar evolution in James Bond's morality to the one we observed regarding his cheating capacities at golf between the novel *Goldfinger* and its filmic adaptation. If, on the one hand, besides the aforementioned scene, we usually see the cinematographic Bond winning at any given game without having to resort to cheating, he may have become, on the other, a tad more of a sadist than his literary counterpart. In *The Man with the Golden Gun* (novel), Bond discards a perfectly good opportunity to assassinate Scaramanga — which is his mission — out of a reluctance to kill a man in cold blood. In "From a View to a Kill" (short story), his very assignment, that of killing a sniper, depresses him so that he eventually decides to botch the job. This particular short story presents a rather gloomy Bond, vaguely dissatisfied with his situation, and hints towards a questioning of his occupation's validity, a rare moment of doubt in the textual Bond, which has all but disappeared on the screen where moral pragmatism for the masses greatly favors action over reflection. The cinematographic Bond seems to have accepted his condition of administrative assassin and seems perfectly at ease with cold-blooded executions, a tendency that has been increasing over the years to reach its peak with Daniel Craig's interpretation.

In *The Spy Who Loved Me*, Bond kills a defenseless Stromberg by shooting him repeatedly in the chest; in *Tomorrow Never Dies*, he executes Dr. Kaufman at very close range, ignoring his victim's pleas for mercy, for, just like Dr. Kaufman himself, who was about to kill him a few seconds earlier, Bond is merely doing his work (0:56:18–0:56:27). 007's second kill, as it is represented at the beginning of *Casino Royale*, is probably the most sadistic of them all, for we see Bond playing with his victim, apparently relishing the prospect of murdering a disarmed and cornered man, and his impassivity shows as he comments upon the sentence that his victim does not live to finish:

> DRYDEN: How did he die?
>
> BOND: Your contact? Not well. [Flashback to Bond's remarkably violent fight in a bathroom with said contact, whom he eventually almost drowns in a sink.]
>
> DRYDEN: Made you feel it, did he? Well, you needn't worry. The second is ... [Bond shoots Dryden at point blank, killing him instantly, and then answers, with the hint of a self-complacent smile on his face]:
>
> BOND: Yes. Considerably [0:02:23 –0:03:29].

The 2006 cinematographic version of *Casino Royale* can be seen as a counterpoint to the original novel, for each constitutes the first installment of a series — a rebooting in the case of the film — and hence sets the general tone of the fictitious universe, narratively as well as ideologically. The comparison between both illustrates particularly well the evolution of Bond's morality as it is revealed through his actions. Naturally, the film adaptation benefits from the cultural status acquired by the Bond genre over nearly six decades and inherits an already established narrative authority; however, given the increasingly vertiginous rhythm at which narrative cultural products are currently created, distributed and substituted by new ones, even a recognized popular hero such as James Bond cannot take for granted the good graces of a constantly evolving receptor who may or may not be as sympathetic to 007 as the previous generations have been. *Casino Royale*, although doubtlessly treading on a collective consciousness that has assimilated Bond as a cultural icon, still had to demonstrate the currency of this particular narrative structure, and therefore aimed to present an updated, improved version of 007 for the Modern Times — which, as it turns out, has magnified Bond's criminal tendencies. The narrative tone of the cinematic medium includes all the elements at work during the semiotic exchange, hence the visual and the musical aspects of any cinematographic narration are to be considered integral parts of the narrative syntagm. When considered from this point of view, and in spite of the undeniable weight of James Bond as an already recognized popular hero, *Casino Royale* is indeed a new beginning for the series — not to say an attempted rebirth — and not only because it marks the debut of Daniel Craig in the leading role, but also because it presents a new aesthetic direction, one logically influenced by the recent visual and narrative developments of contemporary cinema and that tends to favor a gritty representation of death and murder.

In the novel, Bond does not kill anyone; to the contrary, he escapes three attempts on his own life, the last one including torture, and appears more of a victim than an executioner. His mitigated feelings regarding killing, which he seems to consider the least glamorous aspect of his profession, are clearly expressed when, in a conversation with Vesper, he evokes the two kills that have earned him the double-O status:

> "The office was very jealous although they didn't know what the job was. All they knew was that I was to work with a Double O. Of course you're our heroes. I was enchanted." Bond frowned. "It's not difficult to get a Double O number if you're prepared to kill people," he said. "That's all the meaning it has. It's nothing to be particularly proud of. I've got the corpses of a Japanese cipher expert in New York and a Norwegian double agent in Stockholm to thank for being a Double O. Probably quite decent people. They just got caught up in the gale of the world like that Yugoslav that Tito bumped off. It's a confusing business but if it's one's profession, one does what one's told. How do you like the grated egg with your caviar?" [68].

Bond's attitude regarding this particular aspect of his occupation is more one of resignation than of triumphalism, and the end of the dialogue clearly shows his eagerness to change subjects. In this particular instance the third level of defamiliarization, that of the Epic adventure, with its occasional killing, is replaced by the second one, that of luxury-oriented pleasant activities; and so the answer regarding the double murder required to integrate the double-O section morphs into a question about caviar.

The film, on the contrary, introduces James Bond as a ruthless murderer from the very start by dedicating the entire pre-title sequence to his first two kills, which were so elegantly glided over in the novel. As if to demonstrate Bond's versatility when it comes to killing, it presents almost simultaneously two very different modalities of murder by framing the exceedingly violent and dirty fight to the death with Dryden's contact within the clean, cold execution of Dryden in a luxurious and modern office. The form in which this basic opposition is presented underlines its content, for the fight with Dryden's contact takes place in a filthy bathroom and is narrated via a quick succession of slightly over-exposed shots in an almost documentary style reminiscent of a TV-reality show,[7] while Dryden's execution, rather economical in terms of shots and movements, takes place in a modern, very posh office and corresponds to the aesthetics of modern commercial cinema. Bond thus demonstrates his ability to kill passionately as well as dispassionately, and at both ends of the spectrum, before the actual narrative syntagm — that is, the adventure itself— even begins: in the heat of a vicious fight, almost in self-defense, and as a cold-blooded, deliberate executioner. It could, of course, be argued that the narrative syntagm of any installment begins at the same time as the narration, and therefore the pre-title sequence is an integral part of the latter; this is structurally valid, but we must nonetheless take into account the different types of relationships that exist between the pre-title sequence and the primary conflict. When the pre-title sequence presents the end of a previous mission, its relationship to the main syntagm is indirect and has the function of narrative background; when, on the contrary, the pre-title sequence is directly related to the basic conflict, such as in *GoldenEye*, *Die Another Day* or *Quantum of Solace*, it acquires a different value vis-à-vis the narrative syntagm. The pre-title sequence of *Casino Royale* obviously belongs to the first category of narrative background, and informs us about the character and his context rather than about the primary conflict. We are, of course, provided with the reason why Dryden must be eliminated — he has sold secrets to the enemy and therefore endangered the integrity of the Order — and this motivation, unquestionable according to the dominating ideology of the Bond genre, is truly the only thing that distinguishes Bond's behavior from that of a sociopath. Bond's recently developed sadistic tendencies are illustrated by his cruel smile after Carlos, Le Chiffre's henchman on whom Bond has planted the bomb originally destined to destroy the skyfleet airliner, literally blows up in front of his eyes on the runway of the Miami airport (0:51:26–0:51:29). When it comes to inflict violent death, today's 007 appears far less scrupulous than his original textual counterpart.

If Bond's cruelty is undeniably present in the novels, it is usually in relation to the nature of the character rather than to the narrative syntagm, and often comes through the gaze of a woman. In *Casino Royale*, Vesper describes him as "... very good-looking. He reminds me rather of Hoagy Carmichael, but there is something cold and ruthless in his..." [41]. Vesper's perception of Bond is very similar to that of Gala Brand in *Moonraker*, as well as to that of Domino in the closing lines of *Thunderball*:

> Because he was certainly good-looking. (Gala Brand automatically reached into her bag for her vanity case. She examined herself in the little mirror and dabbed at her nose with a powder puff.) Rather like Hoagy Carmichael in a way. That black hair falling down over the right eyebrow. Much the same bones. But there was something a bit cruel in the mouth, and the eyes were cold [*Moonraker* 161].

> The girl watched the dark, rather cruel face for a moment. Then she gave a small sigh, pulled the pillow to the edge of the bed so that it was just above him, laid her head down so that she could see him whenever she wanted to, and closed her eyes [*Thunderball* 335–336].

Bond's cruelty is associated with his good looks and so becomes sexually charged, as further demonstrated in the words of Vivienne Michel, the narrator of *The Spy Who Loved Me*:

> The narrowed watchful eyes gave his good looks the dangerous, almost cruel quality that had frightened me when I had first set eyes on him, but now that I knew how he could smile, I thought his face only exciting, in a way that no man's face had ever excited me before [105].

And later:

> And then he took me fiercely, almost cruelly, and once again there came the small scream from someone who was no longer me and then we were lying side by side and his heart was pounding wildly against my breast and I found that my right hand was clenched in his hair [152].

Casino Royale (film) follows the trend of modern commercial cinema towards a darker, grittier representation of reality by developing the cruel traits of the textual Bond; however, bounded by the financial constraints of the medium, which are mostly determined by distribution factors and therefore depend upon the projected perception of the widest possible recipient, it eliminates the sexually attractive connotations of Bond's ruthlessness to benefit spectacularized violence. And so, whereas Bond does not kill anyone in the original novel, he becomes somewhat of a glorified assassin in the film, and his appetite for killing, as well as his sadism, are further developed in *Quantum of Solace*— to the extent that M herself has to beg him not to kill everyone: "And Bond, if you would avoid killing any possible lead, it would be deeply appreciated" (0:34:08–0:34:13). We come full circle at the end of the film when Bond abandons Greene to certain death in the middle of the Bolivian desert with a quart of oil: 007 has effectively become as cruel as any of the Villains he battles by adopting their habit of leaving their victims — usually Bond himself— to die in some elaborate trap. Admittedly, the trap Bond sets up is not as elaborate as those traditionally prepared by the Villains; however, unlike theirs, it is efficient, for Greene does have about a quart of oil in his stomach when his body is found, indicating that Bond's planned torture has indeed functioned and that Greene has resolved to drink motor oil in an attempt to survive before being executed by his own accomplices.

Contrary to the textual Bond, who usually appears excited by the prospect of action rather by the idea of killing, his latest cinematographic incarnation displays a seemingly undying enthusiasm for murdering people, which can be seen as a logical development of the pragmatic ideology inherent in the narration in relationship to a certain change in our perception of the world and of its conflicts. Today's globalized circulation of information implies a new level of consciousness that naturally favors solutions based on pragmatism rather than on moral absolutes; consequently, the ethical value of crime depends more than ever upon its utility as seen through the prism of the Common Good rather than on metaphysical certainties — or uncertainties, for that matter. The balance of power on which the New World Order is grounded is the first one to be so openly publicized, and its integration into the Cultural Spectacle has forced a higher level of lucidity upon the collective consciousness. The recipient of a would-be realistic narration feeding on current international tensions, such as the adventures of James Bond, has become aware, albeit perhaps confusedly, of the failure of absolute values in the 21st century (as illustrated by current historical events), and is ready to welcome an updated hero who is not reluctant to use increasingly criminal measures to eliminate any threat to the Order. As the world becomes crueler, Bond's criminal tendencies are further developed and become increasingly functional paradigms of the narrative syntagm. The motif of Vesper's death introduces a supplementary level of identification between the Hero and the primal conflict, for it fuses personal and official agendas, allowing Bond to further internalize the Cause of the Order and justifying his deadly relentlessness in the pursuit of its enemies. Not only is he the savior of stability, he is also avenging a broken heart. Bond can therefore innocently let his sociopathic tendencies run free in the name of the Greater Good in response to a new, lucid and highly pragmatic perception of the eternal struggle between Good and Evil.

Virtuous Sins

There seems to be a nonspoken consensus regarding the essentially (not to say ontologically) reactionary political value of the Bond genre; and in spite of widespread, if recent, critical attention,[8] its transgressing aspects have not been addressed clearly. James Bond 007 is a representative figure of the naturally conservative Order and is generally perceived as the heroic watchdog of the establishment. However, the overall political message of the narration is more complex, for we find among its primary elements a constant tendency to transgress certain socially accepted moral rules. As observed in Chapter 3, the character of Bond incorporates quite a few moral aspects from his antagonists, and his evolution on the screen has only confirmed his tendency to challenge the moral status quo in a more or less inconspicuous manner — without, however, jeopardizing his heroic status (for, according to the logic of the narration, he remains the most active, and hence the most representative, paradigm of the naturally conservative Order). If the obvious crimes that 007 perpetrates, such as lying, cheating, stealing and murdering, appear justified in the name of the greater good, his self-indulgence towards food, his weakness for gambling and his appetite for sex out of wedlock could be seen as belonging to an entirely different ideology, since not only do they clearly correspond to personal gratification rather than to the Common Wealth, they also connote Disorder rather than Order: Gambling, greed for food (that is, *gourmandise*[9]), and lust are indeed considered personal flaws by the moral majority.

Bond's inclination towards gambling contrasts with the essence of his activity, for it promotes uncertainty and favors luck over planning. Within the narrative syntagm, 007's gambles are signs of textual intentionality, for chance eventually always favors the agent of the Order. Nonetheless, gambling also connotes a moral make-up which does not exactly correspond to the parameters of the moral unconscious. The same can be said regarding Bond's propensity for fine eating, which is lusciously evoked in the novels, often towards the beginning of the narration, as in *Moonraker*, *Goldfinger* and *On Her Majesty's Secret Service*, and which usually occupies the integrality of the narrative space, as if it were enough to establish and sustain narrative authority.[10]

In the films, Bond's propensity for culinary delicacies is metonymically signified by a few chosen items, such as specific brands of champagne and beluga caviar, a taste that can be shared occasionally by the Villains themselves, as at the end of *The Spy Who Loved Me*, when Bond discovers that Stromberg keeps a bottle of 52' Dom Pérignon in his escape pod, and ironically reconciles with the memory of the man that he has just executed: "Maybe I misjudged Stromberg. Any man who drinks Dom Pérignon'52 can't be all bad" (1:56:40–1:56:46).

By putting forward his love of fine food, Bond reveals a deeply individualistic tendency that clashes with his essential mission as the guardian and protector of the collective Order. It is not a coincidence if the archetypical Bond Villain is also an admirer of fine gastronomy,[11] for *gourmandise* truly has nothing to do with the Common Good.

However, neither gambling nor *gourmandise* seem to dissociate Bond from his official and main narrative function as much as sex, and although this tendency is more apparent in the cinematographic Bond, it is already at work in the novels, if more subtly. For instance, in his very first adventure, Bond puts both his mission and himself at risk by attempting to rescue Vesper from Le Chiffre, and only owes his life to blind luck — that is, the timely intervention of a highly disciplined SMERSH operative. Similarly, in the short story "From a View to a Kill," Bond botches his assignment after he discovers that the sniper he has been ordered to eliminate is a rather attractive woman. The fair sex seems the only cause for which 007 would deviate from his logical path as a instrument in the service of his government, and, as we have seen earlier, both causes — Love and MI6 — are ultimately incompatible; true love, as represented by Bond's relationship with Vesper in *Casino Royale* and with Tracy in *On Her Majesty's Secret Service*, potentially signifies the end of Bond's career as a secret agent — that is, the definitive conclusion of the narrative syntagm. 007's apparently irresistible appetite for sex is therefore a statement of individualism as well as of freedom, and stands out as a peculiar inner contradiction, which confers upon it an undeniable semiotic weight.

In the vast majority of the films that precede the recent rebooting of the franchise, the possible conflict between Bond's identity as the servant of Order and his individualistic, counter-productive penchant for fast sex has been resolved by using the traditional narrative figure of *le repos du guerrier* as a recurrent conclusive figure: The Hero can indulge in purely self-serving sexual activity, for not only has he eliminated the threat to the Order, but he has proven his unquestionable integrity by doing so, which, indirectly and quite remarkably, legitimizes a behavior usually frowned upon by the moral majority. Failing to obey the most elementary rules of his profession, Bond usually eludes contact with MI6 at the end of his mission in order to indulge in sexual activity, often in a most cavalier manner, such as at the end of *For Your Eyes Only* (1:59:15–1:59:50) when he hangs his wristwatch on a parrot's perch, letting the bird answer the congratulations of Prime Minister Margaret Thatcher. This open disrespect for his superiors, and in this case for the highest figure of the Order — the Iron Lady herself — as well as for official protocol, is a transgressing move that stands out as an ideological claim against the dominant conservative tone of the narrative universe. Bypassing social conventions, Bond suddenly emerges as an unlikely champion of Self-Determination and Free Love.

In spite of being downplayed throughout the narrative syntagm in favor of the positive progression of the conflict, this transgressive aspect is nonetheless one of the character's distinctive traits and remains perhaps his only real weakness: James Bond 007 can still be fooled by an attractive woman.

Considering the liberation of sexual desire as a determining component of the narrative universe allows us to better conceive the existence of such an "atypical" Bond novel as *The Spy Who Loved Me*, which can be seen as a development of this particular notion to the detriment of the primal conflict between the forces of Good and Evil. Until the fortuitous arrival of 007 at "the Dreamy Pines Motor Court" in chapter 10, and his fight with the gangsters, which fall under the traditional narrative structure of the genre, the opposition Bond/Villain is substituted by that opposing Vivienne Michel's sexual behavior to the narrow public morality of her time, and her brief but intense sexual encounter with Bond demonstrates implicitly that 007 shares the same conception of sex, a fact corroborated in every Bond installment, both textual and cinematographic. *The Spy Who Loved Me* (novel) might indeed be "atypical"; however, it emphasizes an ideological claim present throughout the Bond genre and stands as the most explicit demonstration that free love is good — for fearless secret agents as well as for modern, liberated women.

Under cover of an apparently rigid conservative ideology, the Bond genre advocates gambling, *gourmandise* and sexual liberation, and hence transcends some of the traditional moral values generally associated with the Order that the secret agent is in charge of defending. This subversive effect is all the more pronounced in that James Bond is the ultimate representative figure of Good within the manichean economy of the narration, leaving the recipient no other choice but to accept that free sex is just as good, necessary and morally viable as 007 himself.

Orderly Subversion

We could be tempted to interpret the function of Fire as the concluding figure of the primary conflict from a metaphysical point of view; in the typical James Bond adventure, Fire signifies both the elimination of the threat to the Order and the punishment of the Villain, and hence could be seen as a metaphor for a very Christian Hell. However, such a view proves anti-economical, for it competes with rather than completes the explicit referent of the narration. In the Bond universe, Fire connotes the technological means of destruction that characterizes the atomic age rather than metaphysical damnation, and the final explosion(s) that destroys the Villain's lair is obviously much closer to a bombing than to the wrath of God. In spite of some critics' attempts to fit 007 within some type of Christian tradition,[12] the moral values purported by the Bond genre are unmistakably and irremediably secular. And in spite of its apparently reactionary ideology, the narrative universe includes several subversive moves at a variety of levels.

From an ethical point of view, the Bond genre also contains an implicit subversion of different qualities usually associated with the Hero of a manichean conflict between Good and Evil. James Bond does not fall under the category of the anti-hero, for he has no real defect and (with a few exceptions[13]) presents no inner conflicts, either personal or ethical, which would lead him to question the nature of his occupation. However, his treacherous ways, his cursory methods, and, most of all, his license to kill and his love of uncommitted sex reveal a radically different moral make-up that distinguishes him from the traditional Epic Hero. James Bond, as the modern version of the fearless White Knight, purports values that seem at odds with his narrative function when compared to its preceding models. So, while defending the collective Order, he also attacks the moral bourgeois conceptions of the very society that he is in charge of protecting, automatically legitimizing what is usually considered as non-legitimate behavior. As metaphysics yield to pragmatism, outdated moral absolutes happily dissolve into logistics and epicurean enjoyment, and thus Bond can lie, cheat, kill and have sex, and still remain dauntless and irreproachable. In this sense, 007 *bonds* different ideological tendencies by acting immorally in order to serve what is presented as a higher moral cause, as well as by indulging in sinful behavior without any sense of guilt, just as he internalizes the basic binary opposition between Hero and Villain from a narrative point of view when it comes to some of his dominants traits, such as ruthlessness, murdering instincts and adaptable morals.

By illustrating the inherent contingency of moral imperatives and their subservience to a pragmatic view of reality and human conflicts, the Bond genre precedes some of the basic principles of postmodern thought, such as cultural constructionism and radical relativism. 007's cold and determined psychological make-up, which corresponds perfectly to the practical ideology that his adventures promote, implies the rejection of any objective moral principle beyond those dictated by pragmatism. The modality in which this narrative structure that tells of the eternal manichean conflict between Good and Evil is presented proves revealing of our collective post-existentialist consciousness as well as of our current perception of reality. If it was difficult to sustain any belief in absolute values in the aftermath of World War II, it appears practically impossible to do so in the second decade of the 21st century, and so James Bond is more than ever the ideal hero for a morally disillusioned receptor, for he represents a positivist message grounded in the benefits of Order and the inevitable victory of one specific way of life — Occidental modern capitalism.

The Bond genre promotes capitalistic imperatives narratively as well as ideologically, for while the second level of defamiliarization related to the finer things in life emphasizes consumer goods, the third level, that of the Epic adventure, underlines the necessity of preserving an Order based upon consumption. The paradigmatic axis shows off the material advantages of the New World Order, displaying the advantages of capitalism by complacently exhibiting its finest achievements, and the basic oppositions upon which the main narrative syntagm relies — Bond vs. Villain, MI6 vs. SMERSH, SPECTRE or Quantum, or simply Good vs. Evil — demonstrate the legitimacy of any means utilized to protect it. The unquestionable righteousness of the Epic Hero status provides the ideal alibi for the promotion of fundamentally materialistic values by inextricably associating courage and sacrifice with the cause of the Order as represented by the fearless secret agent. James Bond is thus a perfect and truly heroic salesman dedicated to the universal export of the Free World's way of life, and his narrative universe works as the ultimate display case for the finest products capitalism has to offer, such as clothes, watches and, of course, cars. The car is perhaps the most micro-structurally significant paradigm of them all, for, besides being the undying symbol of modern capitalism, 007's vehicle generally participates in all levels of defamiliarization by being at the same time a luxury item and a secret weapon provided by the Secret Services to be used against his enemies, such as in *Goldfinger*, *The Spy Who Loved Me* (film), *Tomorrow Never Dies* and *Die Another Day*.[14]

The triumph of Bond is that of the capitalistic structures based upon a positive promotion of materialism with universal ambitions, and it is not a coincidence that the Bond franchise has become a privileged platform for product placement: the pragmatic, essentially materialistic ideology inherent in the narration suits to perfection today's utter commercialization of the cultural object in a globalized economy. The Bond narrative universe sells itself by exhibiting a pleasant lifestyle, which depends mostly on the material wonders of the modern capitalistic Order, and seduces the receptor into embracing a pragmatic vision of the reality principle that is lucid, nonsensical, and necessarily cruel and treacherous. In the rudimentary pragmatic code of ethics enforced by 007, there is no sense of honor but only victory. The absence of any metaphysical dimension in the narration benefits its enduring and widespread appeal, for pragmatism is more universal than faith and definitely more in tune with our present consciousness.

John Le Carré's suspicions regarding 007 are perfectly justified: Bond is more of an "international gangster," albeit a legal and likable one, than a "spy," and his affiliation with England might be in the end the result of chance rather than of patriotism: "But at the root of Bond there was something neo-fascistic and totally materialist. You felt he would have gone through the same antics for any country really, if the girls had been so pretty and the martinis so dry."[15] Although to dissociate James Bond 007 from Her Majesty's Secret Service would imply a serious paradigmatic change, Le Carré's accusation is not without grounds, for it points to the Bond genre's dominating pragmatic ideology that allows the narrative structure, which is not exactly localized either in space or in time, to adapt to any major geo-political change. Bond's loyalty is to the Order, which responds to an increasingly globalized, capitalistic consciousness, and the most primal basic opposition at the core of the narrative conflict is not as political as it is philosophical. The archetypical Evil Organization which puts the Order at risk, such as SMERSH or SPECTRE, transcends the geo-political context and becomes an abstract paradigm defined exclusively by its narrative function, one just as symbolic as the Cyrillic character that the SMERSH operative carves on the back of Bond's hand at the end of *Casino Royale* (novel) and which resembles an upside down "M." Quantum is only the latest incarnation of the exact opposite of MI6, a standard agent of Disorder configured to reflect current concerns regarding the environment, just as the threat represented by the Carver Media Group in *Tomorrow Never Dies* reflected the new global information consciousness that characterized the end of the 20th Century. The nature of the Chaotic Factor (i.e., the weapon the Villain wields to attack the Order) is naturally updated to what is perceived a threat in the collective consciousness at one given time in order to insure identification with the recipient at the third level of defamiliarization, that of the actual adventure. And so, whereas missiles and submarines corresponded to our preoccupations regarding the arms race, the control of water responds to today's heightened ecological awareness. The Bond narration is able to survive profound geo-political and cultural changes because the historical elements on which its basic conflict is based function as interchangeable paradigms in a relatively rigid narrative syntagm that celebrates the triumph and the advantages of Order and pragmatism in every installment, instantaneously adapting to the current geo-political climate, whatever it might be.

As a Hero of the Globalized World, Bond obeys the general principle of unifying materialism, and it is no surprise that John Le Carré perceived him as some type of mercenary. Unlike Le Carré's typical heroes, who often struggle with ethical dilemmas that usually lead them to question their own existence, 007 evolves in a strictly physical universe with no moral absolutes, religious or otherwise, and has no other mission than to insure the sustainability of the capitalistic Order, the benefits of which he reaps on a regular basis. In all fairness, we should point out that there exists a hint of a shadow of an implicit existential angst in the Bond universe and in 007 himself: His somewhat distant and lucid gaze upon the world, which is translated in the novels by the objectivity of certain descriptions, usually semiotically related to the main narrative syntagm; his distaste for routine; his desperation for action; and his constant hunger for defamiliarization, all suggest an inability to identify with the "normal" world, which is narratively legitimized by his profession. Bond's main occupation is pretending to be what he is not; therefore, he is always "someone" else, living on the fringes of social and moral norms. His own existence appears in this sense as inapprehensible, vague and undefined as that of Meursault in Camus' *The Stranger* or as that of Dexter, the existentialist serial killer of the eponymous series. The self-consciousness that we have observed in the narration, which manifests itself through its dual semio-narrative mode, can be seen as a formal manifestation of this uncertainty — the expression of a constant negotiation between seriousness and irony — which underlines both the irremediable necessity of believing in the mission and the possibility of losing that very belief. Naturally, this unspoken, always implicit doubt is quickly dissolved within the ultimate crucial activity — that is, saving the world in the name of an irrefutable cause — which allows for a total and uncompromised *engagement*: the Greater Common Order.

The films have naturally tended to ignore this dimension of the textual Bond, and it would indeed be difficult to discern any traces of existential angst in Connery's self-assured, virile demeanor or in Moore's charming nonchalance. Perhaps Bond's problems with the establishment during the Dalton and the Brosnan tenures do point towards some uneasiness vis-à-vis the overall perception of the Order, and Craig's characterization has doubtlessly added a touch of bitterness to James Bond, who just does not seem as happy as he used to be and a bit more tormented. Nonetheless, 007 remains totally devoted to the cause that he defends and is therefore fundamentally sheltered from existential questions; over the subjectivity of self-introspection, Bond chooses the objectivity of action (unlike Le Carré's typical heroes) and reaffirms its positive importance within a world of relative values.

The enduring and widespread appeal of the Bond genre suggests the triumph of a pragmatic view of reality over one conditioned by absolute convictions; pragmatism, as it turns out, is more universal than faith or existential concerns, and definitely more in tune with the materialist consciousness of our time, which might explain why the Spy Who Came from the Cold stayed there, while the one Who Loved Me is still going strong.

Conclusion: The Runaway Narrative Structure

The preceding structural and semiotic analyses of the main elements at work in the Bond narration allow us to better understand the reasons for its widespread appeal and uncanny longevity. Our study of the names of the Order has uncovered the strong correlations between the most recurrent linguistic figures of the narration and the overall referent of the message; we have seen how the sign "James Bond" is both a name and a semiotic marker of the bonding agent of Order, and how his licence number represents both a specific section of MI6 and the Hero's dominant attributes — namely, courage and virility. At the most elementary level, the narrative syntagm never lets us forget that "Bond" contains the sound of a detonation, or that "M" metonymically signifies MI6 as well as the Motherland, and such a direct relationship between form and content naturally strengthens the message, making it semiotically more authoritative. Living up to his cause, James Bond is indeed *universally exportable*, if only at the primal linguistic level.

Our examination of the different binary oppositions according to which the Bond narration is organized has put forward some of its most specific traits and further defined the nature of James Bond beyond Ian Fleming, as the narrative structure proves malleable enough to incorporate a vast array of narratively authoritative oppositions that allow the fictitious universe to sustain itself. It has also revealed the existence of three different levels of defamiliarization — "Secret Paperwork," Pleasant Lifestyle and Epic Adventure — each addressing a particular degree of suspension of disbelief. These three levels of defamiliarization are naturally related to the function of the natural elements in the narrative syntagm, which confers on the Bond genre a universal dimension and prevents the breakdown of narrative authority due to excessive spectacularization. This correspondence between the different levels of defamiliarization, as well as the fluidity of the terms on which the main binary oppositions are grounded, provide a remarkable flexibility to the narrative structure and enable it to evolve along cultural and temporal markers, constantly updating itself in order to better fit the reality of the addressee and making the Bond narration into its own specific genre. Unlike its closest neighbors of the traditional or hard-boiled detective genres, which are incarnated by several leading popular figures, the Bond narration only represents itself. There is a Sherlock Holmes and a Hercules Poirot — or even an Auguste Dupin for that matter; there is a Sam Spade and a Philip Marlowe; but there is only one James Bond. We have also brought to light the generally ambiguous moral positioning of 007, who can be a thug as well as a gentleman, a hero or a cold-blooded assassin. In some way, Bond takes revenge upon the Order he is in charge of defending by living contrarily to its rules; his mission and narrative function are to protect a bourgeois normalcy that he defies constantly by his behavior, achieving a perfect ideological balance which suggests at the same time military ruthlessness and free love.

We can no longer perceive James Bond simply as a fascistic watchdog protecting the values enforced by the establishment and legally entitled to indulge his sociopathic tendencies under the cover of his licence to kill, for he also the promoter of two fundamental notions generally associated with the Enlightenment Century — namely, secularism and progress. As we saw, there are no traces of divine intervention in the Bond genre, and if any superior intentionality is to be observed, it is more related to the internal logics of popular literature — whose Heroes rarely die — than to the hand of the Savior. It is indeed no coincidence that the Vatican advised against seeing *Dr. No*, finding it not edifying enough for the good Christian masses. Each installment of the Bond genre celebrates the triumph of secular Order and of the technological applications of scientific principles, a tendency which is most exemplified by the Brosnan period. If the gadgets, as well as the traditional visit to the Q lab, have been omitted in the two installments of the recent rebooting, technology remains at the heart of the narrative development, as shown, for instance, by the impressive touch-screen interactive satellite software MI6 uses in *Quantum of Solace* in order to trace the origin of the marked bills found in Mitchell's possession (0:16:23–0:17:01). Whether the technological feats of which MI6 is capable are plausible or not does not affect the reliance on progress that they promote, and the Chaotic Factor itself— the base of the threat to the Order that the Secret Agent/Epic Hero must eliminate — is of a technological or physical nature, which situates the eternal struggle between Good and Evil exclusively within the confines of human reality. 007 is an Epic Hero and a Savior, but only in the material world.

Epic Heroes are by definition highly identifiable; hence the Bondian paradox, which turns an allegedly secret agent into a celebrity to the point of being micro-structurally signified by his well-known catch-phrase introduction: "Bond ... James Bond." By representing at the same time secrecy and disclosure, Bond incarnates the anonymity of the spy as well as the fame of a true hero, allowing the recipient to identify with the narrative universe on both levels and contributing to its seemingly irresistible authority.

To speculate about the survival of any popular figure is a risky proposition. The future of the artifacts produced by popular culture depends on a wide variety of factors, in particular on commercial priorities, and James Bond is no exception. During the writing of this book, MGM, the owner of the James Bond franchise, reached the verge of bankruptcy; consequently, the upcoming James Bond installment, *Skyfall*, was put on hold "indefinitely." If we were to believe the rumors,[1] the situation was bleak, and the Bond franchise was most likely to be involved in endless litigations as a highly desirable asset, which would further delay the possible production of what was simply known at the time as *James Bond 23*. As I write these lines, MGM has resolved its financial situation, and our next Bond film is scheduled to be released in November 2012. Once again, James Bond 007 has triumphed over adversity and is gearing up to keep on saving the world from the evil agents of Disorder. It seems that James Bond can survive economical hardship as easily as any Villain's deadly trap, and that he remains a fairly safe gamble in these times of increasing volatility of popular cultural products. Notwithstanding its inherent Britishness, the Bond narration possesses a trans-cultural vocation, if only because it tells the adventures of an international secret agent who travels the world by profession. Traveling is directly related to the three dominant levels of defamiliarization — it is part of a pleasant lifestyle as well as of the Hero's fundamental mission — hence, the Bond universe is narratively obligated to represent the world as we know it. Unlike traditional Epics, Bond's adventures take place within the highly identifiable geo-political configuration of our time.

James Bond's personal tastes also suggest the resolution of a traditional and elementary, as well as highly symbolic, cultural binary opposition — that which opposes England to France — and so already points to a principle of globalization. If James Bond remains inseparable from M, MI6, the Motherland and Her Majesty — albeit with his own, never fully realizable tendency towards independence — his appreciation of food and sex is closer to French than to English culture.[2] The very first installment, *Casino Royale*, not only takes place in an imaginary French resort town but includes a few French sentences in the text, more semiotically than semantically relevant (that is, more suggestive than explicit, since the designated recipient could not — and still cannot — be expected to be fluent in French). One particular dialogue exchange illustrates Bond's kinship with France and French culture, and involves, naturally, the preparation of his drink:

> "A dry martini," he said. "One. In a deep champagne goblet."
> "Oui, monsieur."
> "Just a moment. Three measures of Gordon's, one of vodka, half a measure of Kina Lillet. Shake it very well until it's ice-cold, then add a large thin slice of lemon-peel. Got it?"
> "Certainly, monsieur." The barman seemed pleased with the idea....
> "Excellent," he said to the barman, "but if you can get a vodka made with grain instead of potatoes, you will find it still better."
> "*Mais n'enculons pas des mouches*," he added in an aside to the barman. The barman grinned. "That's a vulgar way of saying 'we won't split hairs,'" explained Bond [52–53].

The expression is indeed quite vulgar and highly idiomatic,[3] and reveals a surprisingly accurate knowledge of dirty French slang on the part of a subject of Her Gracious Majesty, let alone a respectable government employee.

We find, as well, four chapters in the novel with French titles, all equally suggestive and symmetrically arranged, for they are chapters 4 ("L'Ennemi Écoute"), chapter 7 ("Rouge et Noir"), 14 ("'La Vie en Rose?'") and 24 ("Fruit Défendu"), further underlining the importance of French culture within the narrative universe at both formal and semiotic levels. "L'Ennemi Écoute" places France at the heart of the primary conflict; "Rouge et Noir" suggests one of the main narrative motifs of the novel, gambling; "'La Vie en Rose?'" is a metonymy for French popular culture at large; and "Fruit Défendu" ("Forbidden Fruit") refers, of course, to post-revolutionary French consciousness, which embraces the sinful joys traditionally forbidden by the previous moral order. France occupies a privileged place among the usual allies of Bond and MI6, for it represents the pathway to the European continent and stands for ideological values that complement those of the United Kingdom, echoing once again fundamental concerns from the Enlightenment period. From the secularism of the French Revolution to the highly pragmatic materialism of the English industrial revolution, the Bond genre is impregnated with the values of a European Enlightenment Century, which were conceived and designed from the beginning to be universally exportable.

Ian Fleming created a runaway narrative structure particularly well suited to accommodate a new global consciousness in the making, and which has bloomed along with it over the last six decades. We may muse that the notion of elegance as it is represented in the Bond universe might eventually become outdated, causing 007 to become the victim of his wardrobe and of his somewhat traditional notions of luxury and good living. However, Bond, as the ultimate fictional male top-model for mass consumption, has already proven his ability to adapt his looks to current fashionable trends and even to stand against them, as shown in *Diamonds Are Forever* when James Bond, impeccably clad in a white tuxedo, strolls in the Whyte House casino among a much more informally dressed crowd without calling anybody's attention (0:33:18–00:34:25). This narrative structure for all seasons seems to be able to either resist or effortlessly accommodate new fashion directions, and in spite of not being as suave as his predecessors, Daniel Craig still displays an infallible sense of style. There is such a thing as a stereotypical young, dynamic executive elegance that corresponds to corporate aesthetics; hence, chances are that the first administrator of the Order will always be *à la mode*, whatever the *mode* happens to be.

If we are willing to adopt an optimistic perspective, we might speculate that, as a new world consciousness rises, we may move away from materialistic priorities and towards other equally fundamental values of the Enlightenment, such as fraternity and solidarity, privileging inter-subjectivity over pragmatic egotism.[4] James Bond may then some day become a soldier of the past, a heroic defender of antiquated ideals of consumption born out of the post-industrial revolution era. However, the enthusiasm with which emerging countries such as China and India have embraced the capitalistic rule in an increasingly globalized economy would tend to indicate that materialism and pragmatism are in the process of being universally internalized, fulfilling the unspoken objective of *Universal Exports*. As cultural products become more standardized to suit the ever-growing international market, the collective unconscious is more than ever subjected to the influence of the Spectacle and its commercial imperatives. Therefore, to envision the radical change of ideology that would render the ultimate champion of the Capitalistic Order obsolete might seem at this point beyond optimism and closer to wishful thinking. As to the other values promoted by the Bond narration, such as secularism and progress, not to mention guiltless sexual gratification, they are still to be accepted and assimilated on a global scale. It suffices to observe the very current, albeit hardly new tensions that religious extremisms create around the world, as well as the human exploitation born out of sexual repression in many areas of our reality, to realize that this particular mission is far from over. And so Bond lovers everywhere need not worry just yet; the way things are going, it appears that James Bond 007 will still be bonding the New World Order for a few years to come.

Chapter Notes

Introduction

1. Bennett and Woollacott begin by asking this very question in *The James Bond Phenomenon* but prove unable to answer it satisfactorily in spite of, or perhaps due to, their highly conceptualized theoretical apparatus; in their view, the next James Bond film will make a reasonable profit "less because of the cultural and ideological resonances of the hero or because of the Bond formula than because it is, simply, a Bond film" (294). In comparison to this non-committal stand, even Amis' uncomplicated position which consists in attributing the success of James Bond to its capacity to induce the identification of the reader with the narrative universe appears more convincing, although perhaps not entirely, for inducing identification is far from being exclusive to James Bond and applies to most narrative universes in the realm of popular culture.

2. As I revise these lines, the information regarding the next James Bond film, *Skyfall*, due in November 2012, has just been released.

3. See also Ibáñez's long series of comic books *Mortadelo y Filemón*, a parody of the TV series *The Man from U.N.C.L.E.*, which itself should be considered as a direct spin off of the James Bond universe, conceived in part by Fleming himself.

4. *Steve Pops contre Dr. Yes* and *Opération éclair*, published in 1966 and 1967, respectively, were supposed to be followed by a third installment, *Steve contre les soucoupes volantes* [*Steve VS. The Flying Saucers*]; unfortunately, the original plates for the third book, which we can only assume was to be a parody of *Moonraker*, were stolen before going to press in 1968.

5. The novel *Thunderball* as well as its cinematographic adaptation were untitled *Opération Tonnerre* in French (literally: *Operation Thunder*); in Jacques Devos' comic book, *Opération Éclair* [*Operation Lightning*], the author plays on the double meaning of "éclair": a microfilm containing the blueprint for a formidable weapon is hidden in a pastry, a chocolate *éclair* to be precise, which is accidentally eaten by the secret agent.

6. There is some parallelism to be established among the different interpretations of the James Bond role; thus, the style of George Lazenby's short tenure as 007 was premonitory of Roger Moore's reign whereas Daniel Craig's characterization is somewhat reminiscent of Timothy Dalton's.

7. Stephenie Meyer's *Twilight* could be seen as a follow-up to Anne Rice's treatment of the vampire genre, albeit with younger protagonists: the narrative tension is created by romantic conflicts rather than by the opposition between reality and the supernatural.

8. This is by no means a negative judgment of either Robert Downey, Jr., or Jude Law's superb performances in the 2009 film, *Sherlock Holmes*, nor in its 2011 sequel, *Sherlock Holmes 2: A Game of Shadows*, both directed by Guy Ritchie, but rather a plain structural observation: the mutation of Sherlock Holmes into an action hero would seem to indicate that the original character has lost most of his currency and must mutate into a contemporary

action figure in order for his narrative universe to survive. The BBC series, *Sherlock*, created by Steven Moffat and Mark Gatiss, which transposes the narration into the 21st century, is paradoxically much closer to Conan Doyle's creation for it preserves its most significant paradigms and successfully adapts them to present day.

9. Barthes, "La mort de l'Auteur" ["The Death of the Author"] *Le bruissement de la langue*, 61–67.

10. A shorter version of the first half of this chapter was previously published in the *Popular Culture Review*, under the name "James Bond 007 and the Name of the Order" (Vol. 20, 1, Winter 2009); it is revisited here by kind permission from the editor.

11. Ferreras Savoye, "The Birth of Counter-Theory," 11.

Chapter 1

1. If the second level of "inter-textuality" as described by Bennett and Woollacott concerns the social organization of texts, we might then simply call it "sociology of literature."

2. The notion of "independent film" itself has ironically, and a little sadly as well, become yet another marketing tool for major distribution companies, as demonstrated by the Warner Bros.' "independent" label which simply capitalizes upon the current "anti–Hollywood big block buster" vogue.

3. The social and cultural significance of blaxploitation cinema is indeed far from being reflected in *Live and Let Die*, which by presenting a black villain would tend precisely to convey the opposite message; in the same fashion, to limit the first *Matrix* to its purely visual aspects would appear a singularly reductive approach. (This concerns *Matrix* and not *Matrix Reloaded* or *Matrix Revolutions*, which appear much less meaningful than the first installment, for the narrative conflict has become a mere binary opposition of a Manichean nature, not unlike the *Star Wars* series.)

4. The authors of *Bond and Beyond* insist on referring to any type of narration and reference to Bond as a "text," following in this the trendy terminology that characterizes postmodern theory, often at the expense of the clarity of the exposition.

5. Bennett and Woollacott conceive the traditional structuralist concept of literariness in a very peculiar way: "'Literariness' (...) is not a property which texts have but a particular status and mode of cultural action that is produced for them by means of the classificatory and reading practices brought to bear on them" (254); it seems, however, difficult to conceive how a plane schedule or an income tax form could be read as "literature" even if they were granted a "particular status" and a specific "mode of cultural action."

6. Both Foucault and Lacan, along with Derrida, are indeed considered among the most influential thinkers of post-structuralism, and the importance they have been given in the field has greatly contributed to the dissolution of our object of study, for neither of them was related to literary, let along cinema studies.

7. "*Il n'y a pas de hors-texte*" (Derrida, *De la Grammatologie*, 227); a literal translation of this post-structuralist credo would be "there are no illustrations," for "*hors-texte*" in French refers primarily to the plates or pictures included in a book. Derrida obviously uses this word in a metaphorical manner and his well-known statement is usually translated as "there is nothing outside the text," which adds the word "nothing" to the original; a closer translation in English, along the lines of the postmodern tendency towards polysemy and lyricism, would be "There is no outside the text" or "there no out-text"; albeit stylistically unconvincing in English, both of these translations present the advantage of rendering the poetic license that Derrida takes vis-à-vis the French language.

8. Perhaps a bit carried away by their conception of Bond as an ever mobile vehicle for ideology, Bennett and Woollacott imagine James Bond 007 unionizing espionage workers, campaigning for gay rights, supporting women's liberation and the peace movement, trading his Martini for a beer and his Bentley for a bicycle, and eventually meeting an intellectual woman (283–84).

9. Chapman expands upon these notions in his essay "Bond and Britishness," in Comentale, Watt and Willman, eds. *Ian Fleming & James Bond: The Cultural Politics of 007*, 129–143.

10. Chapman's approach proves much more convincing than most critical analysis for it does not force any preconceived analytical frame onto the corpus of study, but rather proceeds in an empirical manner grounded upon a comprehensive view of the material at hand.

11. James Bond can indeed be seen as the archetype of the young professional, a direct product of modern social mobility, as pointed out by Furio Colombo in his essay "*Le donne di Bond*" ("The Women of Bond"): "*Eco dunque una prima definizione del modello .007, come l'uomo abbronzato delle Lucky Strike, come il giovane businessman nelle noticie-pubblicità de 'Life Magazine,' ha già compiuto, nel momento in cui lo incontriamo, il suo processo di crescita*" ["Here is, therefore, an initial definition of the 007 model, as the Lucky Strike suntanned man, as the young executive from the news-commercials of *Life Magazine*, who has already completed his growth process when we meet him"] (146).

12. The separation from the corpus of study which characterizes most of today theoretical and critical inquiries is addressed more specifically in Ferreras Savoye, "The Birth of Counter Theory."

13. The fundamental distinctions between the structures of the detective story and those of the spy narration are further developed in Ferreras Savoye, "Les aventures de San-Antonio ou la littérature derrière le roman d'espionnage."

14. "The most thorough essay on Bond's literary roots is, ironically, old material. As one of the opening salvos of the collection, Lindner reprints Umberto Eco's influential 'Narrative Structures in Fleming,' first published in the 1960s. Here, this seminal figure shows how Book Bond is not merely a matter of style, but of narrative structure" (83). David Lancaster, *Film & History: An Interdisciplinary Journal of Film and Television Studies*, 34.1 (2004) 82–83.

15. *The James Bond Phenomenon* also includes Woollacott's "The James Bond Films: Conditions of Production" presented as a separate essay, and no mention is made of the fact that this very essay is actually a previous version of the second section from chapter 6 of *Bond and Beyond*, "'Conditions of Production' versus 'Hierarchy of Determinations'" (*Beyond* 184).

16. The fact that both Chapman and Black happened to be the keynote speakers at the conference could also explain in part the apparent aggressiveness of the Manifesto Party, who might have been concerned with marking their territory in terms of cultural appropriation and professional recognition.

17. The current conditions of professional academic publication weight indeed a great deal upon the production itself, as publishing becomes a mere matter of survival; the pressure to publish at all costs tends to clutter any given bibliography with an endless amount of publications that do not always answer to scholarly purposes, but rather serve a very definite function within the academic business, that of fulfilling administrative-like requirements for promotion and tenure. (See Bauerlein, "Social Constructionism: Philosophy for the Academic Workplace" and Ferreras Savoye, "The Birth of Counter Theory.")

Chapter 2

1. Since Umberto Eco's essay "Narrative Structures in Fleming," very little has been done in terms of structural and semiotic approaches to the James Bond narration (see Ladenson's "Pussy Galore" and Stock's "Dial M for Metonym" in *The James Bond Phenomenon*), and never from a comprehensive point of view.

2. Ian Fleming's interview in the *Manchester Guardian*, "The Exclusive Bond: Mr. Fleming on his hero" (April 5, 1958).

3. *The Listerdale Mystery* by Agatha Christie, published in 1934 by Collins for the Crime Club series, including 12 short stories, among which we find "The Rajah's Emerald,"

reprinted in 2002 along with others by Macmillan under the title *The Golden Ball and Other Stories*. The credit for the finding goes to the *James Bond 007 Magazine* online.

4. In spite of the affirmations of the historical author himself, Ian Fleming, his choice for the name James Bond might not be as innocent as he lets on; Fleming's texts exhibit a strong onomastic consciousness, hence, the name "Bond" may have already suggested something else to him beyond "flatness" and "bluntness," which would explain the facility with which the name has quickly acquired radically opposed connotations to those allegedly intended by the original sender; after all, and from his very inception, James Bond was never supposed to behave nor to live in a "flat" manner but more according to his other name, decidedly more exotic and not flat in the least: 007.

5. See "How Ian Fleming Created James Bond" (YouTube video) that shows Fleming describing the process by which he selected the name "James Bond."

6. Eco speaks of "economical" by opposition to "uneconomical" interpretation when the result of the connotative analysis reinforces the semantic value of the syntagm (*Interpretation and Overinterpretation*, 67–71). By adopting as well the notions of complementary and supplementary data, we can distinguish more clearly the type of information that supplements the text, i.e., biographical circumstances, historical context, and that which complements it, i.e., the connotations found within the text which establish a semiotic code complementing the overall narrative referent.

7. See the asteroid named after Ian Fleming's hero, which indeed includes the section number: *9007 James Bond*.

8. Bond does attempt to assassinate M at the beginning of *The Man with the Golden Gun* (novel), but only because he has been brainwashed, and his failed attempt does not alter M's confidence in his favorite agent since 007 is given an opportunity to redeem himself by going after Paco Scaramanga.

9. Although he was the one to abandon Dominic Greene in the desert, Bond denies his involvement when directly interrogated by M: "[M:] They found Green dead, in the middle of the Bolivian desert of all places. Two bullets in the back of his skull. They found motor oil in his stomach. That means anything to you? [Bond:] Wish I could help" (1:36:26–1:36:37).

10. The recent re-booting of the series does seem to emphasize the friction between Bond and his direct superior, however, it remains diegetically legitimized due to the fact that it represents a new start for the character, and hence, young, recently promoted James Bond can naturally display discipline problems without endangering the coherence of the narration, nor raising any doubt concerning his deep loyalty and allegiance to the Order that he represents.

11. The traditional graphic representation of James Bond shows him holding a gun in a vertical, albeit slightly slanted direction, from the covers of the very first French editions of Fleming's novels (Plon, 1964–66) to one of the posters of the recent film *Quantum of Solace*; the only noticeable difference is that the gun has grown much larger.

12. In English, "to be ballsy, to have balls"; in Spanish, "*Tener cojones*; *tener huevos*"; in French, "*Avoir des couilles au cul.*" Equivalent expressions exist in Italian, Polish, Montenegrin, Serbian, Arabic and Chinese. This notion of implicit maleness inherent in the Bond narration might in part explain why Sean Connery remains the "best" Bond yet in the eyes of the public as well as in those of most critics, for he represents physically the virility of the character, if nothing else because of his hairiness.

13. It is indeed significant that when *Casino Royale* was re-published by the American Popular Library in 1955 under the title *You Asked for It*, Fleming originally suggested renaming the novel *The Double-0 Agent*.

14. Although *Never Say Never Again* is not an EON production and could therefore be considered non-canonical, it nonetheless remains a direct adaptation of *Thunderball*, the rights of which were in legal limbo for many years, and is as close as can be from the typical James Bond film: the choice of Sean Connery for the leading role speaks for itself.

15. In the opinion of most critics, *A View to a Kill* failed to live up to the other install-

ments mainly due to an aging, unconvincing Moore; in all fairness, it should be pointed out however that this particular installment presented several redeeming aspects, such as the superb theme song by Duran Duran, the brilliant interpretation of a disturbing Christopher Walken and the energetic intensity of Grace Jones as the converted villain Bond girl.

16. Chapman's often quoted remarks concerning the nostalgic value of Bond who helps to resurrect, or at least to fondly remember the glorious past of the Great Albion are well-taken, however, they do not exactly account for the international success 007 has enjoyed on the screen.

17. The highly commercialized structures of production of popular literature have naturally favored joined and even anonymous authorships; some well-known examples are the French *Fantômas* series, written by Pierre Souvestre and Marcel Allain, the Ellery Queen novels by Frederic Dannay and Manfred Bennington Lee and the current Pendergast books by Douglas Preston and Lincoln Child; as to the very popular series in Europe of *The Adventures of Harry Dickson, the American Sherlock Holmes*, they were originally conceived anonymously by a variety of authors before Belgian writer Jean Ray took over the series in the late 1920s.

18. Some major directors, such as Stanley Kubrick, Martin Scorsese or Quentin Tarantino, could be considered as more individually oriented senders although only to a certain extent; the very nature of cinematic narration implies the presence of other sending entities — actors and writers, among others — who color the narration beyond the director's purely personal intent: ultimately, cinema has to be considered as a collective endeavor by opposition to the individualistic nature of literary authorship, a situation which is magnified by the severe financial impositions that surround any cinematographic endeavor.

19. As documented by Chapman, the release of the early James Bond films corresponded chronologically to the inception of the modern blockbuster, which was aimed to appeal to the widest possible audience (*Licence* 55).

20. The colonialist ideology based on the supremacy of Britain inherent in Fleming's novels has been pointed out by Eco, and echoed since then, associated to the notion of "Britishness," by several critics, including Chapman, Black, Bennett and Woollacott, Baron, and Stock.

21. Eco does point out that Bond enemies are always foreigners, preferably from another race; one could argue that Russians are Caucasians by definition, however, they do represent another political "race," as different as can be from the Anglo-Saxon view of social organization.

22. This is true as well in French, Spanish, Italian, German, or Chinese, and can certainly be associated to the bilabial action of a baby feeding.

23. The openly metafictitious, tongue-in-cheek narrative style that characterizes some of Sam Raimi or Quentin Tarantino's films, such as *Army of Darkness* or *Kill Bill*, is naturally off limits for 007; any more complacency towards ironic distance than that already naturally present in the Bond universe would irremediably precipitate the narration into parody, as it did sporadically in some installments of the Moore tenure.

Chapter 3

1. As Eco points out, the villains often exhibit physical abnormalities, quasi-monstrous traits as external proofs of their corrupt morality: Mr. Big's skin tone is grey-black, Dr. No has hooks in lieu of hands, Goldfinger is a "textbook monster" characterized by a lack of proportion, etc. (148).

2. "[The Bond/Villain dichotomy] embodies all the characteristics of the opposition between Eros and Thanatos, the principle of pleasure and the principle of reality, culminating in the moment of torture in *Casino Royale* explicitly theorized as a sort of erotic relationship between the torturer and the tortured" (153–154).

3. Eco does not deal with the filmic adaptations of Ian Fleming's novels.

4. Since this is hardly the place to analyze in depth the qualities of these two particular cinematographic adaptations in comparison with those of the works on which they are based as well as the semiotic implications of such process, suffice to say that both films condense the original narrative syntagms by selecting and developing specific paradigms; the choice of these paradigms constitutes an interpretation of the original and, in the case of *The Ninth Gate* or of *American Psycho*, the collective interpretation by the sending entity allows for a clearer, semiotically more harmonious and narratively more authoritative version of the same story.

5. The James Bond narration is already self-conscious by nature, as shown by the names of its antagonists and secondary characters, as well as by the predictable organization of its paradigms; however, this self-consciousness must remain suggested rather than explicitly represented in order to preserve a narrative authority based upon the referential story itself rather than upon its parody, which would suppose a second-degree type reading; according to its brand of spectacular realism, the James Bond narration is intended to be received at the immediate level, that is in direct relationship with reality, by opposition to a parody, which implies at least a second level of decoding based upon a preconceived notion of the parodied object: for all its non-believable aspects, the Bond narration still aspires to be realistic.

6. See James Potter's classic work *Elements of Literature*.

7. See in particular Jean-Paul Sartre's short story "L'Enfance d'un chef" ["The Childhood of a Leader"], which develops in a narrative form the importance of total moral and physical dedication (*engagement*) to a cause in order to defeat existential uneasiness (*malaise existentiel*). For an analysis of the concept of *engagement* in relation to contemporary popular culture, see Joshua Mason's "Soap for Sartre: Cleansing the Existential Dilemma in *Fight Club*."

8. We find again here the notion of existential tension resolved by pure action, very much along the lines of the aforementioned Sartre's short story, in which the protagonist establishes that the exploration of his phenomenological consciousness is not the path to happiness and deliberately chooses action over meditation: plainly put, acting rather than thinking will protect us from the throes of existential despair.

9. I call the traditional type of Bond movies those belonging to the Connery, Moore and Brosnan periods; they represent the dominating structure both in terms of numbers and of longevity and have therefore contributed to the construction of the character in a greater measure than alternate, somewhat adventurous installments such as *On Her Majesty's Secret Service* or *Licence to Kill*.

10. Although a theoretical approach of the psychoanalytical persuasion might conceive loving and killing as the manifestation of one single drive, the commonsensical epistemological matrix of the Bond narrative universe naturally does not suggest any type of confusion: in the narrative economy of a Bond adventure, love is the opposite of war, and sex the opposite of battle.

11. The *Dr. Shatterhand's Garden of Death* website offers what might arguably be the most comprehensive description of a possible cinematic Bond formula (http://www.shatterhand007.com/Formula/JamesBondFormula01.html).

12. By now, the adventures of Bond have generated a series of diegetic paradigms that can be considered micro-structurally representative of a narrative superstructure, an essential Bond narrative universe or semiosphere that transcends any of its installments.

13. The constant references to James Bond throughout popular culture in general and in many contemporary film dialogs in particular allude to an entire narrative universe rather than to just his protagonist, who has acquired by now a metonymical status and signifies a whole fictitious dimension by himself.

14. In structural terms, fantasy corresponds to the marvelous, which is too often fused exclusively with fairy tales: *Harry Potter* or *The Lord of the Rings* belong to the Marvelous for they present an alternative universe in which the impossible has been rendered possible; unlike the Fantastic, which is rooted precisely upon the tension between an identifiable

reality and the sudden irruption of a supernatural/unexplainable element, the marvelous — as well as fantasy — accepts the presence of supernatural/unexplainable paradigms as parts of its narrative universe.

15. The historical and political connections between the cinematographic Bond and the evolution of the world's geo-political configuration are abundantly documented, in particular by James Chapman and Jeremy Black.

16. The classical Huxley's *Brave New World* and Orwell's *1984*, for instance. can be considered exemplary works of science fiction, for they express a vision of the future based upon an observation of the present. Their canonical status should not however let us forget the existence of other science fiction authors, such as Phillip K. Dick, Stanislas Lem or Theodore Sturgeon, who are as well deserving of the same type of scholarly attention, even if they have been pigeonholed in a popular genre and hence deprived of academic consideration.

17. Although both genres, science fiction and fantasy/marvelous, present as well alternate realities, that created by science fiction tends to suggest a dystopian note that naturally leads to a reflection upon the flaws of our reality. According to Fernando Moreno, science fiction is to be conceived as prospective fiction and its relationship to reality is grounded in sheer projection (Moreno, *Teoría de la ciencia ficción*, 69–77).

18. Realism is not a genre as much as a mode, susceptible to accommodate different types of narrative forms or genres, such as comedy, tragedy or adventures.

19. We are dealing here with narrative creations by opposition to scientific writings, for, despite some remarkable efforts on the part of some prominent postmodern theorists to painstakingly prove the contrary, the languages of mathematics or physics still aim to express a purely objective representation of reality.

20. The concept of inter-narrativity seems preferable to that of intertextuality, for it allows us to refer to non-textual instances; the trendy postmodern position which consists in considering everything as a "Text" is part of a metaphorical terminology that leads towards speculative rather than pragmatic inquiries.

Chapter 4

1. Having one's arm or leg taken off by a shark, as happens to Bond's CIA associate Felix Leiter in *Live and Let Die* (novel) and in *Licence to Kill*, respectively, corresponds as much to a scuba diving or surfing accident than to the outcome of a Secret Service operation.

2. We find a variation of this paradigm in *The Living Daylights*, when Bond and Kara Milovy elude the villains darting down a snowy valley using the top of a cello case as a sled.

3. For Eco, this paragraph would most likely constitute an example of *école du regard* or even of *nouveau roman* literary styles, for it appears somewhat gratuitous in an action narration; if, on the other hand, we accept the semiotic weight of the natural elements at work within the Bond universe, then said passage fulfills a very clear narrative function by underlining the power of the forces that the agent is in charge of dominating.

4. The *Imaginary* refers to the mental structures that construct cultural products by opposition to raw imagination.

5. The notion of realism here implies solely the absence of excessive special effects; from the point of view of the suspension of disbelief that it elicits, the Bond narration remains as incredible as it has always been.

6. As of this writing, the 23rd cinematographic installment of the James Bond saga, *Skyfall*, has not yet been released.

7. Eco compares it to a game of chess, with specific rules that determine a series of predictable moves.

8. The society of spectacle, as defined by Guy Debord in his ground-breaking essay *La Société du spectacle* [*The Society of Spectacle*], implies a glorification of the spectacle and

its elements as well as the triumph of the imitation over reality, a notion very close to that of the great simulacra made famous by Jean Baudrillard.

9. This fundamental change in status of the actor vis-à-vis his or her character originated during the 19th century with the triumph of the *bourgeois* theatre, which conveyed an ideology mainly based upon the laws of appearance, facilitating the advent of the Society of Spectacle as described by Debord.

10. This is not meant to denigrate Craig's fine acting skills, but to underline the power of James Bond as a still very current and influential figure of popular culture.

11. There have been to date no less than 15 directors involved in the Bond films, including the upcoming *Skyfall*, Sam Mendes, and the very notion of commercial continuity has indeed very little to do with the creative, artistic vision of any director.

12. Anne Thompson. "'Solace' Offers Thinking Person's 007," 10/23/2008, http://www.variety.com/article/VR1117994573?refCatId=2508; retrieved 3/18/2011.

13. See in particular the *Moonraker* pre-title sequence, which shows Bond free falling for long minutes after having been pushed out of a plane before he succeeds in stealing the parachute of a villain.

14. The first level of defamiliarization, that of the Secret Paperwork, has become mostly implicit on the screen; if 007 presents the occasional report, as in *For Your Eyes Only* (film), we never see him writing one — Bond never writes, but only occasionally jots notes of a purely referential nature.

15. From a sheer commercial point of view, the identification of Bond with his watch reached a peak when Brosnan was cast in a TV commercial in 1996 in order to sell the "true" 007's watch.

16. As I write these lines, Japan is still struggling with the aftermath of the nuclear crisis caused by the massive earthquake and the ensuing tsunami in Fukushima on March 11, 2011.

Chapter 5

1. As observed elsewhere, it appears just as arbitrary to dismiss any artifact because it belongs to popular culture than to consider it artistically significant for the same reason (see Ferreras Savoye, "Comic Books and the New Literature").

2. "Ma non lo troviamo mai con un libro in mano o un libro nella valigia, a guardare un cuadro, o a prenotare un posto a teatro, sia pure per lo spazio di una riga" (Colombo, Furio, "Le Donne di Bond" in *Il caso Bond*, 146).

3. Besides achieving international recognition for her playing skills, Amaryllis Fleming (1925–1999) is also known for having resurrected the five-string cello.

4. "*E il suo rapporto con le cose (...) è escusivamente utilitario (...)*" ["His (Bond's) relationship to things (...) is exclusively utilitarian"] (146).

5. As noted by Silhouette Man (http://commanderbond.net/4748/anthony-burgess-on-the-spy-who-loved-me-double-standards.html), Burgess seems to have an ambiguous relationship with the Bond films, which is clearly illustrated by his attempted participation in the elaboration of the script of *The Spy Who Loved Me*.

6. "007's Oriental Eyefuls," *Playboy*, June 1967, p. 87, quoted in Chapman, *Licence*, 109.

7. The Bond universe, as noted earlier, is conceived and expressed in the realistic mode, and any truly meta-fictitious effect would irremediably call the attention of the addressee upon the form to the detriment of the content, thus depriving the narration its ability to establish narrative authority based upon the different levels of defamiliarization that we have encountered; the presence of meta-fictitious elements would irremediably precipitate such a highly structured narration into the parodic mode, for its paradigmatic as well as syntactic predictability cannot stand to be underlined without radically altering the nature of its relationship with the addressee.

8. As of this writing, we only dispose of press release information regarding the next installment, *Skyfall*.

9. Semiotic weakness is to be understood as the inability of any given narration to produce enough meaning — by correlations, connotations, etc. — to establish and maintain narrative authority; besides great spectacularity and an over-representation of natural forces, it seems that *Die Another Day* doesn't have much to tell.

10. *Skyfall* is the title of a "science fiction romance novel" published in 2004 by Catherine Asaro.

11. Alain Robbe-Grillet, along with Claude Simon, Nathalie Sarraute and Marguerite Duras, are usually associated to the so-called *nouveau roman* tendency, which consisted in creating a narration without characters, conflict or background — quite the exact antithesis of the Bondian narration in terms of conception as well as of execution.

12. It should be noted as well that, within the text, Arsène Lupin refers to himself as *Gentilhomme Cambrioleur* and not "gentleman" and the business cards that he leaves on the scene of his burglaries read accordingly: Arsène Lupin is hence a *gentilhomme* rather than a "gentleman," which changes everything, for the connotations of "gentilhomme" in French, the closest translation of the English "gentleman," are irremediably outdated due to France's specific history: gentlemanship was naturally dispatched along with aristocracy during the French revolution.

13. In the novel, the scene takes place in Rosa Klebb's office, located in the underground headquarters of SMERSH, while in the film, it happens in the villa where Grant is kept in between missions by the organization.

14. *Dr. No* remains the only Bond film without a pre-credit sequence.

15. Cybernetic binary language is structured upon this very basic opposition.

16. For Eco, the negation principle contained in Dr. No's name is already by itself an unquestionable proof of his wickedness (*Reader* 162).

17. See Alborg (300–302) and Ferreras Savoye, "Oposiciones binarias y función semiótica: el viaje inacabable de Don Quijote."

18. The orchestration and production of the soundtrack of *Live and Let Die* are credited to George Martin, The Beatles' official producer.

19. The band's line-up for "A View to a Kill" included Simon Le Bon (vocals), Nick Rhodes (keyboards), John Taylor (bass), Andy Taylor (guitar), and Roger Taylor (drums).

20. "A View to a Kill" is the only Bond song that made it to the top of the charts in the United States and to a very respectable number 2 in the United Kingdom.

21. Eco compares a Bond novel to a basketball game between some local team and the Harlem Globetrotters: we know that the Globetrotters will win but we still want to see how they win (*Reader* 160).

22. The Mel Brooks *Get Smart* TV series was produced from 1965 to 1970; *Casino Royale*, released in 1967, can probably be considered as the most important parody of the Bond cinematographic genre from the sixties, notwithstanding *Dr. Goldfoot and the Bikini Machine* (1965) and its Italo-American sequel, *Dr. Goldfoot and the Girl Bombs* [*Le spie vengono dal semifreddo*], which, in spite of Vincent Price's valuable efforts, can hardly considered noteworthy in terms of reception as well as quality.

23. Some of installments of the Moore period, such as *Octopussy* or *Moonraker* in particular, have perhaps exaggerated this self-parodic tendency, upsetting the balance between direct and self-conscious narrative modes and putting the Bond genre at risk of becoming its own parody.

24. Besides representing strongly the referential and poetic functions of language, as described by Jakobson and presented by Terence Hawkes (85), the gun barrel sequences also represents the phatic function for it establishes a particular type of contact with the recipient.

25. This linearity is underlined during the first meeting of Bond and the new M (Judi Dench), as she calls 007 "a relic of the cold war" (*GoldenEye*, 0:46:59).

Chapter 6

1. BBC interview with Malcolm Muggeridge (1966) by Anita Singh in *The Telegraph*, 8/17/2010, http://www.telegraph.co.uk/culture/film/jamesbond/7948363/James-Bond-was-a-neo-fascist-gangster-says-John-Le-Carre.html.

2. As stated in one of the most famous paragraphs of *Leviathan*, "Whatsoever therefore is consequent to a time of war, where every man is enemy to every man; the same is consequent to the time, wherein men live without other security, than what their own strength, and their own invention shall furnish them withal. In such condition, there is no place for industry; because the fruit thereof is uncertain: and consequently no culture of the earth; no navigation, nor use of the commodities that may be imported by sea; no commodious building; no instruments of moving, and removing, such things as require much force; no knowledge of the face of the earth; no account of time; no arts; no letters; no society; and which is worst of all, continual fear, and danger of violent death; and the life of man, solitary, poor, nasty, brutish and short" (*Leviathan*, chap. 13, "Of the Natural Condition of Mankind as Concerning Their Felicity, and Misery," (http://oll.libertyfund.org/index.php?option=com_staticxt&staticfile=show.php%3Ftitle=585&layout=html#chapter_89842). Donatien Alphonse François de Sade shares the same fundamental, rather pessimistic, philosophical view of human nature and of Nature at large, but embraces the freedoms it implies rather than deploring its forcefully pernicious effects, and celebrates strength and determination in a world where Order can only be illusory; the name of de Sade indeed appears in the text of *You Only Live Twice* in reference to Blofeld's garden of death (220).

3. See in particular Bond's fight with Drax's henchman, Chang, in the museum of antique glass in *Moonraker* (0:44:15–0:45:30) or Bond fencing match with Gustav Graves at the London fencing club in *Die Another Day* (0:54:25–0:56:25).

4. Bond's cars are usually "normal" cars in the novel, with the notable exception of the Aston Martin he drives in *Goldfinger*, which is still far from including all the options made available in the eponymous film, such as revolving licence plates or an ejection passenger seat:

> But the DB III had the advantage of an up-to-date triptyque, an inconspicuous colour — battleship grey — and certain extras which might or might not come in handy. These included switches to alter the type and colour of Bond's front and rear lights if he was following or being followed at night, reinforced steel bumpers, fore and aft, in case he needed to ram, a long-barrelled Colt .45 in a trick compartment under the driver's seat, a radio pick-up tuned to receive an apparatus called the Homer, and plenty of concealed space that would fox most Customs men [*Goldfinger*, 91].

5. The only constant semiotic relationship that could be established between Bond's cars and his profession in the novels might be simply the color, "battleship gray," which evokes naturally the military past of his direct superior, M.

6. M reminds Bond of an expensive weeklong course in "card-sharping" paid for by the Service, during which Bond was taught every cheating trick in the book by a shady character named Steffi Esposito (*Moonraker* 27).

7. The almost seemingly improvised angles and camera movements of Bond's fight with Dryden's contact in the *Casino Royale* pre-title sequence are formally very close to the usual chase and apprehension of a culprit in any given episode of a program such as *Cops*.

8. See in particular *Ian Fleming & James Bond: The Cultural Politics Of 007*, which, in spite of the great variety of approaches it represents, does not seem to reach clear conclusions regarding the essential message of the Bond narration, perhaps due to the abuse of over-conceptualized rhetoric and to a somewhat fragmented grasp upon the corpus of study, that is the Bond genre itself in its diverse manifestations.

9. The French language makes a distinction between *gourmandise* (greed for food) and gluttony; *gourmandise* is perceived in the bourgeois collective consciousness as a fault, expressed in a common proverb: "*La gourmandise est un vilain défaut*" ["Greed for food is an unbecoming flaw"].

10. See in particular the description of the meal Bond shares with Mr. Du Pont at the beginning of *Goldfinger*:
With ceremony, a wide silver dish of crabs, big ones, their shells and claws broken, was placed in the middle of the table. A silver sauceboat brimming with melted butter and a long rack of toast was put beside each of their plates. The tankards of champagne frothed pink [26].
11. As shown for instance by Scaramanga's lifestyle in *The Man with the Golden Gun* (film).
12. See in particular Pratt's unconvincing efforts to turn Bond into the champion of Christian values.
13. The short story "From a View to a Kill" is one of the rare examples of Bond questioning the ultimate validity of his occupation, albeit confusedly and in a non-explicit manner.
14. http://www.jamesbondlifestyle.com is dedicated exclusively to the commercialization of any identifiable consumer product from the Bond narration, from champagne and cars to clothes and watches.
15. 1966 BBC interview with Malcolm Muggeridge.

Conclusion

1. *Entertainment Weekly*, Aug. 13, 2010, 34–39.
2. We are left wondering about the possible irony of Bond's statement regarding English gastronomy during his dinner at Blades with M in *Moonraker*: "The best English cooking is the best in the world — particularly at this time of the year" (61).
3. The verb "*enculer*" means literally "to sodomize," but belongs to the same linguistic register as "to fuck." In the spirit of full disclosure, we must add that the French would actually use the definite article "*les*" rather than the indefinite "*des*" in this particular context.
4. The cancellation of some developing countries' debts could be, for instance, a step towards less materialistic priorities; regardless of the motivations behind such cancellations, which may very well be seen as self-serving on the part of the lenders who understand the necessity of preserving the liquidity of prospective markets, this type of move indicates a higher consciousness of the global economical structures beyond the notion of immediate profit.

Works Cited

Alborg, Juan Luis. *Sobre Crítica y críticos*. Madrid: Gredos, 1991.
Allen, Dennis W. "'Alimentary, Dr. Leiter': Anal Anxiety in *Diamonds Are Forever*." *Ian Fleming & James Bond: The Cultural Politics of 007*. Eds. Edward P. Comentale, Stephen Watt and Skip Willman. Bloomington: Indiana University Press, 2005: 24–41.
American Psycho. Dir. Mary Harrow. Lion Gate Films, 2000.
Amis, Kingsley. *The James Bond Dossier*. London: Jonathan Cape, 1965.
Barthes, Roland. *Le bruissement de la langue*. Paris: Seuil, 1984.
Bauerlein, Mark. "Social Constructionism: Philosophy for the Academic Workplace." *Theory's Empire*. New York: Columbia University Press, 2005: 341–353.
Bennett, Tony, and Janet Woollacott. *Bond and Beyond: The Political Career of a Popular Hero*. New York: Methuen, 1987.
_____, and _____. "The Moments of Bond." *The James Bond Phenomenon: A Critical Reader*. Ed.
Benson, Raymond. *The James Bond Bedside Companion*. Seattle: PublishingOnline, 2001.
Black, Jeremy. *The Politics of James Bond: From Fleming's Novels to the Big Screen*. Lincoln: Bison Books, 2005.
Bond, James. *A Guide to the Birds of the West Indies*. New York: Houghton Mifflin, 1999.
Bons Baisers de Hong Kong [*From Hong Kong with Love*]. Dir. Yvan Chiffre, Les Films Christian Fechner, 1975.
Bouzerau, Laurent. *The Art of Bond*. New York: Harry N. Abrams, 2006.
Burgess, Anthony. "The James Bond Novels: An Introduction." *Dr. No*. London: Coronet Books, 1988.
Le Caire, nid d'espions. Dir. Michel Hazanavicius. Mandarins Films, 2006. Christoph Lindner. Manchester: Manchester University Press, 2003: 13–33.
Casino Royale. Dir. Val Guest, Ken Hugues, John Huston, Joseph McGrath, Robert Parrish, Richard Talmadge. MGM, 1967.
Casino Royale. Dir. Martin Campbell. Eon Productions, 2006.
Chancellor, Henry. *James Bond: The Man and His World: The Official Companion to Ian Fleming's Creation*. London: John Murray, 2005.
Chapman, James. "Bond and Britishness." *Ian Fleming & James Bond: The Cultural Politics of 007*. Eds. Edward P. Comentale, Stephen Watt and Skip Willman. Bloomington: Indiana University Press, 2005: 129–143.
_____. *Licence to Thrill: A Cultural History of the James Bond Films*. London: I.B. Tauris, 2007.
_____. "A Licence to Thrill." *The James Bond Phenomenon: A Critical Reader*. Ed. Christoph Lindner. Manchester: Manchester University Press, 2003: 91–98.

Christie, Agatha. *Death on the Nile*. New York: Berkley, 2004.
____. *The Golden Ball and Other Stories*. New York: Macmillan, 2002.
____. *Murder on the Orient Express*. New York: Berkley, 2004.
Colombo, Furio. "Le donne di Bond." *Il caso Bond*. Eds. Oreste Del Buono and Umberto Eco. Milan: Bompiani, 1965: 141–166.
Comentale, Edward P., Stephen Watt and Skip Willman, eds. *Ian Fleming & James Bond: The Cultural Politics of 007*. Bloomington: Indiana University Press, 2005.
Cork, John, and Collin Stutz. *The James Bond Encyclopedia*. London: DK, 2009.
d'Abo, Maryam, and John Cork. *Bond Girls Are Forever: The Women of James Bond*. New York: Harry N. Abrams, 2003.
Debord, Guy. *La Société du spectacle*. Paris: Gallimard, 1992.
Del Buono, Oreste, and Umberto Eco, eds. *Il caso Bond*. Milan: Bompiani, 1965.
Denning, Michael. "Licensed to Look: James Bond and the Heroism of Consumption." *The James Bond Phenomenon: A Critical Reader*. Ed. Christoph Lindner. Manchester: Manchester University Press, 2003.
Derrida, Jacques. *De la Grammatologie*. Paris: Éditions de Minuit, 1967.
Devos, Jacques. *Opération Éclair*. Tournai [Belgium]: Casterman, 1967.
____. *Steve Pops contre Dr. Yes*. Tournai [Belgium]: Casterman, 1966.
Diamonds Are Forever. Dir. Guy Hamilton. Eon Productions, 1971.
Die Another Day. Dir. Lee Tomahori. Eon Productions, 2002.
Dr. Goldfoot and the Bikini Machine. Dir. Norman Taurog. MGM, 1965.
Dr. Goldfoot and the Girl Bombs [*Le spie vengono dal semifreddo*]. Dir. Mario Bava. American International Pictures, Italian International Film, 1966.
Dr. No. Dir. Terence Young. Eon Productions, 1962.
Dougall, Alastair. *James Bond: The Secret World of 007*. London: DK Children, 2000.
Eco, Umberto. *Interpretation and Overinterpretation*. Cambridge: Cambridge UP, 1992.
____. "Narrative Structures in Fleming." *The James Bond Phenomenon: A Critical Reader*. Ed. Christoph Lindner. Manchester: Manchester University Press, 2003: 34–55.
____. *The Role of the Reader*. Bloomington: Indiana University Press, 1979.
Ferreras Savoye, Daniel. "Les Aventures du Commissaire San-Antonio ou la littérature derrière le roman d'espionnage." *French Literature Series*, vol. XX (1993): 127–139.
____. "The Birth of Counter Theory." *Popular Culture Review*, vol. 20, 2 (Summer 2009): 5–15.
____. "Comic Books and the New Literature" *Popular Culture Review*, vol. 22, 1 (Winter 2011): 25–36.
____. "Oposiciones binarias y función semiótica: el viaje inacabable de Don Quijote." *Lectura y Signo*, vol. 1. León: Prensas de la Universidad de León, 2005: 89–103.
Fleming, Ian. *Casino Royale*. London: Penguin Group, 2002.
____. *Diamonds Are Forever*. London: Penguin Group, 2002.
____. *Dr. No*. London: Coronet Books, 1988.
____. *Dr. No*. London: Penguin Group, 2002.
____. *For Your Eyes Only*. London: Penguin Group, 2002.
____. "For Your Eyes Only." *For Your Eyes Only*. London: Penguin Group, 2002.
____. "From a View to a Kill." *For Your Eyes Only*. London: Penguin Group, 2002.
____. *From Russia with Love*. London: Penguin Group, 2002.
____. *Goldfinger*. London: Penguin Group, 2002.
____. "The Hildebrand Rarity." *For Your Eyes Only*. London: Penguin Group, 2002.
____. "James Bond in New York." *Octopussy & The Living Daylights*. London: Penguin Group, 2002.
____. *Live and Let Die*. London: Penguin Group, 2002.
____. "The Living Daylights." *Octopussy & The Living Daylights*. London: Penguin Group, 2002.

_____. *The Man with the Golden Gun*. London: Penguin Group, 2002.
_____. *Moonraker*. London: Penguin Group, 2002.
_____. *Octopussy & The Living Daylights*. London: Penguin Group, 2002.
_____. "Octopussy." *Octopussy & The Living Daylights*. London: Penguin Group, 2002.
_____. *On Her Majesty's Secret Service*. London: Penguin Group, 2002.
_____. "The Property of a Lady." *Octopussy & The Living Daylights*. London: Penguin Group, 2002.
_____. "Quantum of Solace." *For Your Eyes Only*. London: Penguin Group, 2002.
_____. "Risico." *For Your Eyes Only*. London: Penguin Group, 2002.
_____. *The Spy Who Loved Me*. New York: Penguin Group, 2003.
_____. *Thunderball*. London: Penguin Group, 2002.
_____. *You Only Live Twice*. London: Penguin Group, 2002.
For Your Eyes Only. Dir. John Glen. Eon Productions, 1981.
From Russia with Love. Dir. Terence Young, 1963.
Gardiner, Philip. *The Bond Code: The Dark World of Ian Fleming and James Bond*. Franklin Lakes, NJ: New Page Books, 2008.
GoldenEye. Dir. Martin Campbell. Eon Production, 1995.
Goldfinger. Dir. Guy Hamilton. Eon Productions, 1964.
Hawkes, Terence. *Structuralism and Semiotics*. London: Methuen, 1977.
Hovey, Jaime. "Lesbian Bondage or Why Dykes Like 007." *Ian Fleming & James Bond: The Cultural Politics of 007*. Eds. Edward P. Comentale, Stephen Watt and Skip Willman. Bloomington: Indiana University Press, 2005: 42–54.
Ibáñez, Francisco. *Mortadelo y Filemón*. Barcelona: Bruguera, 1958–2012
Johnny English. Dir. Peter Howitt. Universal, 2003.
Johnny English Reborn. Dir. Oliver Parker. Universal Pictures, 2011.
Ladenson, Elisabeth. "Pussy Galore." *The James Bond Phenomenon: A Critical Reader*. Ed. Christoph Lindner. Manchester: Manchester University Press, 2003: 184–201.
License to Kill. Dir. John Glen. Eon Productions, 1989.
Lindner, Christoph, ed. "Criminal Vision and the Ideology of Detection in Fleming's 007 Series." *The James Bond Phenomenon: A Critical Reader*. Ed. Christoph Lindner. Manchester: Manchester University Press, 2003: 76–90.
_____. "Why Size Matters." *Ian Fleming & James Bond: The Cultural Politics of 007*. Eds. Edward P. Comentale, Stephen Watt and Skip Willman. Bloomington: Indiana University Press, 2005: 223–237.
Live and Let Die. Dir. Guy Hamilton. Eon Productions, 1973.
The Living Daylights. Dir. John Glen. Eon Productions, 1987.
Lotman, Juri. "On the Semiosphere." *Sign System Studies* 33.1 (2005): 205–226. (Translated by Wilma Clark.)
Macintyre, Ben. *For Your Eyes Only: Ian Fleming and James Bond*. London: Bloomsbury, 2008.
The Man with the Golden Gun. Dir. Guy Hamilton. Eon Productions, 1974.
Mason, Joshuah. "Soap for Sartre: Cleansing the Existential Dilemma in Fight Club." *Popular Culture Review*, vol. 21, 2 (Summer 2010): 91–97.
Miller, Toby. "James Bond's Penis." *The James Bond Phenomenon: A Critical Reader*. Ed. Christoph Lindner. Manchester: Manchester University Press, 2003: 232–247.
Moonraker. Dir. Lewis Gilbert. Eon Productions, 1979.
Moreno, Fernando Ángel. *Teoría de la literatura de ciencia ficción*. Vitoria: Portal Editions, 2010.
Never Say Never Again. Dir. Irvin Kershner. Warner Brothers, 1983.
Octopussy. Dir. John Glen. Eon Productions, 1983.

On Her Majesty's Secret Service. Dir. Peter R. Hunt. Eon Productions, 1969.

Pfeiffer, Lee, and Dave Worral. *The Essential Bond: The Authorized Guide to the World of 007.* New York: Macmillan, 2003.

Potter, James L. *Elements of Literature.* New York: The Odyssey Press, 1967.

Pratt, Benjamin. *Ian Fleming's Seven Deadlier Sins & 007's Moral Compass.* Canton, MI: David Crumm Media, LLC, 2008.

Quantum of Solace. Dir. Marc Forster. Eon Productions, 2008.

Rio ne répond plus [*Lost in Rio*]. Dir. Michel Hazanavicius. Mandarin Films, 2009

Sebreli, Juan José. *El olvido de la razón* [*Forgetting Reason*]. Barcelona: Random House Mondadori, 2007.

The Secret Life of Ian Fleming. Dir. Ferdinand Fairfax. Turner Pictures, 1990.

Sherlock. Dir. Toby Haynes, Euros Lyn, Paul Mc Guigan. Hartswood Films, BBC Wales, 2010. (on-going series.)

Sherlock Holmes. Dir. Guy Ritchie. Warner Bros. Pictures, 2009.

Sherlock Homes 2: A Game of Shadows. Dir. Guy Ritchie. Warner Bros. Pictures, 2011.

Simpson, Paul, ed. *The Rough Guide to James Bond.* London: Rough Guides, 2003.

South, James B, and Jacob M. Held, eds. *James Bond And Philosophy.* Chicago: Open Court, 2006.

The Spy Who Loved Me. Dir. Lewis Gilbert. Eon Productions, 1977.

Stock, Paul. "Dial M for Metonym: Universal Exports, M's Office Space and Empire." *The James Bond Phenomenon: A Critical Reader.* Ed. Christoph Lindner. Manchester: Manchester University Press, 2003: 215–231.

Stowe, William W., and Glenn W. Most, eds. *The Poetics of Murder: Detective Fiction and Literary Theory.* New York: Harcourt, 1983.

Thunderball. Dir. Terence Young. Eon Productions, 1965.

Tomorrow Never Dies. Dir. Roger Spottiswoode. Eon Productions, 1997.

Vázquez Gallego, Manuel. *Anacleto, agente secreto.* Barcelona: Bruguera, 1964.

A View to a Kill. Dir. John Glenn. Eon Productions, 1985.

Windler, Simon. *James Bond: The Man Who Saved England.* New York: Farrar, Straus and Giroux, 2006.

Woollacott, Janet. "The James Bond Films: Conditions of Production." *The James Bond Phenomenon: A Critical Reader.* Ed. Christoph Lindner. Manchester: Manchester University Press, 2003: 99–117.

The World Is Not Enough. Dir. Michael Apted. Eon Productions, 1999.

Yeffet, Glenn, ed. *James Bond in the 21st Century: Why Do We Still Need 007.* Dallas: Benbella, 2006.

You Only Live Twice. Dir. Lewis Gilbert. Eon Productions, 1967.

Index

Alborg, Juan Luis 181*n*17
Alec Trevelyan *see* Trevelyan, Alec
Allain, Marcel 185*n*17
Allen, Dennis W. 26
Amasova, Ania 68, 99
American Psycho 58, 186*n*4
Amis, Kingsley 12–13, 20, 79, 181*n*1
Amritraj, Vijay 68
Anacleto, agente secreto 4
Army of Darkness 185*n*23
Arsène Lupin *see* Lupin, Arsène
The Art of Bond 12
Atala 117

Barthes, Roland 6, 182*n*9
Batman 20
Baudrillard, Jean 188*n*8
Bauerlein, Mark 183*n*17
Bennett, Tony 1, 8, 14–19, 21, 29, 181*n*1, 182*n*1, 185*n*20
Benson, Raymond 12, 79
Bey, Kerim 27
Bill Tanner *see* Tanner, Bill
Black, Jeremy 20–21
blaxploitation 16
Blofeld (Ernst Stavro) 23, 26, 35, 38, 43, 49, 56, 66, 68, 77, 83, 93, 105, 108, 117, 134, 136, 142, 190*n*2
Blunt, Irma 49
Bond, James (ornithologist) 34, 27, 124, 142, 155
Bond, Samantha 46, 73
Bond, Trevor 46, 73
Bond and Beyond: The Political Career of a Popular Hero 1, 14–19
The Bond Code: The Dark World of Ian Fleming and James Bond 36, 37

Bond Girls Are Forever: The Women of James Bond 12
Bons baisers de Hong Kong (*From Hong Kong with Love*) 4
Bouvier, Pam 99, 100
Bouzerau, Laurent 12
Brand, Gala 24, 36, 75, 93, 143, 165, 166
Bray, Hilary 23, 136
Brosnan, Pierce 5, 16, 39, 45, 46, 47, 48, 50, 54, 55, 64, 67, 81, 87, 98, 99, 102, 122, 124, 128, 149, 174, 177, 186, 188
Le Bruissement de la langue 182*n*9
Burgess, Anthony 37, 120–121, 141, 188*n*5
Burroughs, Edgar Rice 3

C.C. 26, 27, 148
Le Caire, nid d'espion (*Cairo, Nest of Spies*) 4
Camille Montes *see* Montes, Camille
Cara Milovi *see* Milovi, Cara
Carver (Elliot) 68 71, 98, 173
Carver, Rosie 68
Case, Tiffany 34, 35, 142, 144
Casino Royale (film, 1967) 4, 16, 38, 59, 79, 121, 169, 185*n*25
Casino Royale (film, 2006) 3, 21, 32, 35, 39, 42, 50, 61, 63, 69, 71, 97, 100, 109, 110, 113, 116, 120, 122, 125, 126, 140, 145, 163–166, 169, 178, 184*n*13, 184*n*3, 190*n*7
Casino Royale (novel) 1, 35, 37, 38, 41, 43, 46, 52, 57, 59, 77, 83, 88, 89, 96, 102, 104, 107, 112, 139, 173
Il caso Bond 24, 188
Cervantes, Miguel 5, 139
Chapman, James 1–2 (foreword), 13, 14, 15, 19–20, 21, 26, 29, 30, 66, 88, 121, 138, 145, 183, 185, 187, 188*n*6

197

Index

Chateaubriand, René de 117
Child, Lincoln 185n17
Christie, Agatha 33–34, 183n3
El Club Dumas 58
Colombo, Furio 116, 183n11, 188n2
Comentale, Edward P. 183n9
Conan the Barbarian 81
Connery, Jason 152
Connery, Sean 16, 32, 38, 49, 50, 54, 64, 99, 128, 174, 184, 186
Cork, John 12
Craig, Daniel 3, 5, 6, 16, 19, 21, 42, 45, 50, 55, 99, 100, 128, 147, 149, 163, 164, 174, 180, 181n6, 188n10

Dalton, Timothy 38, 48, 49, 50, 55, 64, 99, 124, 128, 147, 149, 174, 181n6
Dannay, Frederic 185n17
Darko Kerim see Kerim, Darko
Day, May 68
Death on the Nile 34
Debord, Guy 187n8, 188n9
Derrida, Jacques 17, 18, 182n6
detective fiction 28, 39, 79–80, 149, 150
Devos, Jacques 4, 181n5
Dexter 174
Diamonds Are Forever (film) 49, 50, 123, 124, 143, 156, 180
Diamonds Are Forever (novel) 22, 35, 93, 116, 132, 134, 142, 148
Dickson, Harry 185n17
Die Another Day 6, 16, 39, 46, 67, 68, 81, 86, 97–100, 111, 116–118, 124–126, 131, 147, 165, 172, 189n9, 190n3
Die Hard 20, 39
Dr. Goldfoot and the Bikini Machine 189n25
Dr. Goldfoot and the Girl Bombs (*Le spie vengono dal semifreddo*) 189n25
Dr. Kaufman 71, 163
Dr. No 34, 35, 94, 95, 98, 139, 142, 146
Dr. No (film) 1, 26, 32, 38, 40, 42, 46, 59, 69, 86, 97, 100, 106, 107, 121, 122, 124, 137, 138, 140, 145, 155, 156, 177, 185n1, 189n14
Dr. No (novel) 34, 35, 38, 41, 42, 69, 71, 93, 94, 96, 97, 105, 106, 116, 117, 139, 155
Dr. Shatterhand's Garden of Death 186n11
"007 in New York" 61, 62, 77, 132
Dougall, Alastair 12
Drax (Hugo) 35, 38, 66, 67, 93, 108, 117, 125, 139, 160, 161, 162

dual semio-narrative mode 145, 174
Duras, Marguerite 189n11

Eco, Umberto 1, 6, 7, 13, 21, 29–30, 34, 56–57, 59, 64, 65, 66, 67, 68, 70, 74, 75–76, 81, 83, 112, 121, 128, 129, 130, 132, 133, 134, 135, 142, 183, 184, 185, 187n3, 189n16, 189n21
Elements of Literature 186n6
Ellis, Brett Easton 58
Emilio Largo see Largo, Emilio
Enter the Dragon 16
The Essential Bond: The Authorized Guide to the World of 007 12

the Fantastic 84, 129, 186n14
fantasy 80–81, 186n14
Fantômas 185n17
Fat, Hai 69
Felix Leiter see Leiter, Felix
For Your Eyes Only (film) 92, 111, 188n14
"For Your Eyes Only" (short story) 77
For Your Eyes Only: Ian Fleming and James Bond 12
Foucault, Michel 17, 182n6
Freud, Sigmund 26, 27, 43
"From a View to a Kill" 62, 162, 169, 191n13
From Russia with Love (film) 27, 46, 68, 106, 108, 122, 125
From Russia with Love (novel) 57, 68, 74, 94, 108, 116, 125, 132–133, 153

Gala Brand see Brand, Gala
Galore, Pussy 23, 34, 104, 142, 143, 146
Gardiner, Philip 37
Glen, John 50
Goethe, Johann Wolfgang von 117
The Golden Ball and Other Stories 184n3
GoldenEye 45, 47, 48, 50, 67, 78, 102, 111, 124, 126, 143, 146, 165, 189n24
Goldfinger (Auric) 34, 35, 42, 52, 66, 68, 77, 98, 108, 111, 142, 146, 161, 162, 185n1
Goldfinger (film) 43, 46, 47, 52, 101, 107, 108, 111, 119, 122, 125, 161
Goldfinger (novel) 34, 42, 46, 57, 83, 93, 104, 106, 107, 108, 147, 152, 161, 168, 172, 190n4, 191n10
Goodnight, Mary 34, 36, 105, 107, 142
Grant, Red 74, 108, 132–134, 189n13
Graves, Gustav 67, 68, 98, 117, 118, 124, 190n3
Griffon Or see Or, Griffon
A Guide to the Birds of the West Indies 124

Index

gun barrel sequence 4, 140, 145–147, 189n23
Gustav Graves *see* Graves, Gustav

Hai Fat *see* Fat, Hai
Hamilton, John 50
Hammer, Mike 79
Harron, Mary 58
Harry Dickson *see* Dickson, Harry
Hawkes, Terence 189n23
Hercules Poirot *see* Poirot, Hercules
Hilary Bray *see* Bray, Hilary
"The Hildebrand Rarity" 34, 77, 94
Hobbes, Thomas 152, 155
The Hobbit 129
Holmes, Sherlock 3, 5, 78, 115, 127
Honey Rider *see* Rider, Honey
Honeychile Rider *see* Rider, Honeychile
Hovey, Jaime 25, 29

Ian Fleming & James Bond: The Cultural Politics of 007 25–29, 190n8
Ian Fleming's Seven Deadlier Sins & 007's Moral Compass 154
Ibáñez, Francisco 181n3
Indiana Jones *see* Jones, Indiana
Indiana Jones 20
El Ingenioso Hidalgo, Don Quijote de La Mancha 5
Interpretation and Overinterpretation 184n6
Irma Blunt *see* Blunt, Irma

Jack Spang *see* Spang, Jack
The James Bond Bedside Companion 12
The James Bond Dossier 13, 20
James Bond 007 Magazine (on line) 184n3
The James Bond Encyclopedia 12
James Bond in the 21st Century: Why Do We Still Need 007 13
The James Bond Phenomenon: A Critical Reader 21–25
James Bond: The Man and His World: The Official Companion to Ian Fleming's Creation 12
James Bond: The Man Who Saved England 12
James Bond: The Secret World of 007 12
Jaws 86, 149
Jinx (Giacinta Johnson) 42, 68, 99
John Strangways *see* Strangways, John
Johnny English 4
Johnny English Reborn 79
Johnson, Tee Hee 124
Jones, Indiana 3, 20

Kananga 43
Kerim, Darko 74, 133
Kerim Bey *see* Bey, Kerim
Kill Bill 185n23
Kissy Suzuki *see* Suzuki, Kissy
Klebb, Rosa 133, 189n13
Kristatos 77
Kubrick, Stanley 185n18

Lacan, Jacques 17, 18, 182n6
Lancaster, David 24, 183n4
Largo, Emilio 77
Lazenby, George 38, 48, 49, 50, 64, 128, 146, 181n6
Leblanc, Maurice 130
Le Carré, John 151, 173, 174
Le Chiffre 38, 43, 45, 52, 59, 69, 77, 83, 88, 96, 97, 107, 109, 110, 125, 142, 169
Leiter, Felix 39, 50, 70, 97, 135, 187n1
Lethal Weapon 39
Leviathan 190n2
License to Kill 38–40, 48, 49
Lin, Wai 99
Lindner, Christoph 20, 21, 23, 28, 183n14
Live and Let Die (film) 6, 16, 38, 43, 68, 71, 111, 117, 123, 126, 135, 141, 152, 182n3, 187n1, 189n18
Live and Let Die (novel) 22, 35, 38, 49, 74, 75, 92, 93, 96, 104, 105, 108, 110, 112, 155
"Live and Let Die" (song) 140
The Living Daylights (film) 48, 49, 64, 124, 187n2
The Living Daylights (short stories) 30, 117, 118
"The Living Daylights" (short story) 62, 116, 118
Llewellyn, Rhoda 77
The Lord of the Rings 81, 186n14
Lotman, Juri 149
Lucas, George 16
Luke Skywalker *see* Skywalker, Luke
Lupin, Arsène 130, 189n12
Lynn, Vesper 35, 36, 41, 69, 88, 89, 97, 104, 164, 165, 167, 169

Macintyre, Ben 12
Mad Max 130
Maigret 115
The Man with the Golden Gun (film) 6, 16, 39, 47, 65, 69, 86, 107, 116, 123, 124, 152, 191n11
The Man with the Golden Gun (novel) 12,

22, 26, 35, 36, 42, 51, 53, 57, 66, 88, 93, 105, 108, 148, 152, 162, 184n8
Marlowe, Philip 79, 177
the Marvelous 186n14, 187n17
Mary Goodnight *see* Goodnight, Mary
Mason, Joshuah 186n7
Masters, Philip 77
Matrix 6, 16, 182n3
May Day *see* Day, May
Mendes, Sam 11
Meyer, Stephenie 5, 181
Michel, Vivienne 64, 65, 78, 100, 166, 170
Mike Hammer *see* Hammer, Mike
Miller, Toby 24, 40, 41
Milovi, Cara 119
Mr. Big 22, 38, 43, 56, 92, 93, 96, 98, 105, 108, 112, 124, 131, 135, 142, 185n1
Mr. Kidd 134, 156
Mr. Wint 134, 156
Molony, Sir James 50, 51
Montes, Camille 55, 70, 98, 99, 100, 143
Moonraker (film) 6, 16, 39, 81, 86, 103, 108, 111, 116, 118, 125, 128, 143, 157
Moonraker (novel) 20, 24, 46, 59, 64, 67, 75, 81, 83, 84, 93, 108, 113, 128, 139, 158, 160, 161, 165, 168, 181n4, 188n13, 189n22, 190n3, 191n2
Moore, Roger 5, 6, 16, 19, 38, 48, 50, 54, 58, 64, 72, 87, 99, 123, 128, 140, 147, 149, 174, 181n6, 185n15, 186n9, 189n23
Moreno, Fernando Ángel 187n17
Mortadelo y Filemón 181n3
Most, Glenn W. 24
Mrs. Whistler 156
Murder on the Orient Express 34
music 48, 116, 118, 119, 137, 139–14, 156, 164

Never Say Never Again 43, 44, 126, 184n14
The Ninth Gate 58, 186n4

Octopussy 69, 107
Octopussy (film) 46, 68, 107, 125, 146, 189n22
"Octopussy" (short story) 77, 83, 105, 106, 132
Octopussy & The Living Daylights (short stories) 30
Oddjob 106, 111
El olvido de la razón 118
On Her Majesty's Secret Service (film) 23, 35, 36, 48, 49, 50, 51, 53, 57, 64, 78, 85, 91, 101, 103, 106, 108, 122, 123, 124, 135, 169, 186n9
On Her Majesty's Secret Service (novel) 23, 35, 36, 40, 41, 57, 74, 77, 83, 85, 88, 89, 91, 93, 100, 108, 110, 126, 128, 132, 136, 146, 147, 153, 158, 159, 168, 169
Opération Éclair 4, 181n4
Or, Griffon 23
O'Toole, Plenty 143

Pam Bouvier *see* Bouvier, Pam
Pendergast 185n17
Pérez Reverte, Arturo 58
Pfeiffer, Lee 12
Philip Marlowe *see* Marlowe, Philip
Philip Masters *see* Masters, Philip
Plenty O'Toole *see* O'Toole, Plenty
The Poetics of Murder: Detective Fiction and Literary Theory 24
Poirot, Hercules 78, 177
Polansky, Roman 58
The Politics of James Bond: From Fleming's Novels to the Big Screen 14, 20
Potter, James L. 186n6
Pratt, Benjamin 154-155, 191n12
Preston, Douglas 185n17
"The Property of a Lady" 77, 93
Pussy Galore *see* Galore, Pussy

Quantum of Solace (film) 3, 39, 40, 45, 50, 55, 61, 64, 70, 97, 98, 99, 101, 109, 110, 117, 120, 125, 126, 131, 139, 140, 143, 152, 165, 166, 177, 184n11
"Quantum of Solace" (short story) 47, 77, 78, 111, 132
Quarrel 49, 69, 74, 95

Raimi, Sam 185n23
Ray, Jean 185n17
Red Grant *see* Grant, Red
Renard 23, 67, 102
Rhoda Llewellyn *see* Llewellyn, Rhoda
Rice, Anne 181n7
Rider, Honey 42, 100, 106
Rider, Honeychile 34, 42, 95
Rigg, Diana 41
Rio ne répond plus (*Lost in Rio*) 4
"Risico" 35, 77
Robbe-Grillet, Alain 129, 189n11
Romanova, Tatiana 27, 68
Rosa Klebb *see* Klebb, Rosa
Rosie Carver *see* Carver, Rosie

The Rough Guide to James Bond 12
Rousseau, Jean-Jacques 155

Sade, Donatien Alphonse François de 152, 190n2
Salgari, Emilio 133
Sarraute, Nathalie 189n11
Scaramanga (Paco) 22, 26, 35, 38, 39, 51, 65, 66, 68, 69, 93, 108, 117, 142, 148, 184n8, 191n11
science fiction 6, 79, 80, 81, 128, 129, 187n16, 187n17
Sebreli, Juan José 18
The Secret Life of Ian Fleming 152
semiosphere 149, 150, 186n12
The Seven Deadly Sins 154
Sherlock Holmes *see* Holmes, Sherlock
Sherlock Holmes 181n8
Sherlock Holmes: Games of Shadows 181n8
Simon, Claude 189n11
Simpson, Paul 12
Sinbad the Sailor 129
Sir James Molony *see* Molony, Sir James
Skyfall 126, 178, 181n2, 187n6, 188n11, 189n8
Skywalker, Luke 115
Sluggsy 78, 93
La Société du spectacle 187n8
Solitaire 34, 35, 56, 74, 75, 92, 108, 142, 155
Souvestre, Pierre 185n17
South, James B. 13
space opera 6, 81, 128–129
Spade, Sam 79, 177
Spaghetti Western 5
Spang, Jack 22, 93, 134, 144; *see also* The Spangled Mob
The Spangled Mob 22, 56, 134, 142
The Spy Who Loved Me (film) 16, 68, 86, 99, 111, 117, 124, 125, 163, 168, 172, 188n5
The Spy Who Loved Me (novel) 30, 64–65, 78, 80, 85, 93, 100, 153, 105, 170
Star Wars 16, 81, 123, 128, 182n3
Steve Pops contre Dr. Yes 4, 181n4
Stock, Paul 23, 183n1, 185n20
Stowe, William W. 24
Strangways, John 71, 156

Strawberry Fields 39, 100, 143
Stutz, Collin 12
The Sufferings of Young Werther 117
Superman 20
Suzuki, Kissy 68, 105, 122

Tanner, Bill 44
Tarantino, Quentin 185n23
Tarzan 3
Tatiana Romanova *see* Romanova, Tatiana
Tee Hee Johnson *see* Johnson, Tee Hee
Thunderball (film) 122, 123, 125
Thunderball (novel) 35, 38, 53, 59, 71, 74, 77, 83, 93, 166, 181n5, 184n14
Tiffany Case *see* Case, Tiffany
Tomorrow Never Dies 38, 47, 68, 71, 99, 111, 124, 126, 147, 163, 172
Tracy (Teresa di Vincenzo) 35, 36, 41, 100, 159, 169
Trevelyan, Alec 47, 67, 68
Trinita 5
Twilight 5

Vázquez Gallego, Manuel 4
Verne, Jules 133
Vesper Lynn *see* Lynn, Vesper
A View to a Kill 18, 35, 66, 92, 184, 196
"A View to a Kill" (song) 189
Vivienne Michel *see* Michel, Vivienne

Wachowski, Lana, and Andy 16
Wai Lin *see* Lin, Wai
Watt, Stephen 183n9
Willman, Skip 183n9
Windler, Simon 12, 13
Wolverine 115
Woollacott, Janet 1, 8, 14–19, 21, 29, 181n1, 182n1, 183n15, 185n20
The World Is Not Enough 16, 23, 67, 92, 102, 111, 124, 126
Worral, Dave 12

Yeffet, Glenn 13, 14, 130
You Only Live Twice (film) 68, 122–123, 124, 125, 126
You Only Live Twice (novel) 43, 44, 50, 57, 68, 83, 93, 105, 117, 190n1

www.ingramcontent.com/pod-product-compliance
Ingram Content Group UK Ltd.
Pitfield, Milton Keynes, MK11 3LW, UK
UKHW042008140426
5217IPUK00015B/1050

9 780786 470563